The cinema of Cecilia Bartolomé

Manchester University Press

SPANISH AND LATIN AMERICAN FILMMAKERS
Series editors:
Núria Triana Toribio, University of Kent
Andy Willis, University of Salford

Spanish and Latin American Filmmakers offers a focus on new filmmakers; reclaims previously neglected filmmakers; and considers established figures from new and different perspectives. Each volume places its subject in a variety of critical and production contexts.

The series sees filmmakers as more than just auteurs, thus offering an insight into the work and contexts of producers, writers, actors, production companies and studios. The studies in this series take into account the recent changes in Spanish and Latin American film studies, such as the new emphasis on popular cinema, and the influence of cultural studies in the analysis of films and of the film cultures produced within the Spanish-speaking industries.

To buy or to find out more about the books currently available in this series, please go to: https://manchesteruniversitypress.co.uk/series/spanish-and-latin-american-filmmakers/

The cinema of Cecilia Bartolomé

Feminism and Francoism

Sally Faulkner

MANCHESTER UNIVERSITY PRESS

Copyright © Sally Faulkner 2024

The right of Sally Faulkner to be identified as the author of this work has been asserted in accordance with the Copyright, Designs and Patents Act 1988.

Published by Manchester University Press
Oxford Road, Manchester, M13 9PL

www.manchesteruniversitypress.co.uk

British Library Cataloguing-in-Publication Data
A catalogue record for this book is available from the British Library

ISBN 978 1 5261 6971 6 hardback
ISBN 978 1 5261 9481 7 paperback

First published 2024
Paperback published 2026

The publisher has no responsibility for the persistence or accuracy of URLs for any external or third-party internet websites referred to in this book, and does not guarantee that any content on such websites is, or will remain, accurate or appropriate.

EU authorised representative for GPSR:
Easy Access System Europe – Mustamäe tee 50,
10621 Tallinn, Estonia
gpsr.requests@easproject.com

Typeset
by Deanta Global Publishing Services, Chennai, India

For my mother, Helen Faulkner, and in memory of my mother-in-law, Kaye McDowell

Contents

List of figures	*page* viii
Acknowledgements	x
Textual note	xii
Introduction: feminism and Francoism	1
1 Film School shorts: *La noche del doctor Valdés* and *Carmen de Carabenchel*	15
2 Feminism and Francoism, *Margarita y el lobo*	37
3 The unfilmed scripts: *Qué tal Margarita... pero bien* and *La linda Casilda*	59
4 Putting Bárbara into ¡*Vámonos, Bárbara!*: Girlhood Studies and 'Spain's first feminist film'	76
5 Filming between the jaws of the wolf: documentary and denunciation in the diptych *Después de...*	108
6 'Es que no sabéis mirar': colony and memory in *Lejos de África*	145
7 The Admiral and the Alcántaras: political biopic meets popular soap in 'Especial Carrero Blanco: El comienzo del fin', *Cuéntame cómo pasó*	172
Conclusion: Cecilia Bartolomé and the incomplete history of Spanish cinema	199
Appendix: Cecilia Bartolomé interview	205
Filmography	222
Bibliography	224
Index	239

List of figures

1.1	Lucía (Coral Pellicer)'s enigmatic smile in *La noche del Dr Valdés* (1964)	*page* 27
1.2	Carmen (Pilar Romero) with a family that exceeds the frame in *Carmen de Carabanchel* (1965)	31
2.1	Marital separation in Franco's Spain. Margarita (Julia Peña), centre, in *Margarita y el lobo* (1969). Photograph courtesy of the Filmoteca Española	46
2.2	The film crew, including Cecilia Bartolomé (centre) in *Margarita y el lobo* (1969). Photograph courtesy of the Filmoteca Española	52
4.1	Ana (Amparo Soler Leal), standing, and the housewives in *¡Vámonos, Bárbara!* (1978)	95
4.2	Bárbara (Cristina Álvarez), the 'hinge' between Ana (Amparo Soler Leal), left, and tía Remedios (Josefina Tapias), right, standing, in *¡Vámonos, Bárbara!* (1978)	96
5.1	Anonymous older lady at the 1 May 1979 Workers Day: '¿Os cuento más?' (Shall I go on?). In *Después de… primera parte: No se os puede dejar solos* (1983)	125
5.2	Anonymous lady clears up after street riots in *Después de… segunda parte: Atado y bien atado* (1983)	131
6.1	Susana (Alicia Hernández Díaz) and Rita (Isabel Derrick) at school in Fernando Poo in *Lejos de África* (2006)	149
6.2	Diego (Patricio Wood) (left), Susana (Alicia Bogo) (centre) and Rita (Ademilis Hernández) (right)'s reconciliation in *Lejos de África* (2006)	167

List of figures

7.1 Gloria Berrocal, Elena Arnao, and Julia Peña, 'El comienzo del fin', *Cuéntame cómo pasó* (2005)   187

7.2 Emilio Ruiz in the model he constructed for *Operación Ogro* (Pontecorvo 1979) in 'El comienzo del fin', *Cuéntame cómo pasó* (2005)   193

Acknowledgements

Cecilia Bartolomé herself must come first in these acknowledgements, as she very kindly agreed to be interviewed by Núria Triana Toribio and me on a very hot summer's day in Madrid, on 9 June 2022. Núria herself is a very close second. Both her own outstanding research on Spanish cinema and her generosity as a scholar have been an inspiration. She first encouraged me to watch Bartolomé's films, shared materials with me that are difficult to access and introduced me to Bartolomé scholars in Spain. And key among those scholars in Spain, and a close third in these acknowledgements, is the Madrid Instituto Cervantes Film Curator, Marina Díaz López, who has been ever supportive and sympathetic to a Spanish cinema scholar working from a distance – a distance that became especially wide during the pandemic.

My thanks to the editors of *Feminist Media Studies* for granting permission for me to include a revised version of 'Spain's "First Feminist Film": Feminism and Francoism, *Margarita and the Wolf* (Cecilia Bartolomé, 1969)' (2022) in Chapter 2. Thanks also to Ana Vera and Sacramento Roselló-Martínez, for the invitation to speak at 'Conversations on Iberian Studies: Challenges and Opportunities', Department of English, Germanic and Romance Studies, University of Copenhagen, Denmark, where I presented a version of Chapter 4. I also acknowledge the University of Exeter's support in enabling me to travel to Spain to interview Bartolomé and consult materials in the Madrid Film Archives and National Library.

At Exeter, my colleagues Katie Brown, Fiona Handyside, Helen Hanson, Will Higbee, Danielle Hipkins, Eliana Maestri, Muireann Maguire, Katharine Murphy, Natália Pinazza, Linda Williams and Ulrike Zitzlsperger have been consistently supportive, cheerful and insightful. My recent PhD students Rachel Beaney and Delphi May have been a joy to work with, and their own scholarship on gender, race and the child helped me think through these questions in Chapters 4 and 6. I have also benefitted from the support of research assistants Jara Fernández Meneses and Rachel, again.

Working with Núria, again, as well as Hilary Owen, on our Arts and Humanities Research Council project 'Invisibles e insumisas / Invisíveis e insubmissas: Leading Women in Portuguese and Spanish Cinema and Television, 1970–1980' provides support and stimulation. In Spain, colleagues at Carlos III, Conchi Cascajosa Virino, Sonia García López, Elena Galán Fajardo, Asier Gil Vázquez and Alejandro Melero, the Complutense's Fernando Ramos Arena and Natalia Martínez Pérez of the University of Burgos, have been generous in sharing materials as well as their own excellent work on gender. In Portugal, I am grateful to Mariana Liz (University of Lisbon) for her insights, especially in the context of our work, with Hilary again, on Portuguese women's cinema. Many thanks to the staff at Manchester University Press and to the series editors for their care and attention.

I dedicate this book to two women in my family, but it is also for my 'chicos': I thank Nick McDowell for his endless support and I thank our two sons, Rowan and Cameron McDowell, who bring us endless joy. 'When love comes to me and says / What do you know, I say This boy, this boy' (Sharon Olds, 'Looking at them Asleep', 1987, adapted).

Textual note

All translations from Spanish are my own, with the exception of the Appendix Interview (Mar Diestro-Dópido) and the dialogue of *Carmen de Carabanchel*, *Margarita y el lobo* and *¡Vámonos Bárbara!* (see 'Subtitling World Cinema' project, Introduction, note 9). I have included both the original title and an English translation, as well as the year of release, on first mention of each film (for the titles under discussion, on first mention in the relevant chapter too); thereafter I have used the Spanish title, occasionally shortened. I have taken English titles from the International Movie Database (www.imdb.com) where possible. Audience figures are taken from the database of the Spanish Ministry of Culture and Sport website, https://sede.mcu.gob.es/CatalogoICAA.

Introduction: feminism and Francoism

Fusing a distinctive feminist aesthetic with a startling vision of twentieth-century Spain, the work of Cecilia Bartolomé casts a new light on the histories of both Spanish national film and transnational women's cinema. This book, the first in English on the director, and only the second in any language,[1] analyses her shorts, medium- and feature-length films, television work, as well as her unfilmed scripts, in order that she may take her place among other key auteurs of Spanish and feminist cinema. However, while an auteurist framework allows for an analysis of the aesthetics and vision of her filmed work, the nature of Bartolomé's career subjects it to severe strain. What follows, then, might be described as a mindful auteurist approach. Readers will find in these pages close readings of commercially released films, but also sustained analysis of the director's Film School pieces as finished work, rather than merely developmental. I also include creative exploration of her unfilmed scripts, where we only have the word, and must imagine the image and sound. The nature of Bartolomé's career forces us critically to adapt, to fill gaps, to read between the lines and to imagine: it aims to show that such a critical approach is thereby stronger for the adaptation.

For Bartolomé's work has, until recent acts of recovery in Spain, been lost. As I have written these pages, one book in particular, Giuliana Bruno's *Streetwalking on a Ruined Map: Cultural Theory and the City Films of Elvira Notari*, has been a companion. I initially disregarded Bruno's exploration of a much earlier female director, Notari, who was born in 1875 and died in 1946, as less relevant to Bartolomé, born in 1940, and her far later career. While her Italian predecessor had created a wide body of films, though, the archive of this work had been 'ruined' by her subsequent rejection by Mussolini's fascism. Bartolomé is a cognate case, whose body of work was in fact 'ruined' before, as and after it came into existence. Both her extant and intended work were censored under Spain's far lengthier period of authoritarianism, which began, as in Italy, in the context of 1930s European fascism, but lasted, unlike Italy, until dictator Francisco Franco's death in 1975 and the signing of the democratic constitution in 1978, events that occurred early to mid-way through our director's career. Despite these differences in the careers of the directors we analyse, where Bruno's approach inspires my own is in the creative, feminist counter-history that she writes in response to 'ruin'.

Bartolomé's work may be approached through the metaphor of the 'ruined map' for several reasons. Her extant work is comprised of six Film School[2] shorts, to which I devote Chapter 1, with a particular focus on *La noche del Dr Valdés / Doctor Valdés's Night* (1964) and *Carmen de Carabanchel / Carmen from Carabenchel* (1965); a Film School medium-length work, *Margarita y el lobo / Margarita and the Wolf* (1969) (Chapter 2); the features *¡Vámonos, Barbara! / Bárbara, Let's Go!* (1978) and *Lejos de África / Far from Africa* (1995) (Chapters 4 and 6); the documentary diptych *Después de... / Afterwards...* (Chapter 5); and the *Cuéntame cómo pasó / Tell Me How It Happened* television episode 'El comienzo del fin' / 'The Beginning of the End' (Chapter 7). I turn to the archive materials of Film School documentation and press reviews to track the processes by which this work appeared, or was prevented from appearing at all, on the map of Spanish audiovisual media. These archive materials also reveal the obstacles that prevented each piece from leading in new directions. From interviews with the director, we know that these directions would have led to countless other projects. Those which have names include the extension of the medium-length *Margarita y el lobo* to a feature-length film, to be called *Qué tal Margarita... pero bien / What's Up, Margarita...? Not Bad*[3] (see Chapter 3); the documentary about the attempted coup d'état of 1981, *¡Todos al suelo! / Everyone Down on the Floor!*,[4] the third part of *Después de...*, a trilogy of which we only have an extant diptych; and an adaptation of Adelaida García Morales's novel of 1985, *El silencio de las sirenas / The Silence of the Sirens*.[5]

The map is ruined, second, then, as this unfilmed work is missing. Relying on the archive once again, in Chapter 3 I closely read two scripts. These scripts were written in the nine-year missing fragment of the map, the period from 1969 to 1978, when the censors' banning of *Margarita y el lobo* led to the director's blacklisting. One of the places where we find her creativity in this period, then, is not in extant films, but in the authorship of these scripts that the authorities rejected for filming.[6] In this chapter, I consider updates to Bruno's 'ruined map' and investigate the potential of recent reflections on the 'incomplete'. I consider how incompleteness strains the Film Studies critical approaches that have been developed in response to completed work, and how incompleteness forces us to acknowledge the epistemological mirage of the 'complete'. This chapter could only be written because of the existence of an archive that curates these scripts (Spain's National Library, the Biblioteca Nacional). The mapping of Bartolomé's work in this book thus remains incomplete, for I have excluded work for which there is no archived script (see note 5).

Yet this existence of Bartolomé's work in archives alone is the third reason we find the map of her work 'ruined'. While such work may have been accessible in these archives to those who knew where to look (and to those who possessed the resources to pay for their time and travel as they looked), there has, until recently, been little public access to it. This has meant that the traces of this work on the map have been allowed to fade. While Film School work is a separate case, as assessment pieces were rarely screened publicly, obstacles in distribution and exhibition frequently prevented Bartolomé's commercially focussed films from reaching the wide public they sought. Stumbling, as it were, as each film left the blocks, they failed to reach Spanish audiences through wide national distribution, let alone international ones through festivals. Returning to Bruno's metaphor, Bartolomé's mark on the maps of both Spanish and women's world cinemas, is, therefore, at best, faint.

In the new millennium, we may note that three elements have contributed to the recovery of Bartolomé's work, or to the colouring in of the marks that are so faint on the map. First, the director's own innovation in technology has meant she has bypassed the cultural gatekeepers that monitor distribution and exhibition where she can (in other words, copyright-permitting), to create her own archive. At present, *La noche del Dr Valdés*, *Carmen de Carabanchel* and *Margarita y el lobo* are all free to stream, unsubtitled, on the author's personal webpage and Vimeo channel.[7] A second motor for the critical recovery of this director has been the temporal coincidence of the end of her career with Spain's desire to recover lost memories of its Civil War-torn, then dictatorship-dominated, twentieth century. While this sustained interest in her work towards the end of her career scarcely makes up for its subjection to Francoist repression in its early and middle stages, it has at least meant that Bartolomé is now receiving sustained, if tardy, recognition. Starting with the first public screening of *Margarita y el lobo* at the San Sebastián Film Festival in 2004, followed by its inclusion at the thirteenth Mostra Internacional de Films de Dones (Festival of International Film by Women) the following year, Bartolomé's work now frequently appears in festivals, where she often receives prizes in recognition of the achievements of her career.[8] Such accolades must be bitter-sweet for the director, though, as the attention to her work through festival exhibition, and the acknowledgement conferred on it by prizes, constitute precisely the recognition that was needed when the films themselves were released, to ensure wider distribution and access. Finally, the subtitling project that accompanies the publication of this volume in English seeks, modestly, to foster international discovery of Bartolomé's work, for Anglophone audiences at least. By subtitling her work for the first time in English, the project aims to allow her name in particular, and Spanish feminist cinema in general, to begin to find a place among transnational histories of women's cinema.[9]

Spain's feminist filmmaking under dictatorship and democracy

While the first academic monograph to analyse Spanish cinema from a sustained feminist perspective was Susan Martin-Márquez's 1999 English-language *Feminist Discourse and Spanish Cinema: Sight Unseen*, in the areas of activism, journalism and events, the volume had a number of important precedents in Spain, as its author acknowledges (1999, 11–12). In Barcelona in 1970, Marta Selva and others and Anna Solà formed Drac Màgic, a collective that championed the role of film in children's education, at both primary- and secondary-school levels, and also questions of gender.[10] In 1993, Drac Màgic founded the ongoing annual Mostra Internacional de Films de Dones de Barcelona (Barcelona Festival of International Film by Women), which featured Bartolomé's work in its thirteenth edition (2005), as we have seen, as well as its fourteenth (2006), twenty-sixth (2018) and twenty-seventh (2019) editions. In Madrid, the Ateneo Feminista de Madrid had previously established the annual Festival internacional de cine realizado por mujeres (International Festival of Film by Women), in 1985, and in fact screened ¡Vámonos, Bárbara! in its seventh edition (1991), but this organisation folded when government funding was cut in 2001. Returning to the 1970s, too, the feminist monthly magazine *Vindicación Feminista* (Feminist Vindication, 1976–9), founded by lawyer and feminist activist Lidia Falcón (who also founded the Partido Feminista de España (Spanish Feminist Party) in 1979), published a series of articles on women in Spanish film by Gumer Fuentes: the first such journalistic work in print.[11]

Martin-Márquez's monograph, though, was the first work to fuse broad temporal mapping and the application of transnational feminist theory to the Spanish case. More recent discoveries, like the Spanish Film Archives (Filmoteca Española)'s unearthing in 2020 of the first sound film directed by a Spanish woman – previously it had wrongly been attributed to a male director – would still sit within Martin-Márquez's framework. María Forteza's eight-minute documentary short *Mallorca* (1932–4) might be a further example of the 'Women and Agency' that Martin-Márquez charts in her Part I, which, in 1999, had focussed on Rosario Pi, whose *El gato montés / The Mountain Cat* (1935) was previously thought to be the first Spanish sound film by a woman. While little is known about Forteza, Pi's directorial career ended with the fall of the Second Republic, which, from 1931 to 1936, had advanced gender equality by, for example, legalising women's work outside the home. Martin-Márquez's second case study, Ana Mariscal, had managed to enter the male-dominated industry owing to her contracts as an actor, and directed eleven films from 1953 to 1968. Those contacts protected her, to an extent, from the patriarchal authoritarianism of Franco's regime. A dictatorship (1939–78) that seized power after the Civil War of 1936 to 1939 that illegally deposed the democratically elected Republic, it negated gender equality by reconstructing the patriarchy that the Second Republic had attempted to dismantle, thus banning women's work outside the home. Martin-Márquez's third case study, Pilar Miró, a contemporary of Bartolomé, was able to find a place as a director in the context of the 1960s to 1970s 'apertura' (opening up) of that regime, a time when women accessed education, including university education, in soaring numbers (Longhurst 1999). But only minute numbers of women entered the film industry in the 1970s. To be precise, in the area of direction, there were just three, Bartolomé, Miró and Josefina Molina, who authored the 'feminist trilogy'. This monograph will show, however, the far greater difficulties faced by Bartolomé than Miró, being both openly feminist (a term Miró always rejected) and more politically radical (to the Left of the Partido Socialista Obrero Español (Spanish Labour Party), the party for which Miró became Director General of Cinema).[12]

Martin-Márquez's focus on women directors from the 1930s to the 1960s thus showed that the 'feminist trilogy' of films of the following decade did not emerge in a vacuum. Released during the Transition, the historical period in which Spain shifted from dictatorship back to democracy – usually dated from 1973, the assassination of Franco's successor Admiral Carrero Blanco (the subject of Bartolomé's only non-anonymous television work)[13] to 1986, the year Spain joined the then European Economic Community – the 'trilogy' was made up of the first, third and first feature-length films, respectively, of the first three women to graduate from Film School. Bartolomé and Molina were the first two women to graduate in film direction from the School.[14] When the opportunity to make her first feature-length film finally arose for Bartolomé in 1976, she turned producer Alfredo Matas's commission to make a Spanish version of *Alice Doesn't Live Here Anymore* (Scorsese 1974) into a feminist road movie: it was hailed as Spain's first feature-length feminist film, *¡Vámonos, Bárbara! / Bárbara, Let's Go!* (1978) (Chapter 4).[15] After gaining experience in both television and film during the 1960s and 1970s, Miró, who graduated in scriptwriting from the school the year before in 1968, formed her own production company (Pilar Miró P.C.) to offer an autobiographical portrait of professional women working in television direction in *Gary Cooper, qué estás en los cielos / Gary Cooper, Who Art In Heaven* (1980), her third feature. In what we might today call an act of transmedia storytelling (Jenkins 2006), Molina, meanwhile, who also worked in television during the 1960s and 1970s, offered a *cinéma vérité*-influenced documentary about the production of a play based on a novel (*Cinco horas con Mario / Five Hours with Mario* (Delibes 1966)) in her *Función de noche / Night Performance* (1981).

Important as these three works are, in a national cinema with so few female directors, and thus only a handful of commercially distributed, feature-length films by women directors before the 1990s boom, it is also crucial that we look elsewhere for its feminist cinema. Martin-Márquez proposed in Part II of her monograph (1999) that scholars identify 'feminist discourse' in films directed by both men and women that may have previously been overlooked (part of the 'sight unseen' of her clever subtitle).[16] Gendered readings of 'feminist discourse' in genres such as the historical epic (Labanyi 2000) and melodrama in the 1940s and 1950s (Martín 2005), and 1960s (Faulkner 2017), followed. Still focussing on the Franco and Transition periods, female authorship is also being recovered by considering creative roles in feature-length films beyond the director, such as actors (Labanyi 2000), scriptwriters (Martínez Pérez and Gómez 2022) and below-the-line roles (Faulkner, Owen and Triana Toribio 2021).

However, the news that the number of Spanish women directors tripled from ten, in 1988, to thirty-four, by 2000 (Camí-Vela 2001, 13–14), suggested a history of uninterrupted feminist progress that allowed Martin-Márquez to conclude her 1999 volume by describing the 'dramatic recent upsurge in the number of women film-makers' (291). But if these assessments at the turn of the century seemed to herald a new millennium when gender parity would be reached, this has not come to pass. Twenty years on, we can see that the Whig version of an uninterrupted history of gender progress that we thought we had glimpsed, was a mirage. In 2006, the establishment of CIMA (Asociación de mujeres cineastas y de medios audiovisuales (Association of Women in Film and Audiovisual Media)), of which Bartolomé is a founding member, responded to this situation through awareness-raising, mentorship schemes and the commissioning of reports to track data (available annually from 2015 on its website).[17] Academic publications also turned to statistics, decrying the fact that while in 1996, 13 per cent overall of Spanish films were directed by women (Zecchi 2004, 338), the figure fell to 8.1 per cent for the period 2000 to 2005, then 9.8 per cent from 2006 to 2010 (Arranz 2013). Cutting the data another way, we can see that at the high point of the 1990s, 17 per cent of first-time directors were women; the halving of that number in the 2010s for overall film direction shows that those women were unable to make a second film and sustain a career in the industry. Taking stock ten years on, Annette Scholz demonstrates that the situation has not improved in her pointedly titled article, 'invisible women' (2018).

Choosing a different angle, Núria Triana Toribio's 2013 chapter 'Igualdad. En torno a la paridad y la visibilidad' (Equality. On Parity and Visibility) takes as its wider starting point Spain's 2007 Equality Law, and, saluting the activist role played by CIMA from 2006, she thus moves from legislation, to activism, to historiography in a call to action for scholars to rewrite Spanish film history from a feminist perspective (2013, 99). Drawing on Martin-Márquez's defence of studying overlooked work, she suggests a new metaphor for that film historiography, one that turns 'peaks into valleys' and 'valleys into peaks' (2013, 95–6; 99; 100).

The cinema of Cecilia Bartolomé: feminism and Francoism

This book aims to contribute to answering this call for a feminist rewriting of Spanish film history. It avoids Triana Toribio's celebrated 'peaks', which I interpret as the critically consecrated canon of work by auteurist male directors of the period, and searches, instead, in the 'valleys'. Looking, like Martin-Márquez, for the overlooked, *The Cinema of Cecilia Bartolomé* brings little-known Film School work out of the archive, creatively imagines the work that may have sprung from unfilmed scripts, and assesses work whose commercial release was restricted, as well as television. It names the opposite ideologies of feminism and Francoism in its subtitle to identify them as the twin poles around which the director's work turns. These two, then, make up the ideological bearings for the reader as we navigate the 'ruined map' of Bartolomé's work.

Hidden behind Film School walls and forgotten in the archives until recently,[18] the shorts and medium-length films I analyse in Chapters 1 and 3 contribute, therefore, to answering the question: what was the impact on Spanish film in the 1960s of international Second Wave feminism?[19] *La noche del Dr Valdés* charts the confrontation of an independent young woman with stifling Catholic repression in the provinces; *Carmen de Carabanchel* denounces urban working-class women's lack of access to family planning, under a patriarchal dictatorship that was also sanctioned, especially at its start, by the Catholic Church. Reaching beyond the suffocating context of women's repression in Francoist Spain, the longer running time of the medium-length *Margarita y el lobo* allowed Bartolomé to place her denunciation of the lack of women's rights in Spain in the wider contexts of international feminism. Drawing on an original novel by French writer Christiane Rochefort, and harnessing a panoply of further international film, television, literary and musical sources, Chapter 2 argues that *Margarita* offers a denunciation of the lack of divorce that is specific to Spain, but also a widely applicable feminist re-interpretation of the fairy tale, which anticipates British writer Angela Carter's work a decade later. Chapter 3 suggests that such concerns continued to dominate Bartolomé's creative work across the years when she was blacklisted, though the investigation of female mental health, including post-natal depression and suicide, in the unfilmed scripts that I analyse, also indicate tantalising new ventures that never made it to screen.

The opportunity to make her first feature came in 1976, the year after Franco's death, in the form of the Matas commission, *¡Vámonos, Bárbara!* The limited critical attention that this largely forgotten film has thus far attracted focus on the adult protagonist, Ana. Her bid for freedom in the dying days of the dictatorship, for these critics, stands for the opportunities of the new socio-political moment of the Transition. Drawing on Girlhood Studies, my Chapter 4 argues, alternatively, that we place the teenage girl Bárbara at the centre of the frame. It thereby proposes that Bartolomé's brilliant metaphor for the possibility and anxiety of this historical moment may be found, instead, in her exploration of female adolescence. With a more uneven result, it is again to the figure of the Girl that Bartolomé turns in order to offer a nonetheless unique portrait of Spain's colonial occupation of West Africa in *Lejos de África* (Chapter 6). The *Después de...* diptych, co-directed with her brother José Juan Bartolomé (Chapter 5), and the 'El comienzo del fin' *Cuéntame cómo pasó* episode for Televisión Española (Spanish National Television) (Chapter 7), meanwhile, turn to documentary to interpret the Transition as it happened (*Después de...*) and in retrospect ('El comienzo del fin'). These two chapters show that the documentary genre, in Bartolomé's hands, is one that pays particular attention to the everyday to fashion its feminist address.

Throughout this fiction and non-fiction work, at Film School and within the industry, commissioned or original, in film or television, or, even, filmed and unfilmed, the encounter with Bartolomé's work rewards us not only with themes that are pressing, yet scarcely seen, on Spanish screens – women's rights under dictatorship, the experience of the Transition on the streets and Francoist colonialism and de-colonialisation from the perspective of a girl. It is also an encounter that always seeks to be accessible to wide audiences by working with recognisable genres. The encounter is often also darkly humorous, drawing on the Spanish theatre tradition of exaggeration, the *esperpento*,[20] and the comedy often arises from the attention Bartolomé pays to the often-overlooked experience of the everyday, or from her endlessly playful use of diegetic and extradiegetic music – the faint sounds of which we may even hear in the written lyrics of songs that are included in the unfilmed scripts. The map of feminist filmmaking in Spain does not only contain more details when we include Bartolomé, this volume aims to show that it is also all the more colourful for the inclusion too.

Notes

1 See Cerdán and Díaz (2001).
2 This was the Film School of the Spanish state. Originally named the 'Instituto de Investigaciones y Experiencias Cinematográficas' (School of Cinematographic Experience and Research) and renamed the 'Escuela Oficial de Cinematografía' (Official Film School) in 1962, the

Film School taught future film professionals in Spain from 1947 to 1976.
3 I take this great translation from García López (2023).
4 This, famously, was Lieutenant-Colonel Antonio Tejero's cry as he, along with approximately three hundred (estimates range from two to four hundred) armed members of the Guardia Civil (Civil Guard), entered the Spanish parliament in Madrid on 23 February 1981. In coordinated action, Army General Jaime Milans del Bosch, whom we will meet in Chapter 5, declared a state of emergency, and led tanks onto the streets of Valencia.
5 See this volume's interview by Núria Triana Toribio and the author for references to Bartolomé's advertising and documentary work, including a 'making-of' documentary of Antonio Aisasi-Isamendi's *El perro / A Dog Called... Vengeance* (1977), which eventually folded (Devesa and Potes 1999, 39). In the 2001 filmography compiled by Rafael Gómez Alonso, as well as the García Morales adaptation, films titled *Negro / Black* and *La niña bonita / The Pretty Girl* are included, the latter having at that stage even secured Ministry of Culture funding (2001, 48). In a 2018 interview on the occasion of the twenty-sixth Mostra Internacional de Films de Dones de Barcelona, the director recalls the frustrations she experienced when three further projects collapsed: alongside the García Morales adaptation and *La niña bonita*, she mentions a film about immigration, based on her own experience of colonialism; a programme on Al Andalus; she also describes an ongoing project on the superiority of women (Pérez Guevara 2018).
6 For other places, see this volume's Appendix Interview, where the director discusses details of the television advertising and documentary work that she completed in this period (p. 210).
7 See the 'web pionera' (pioneering web) section of http://www.ceciliabartolome.com, and the link to what the director describes as the first example of the promotion of a film via the internet, noting also the translation of information on the site into nine languages: https://ua838608.serversignin.com/ceciliabartolome/islanegra/IslaNegraE.html. This multilingualism contrasts with the lack of availability of the film with subtitles in any language.

The overall site also includes a two-and-a-half-minute silent piece, *Cecilia*, which focusses on unnamed young Black children and a white adolescent girl (possibly the director herself); this is described as recovered 8 mm clips shot by the director in Equatorial Guinea in the 1950s. See also Bartolomé's Vimeo channel, https://vimeo.com/user12132296. Websites accessed 12 April 2023.

8 The work was included in the 'Incorrect@s' Section, for its thirty-five years-delayed première at San Sebastián in 2004. There followed: Bartolomé's award of the Gijón Film Festival's 'Mujer de Cine' (Woman in Film) in 2012; the 'Medalla de Oro al Mérito en las Bellas Artes' (Gold Medal for Merit in Fine Arts) in 2014; the Award of Honour at the 2017 Mostra Viva del Mediterrani; an act of homage at CIMA, in 2019 (Asociación de mujeres cineastas y de medios audiovisuales (Association of Women in Film and Audiovisual Media): https://cimamujerescineastas.es/); inclusion in the Reina Sofía museum 'Fuera del canon' series in 2020; the 2022 season of her work at the Filmoteca Española, 'Deseos (re)velados/ Cecilia Bartolomé. Contra la amnesia' (Concealed/Revealed Desires. Cecilia Bartolomé. Against Amnesia) (https://entradasfilmoteca.gob.es/listaPeliculas.aspx?idciclo=217); and the award of the 'Premio Feroz de Honor' (Feroz Honorary Award) in 2022. Bartolomé was amused that the name of this last prize connected with an earlier title she planned for *Margarita el lobo*, where 'el lobo' (the wolf) was 'el lobo feroz' (the big, bad wolf) (García López 2023). Websites accessed 12 April 2023.

9 See the Subtitling World Cinema Project, co-led by the author with Will Higbee and Danielle Hipkins, at https://subtitlingworldcinema.com. In collaboration with the AHRC project 'Invisibles e insumisas / Invisíveis e insubmissas: Leading Women in Portuguese and Spanish Cinema and Television, 1970–1980' that I lead (https://leadingwomenproject.com), the UK Manchester HOME cinema, and the UK ¡Viva! Spanish and Latin American Film Festival 2023, Núria Triana Toribio and I premièred *Carmen de Carabanchel*, *Margarita y el lobo*, and *¡Vámonos, Bárbara!*, all with English subtitles, to an international audience for the first time on 25–26 March 2023. Núria and I thank the University of Exeter MA Translation Studies students, Amy Watts and Flor Fernández, along with Rachel Beaney, Jara Fernández Meneses and Eliana Maestri, for their work on the subtitling, and Marina Díaz and Jessie Gibbs for their help in securing copyright. We are especially grateful to Rachel Hayward and Jessie, again, both of HOME, Manchester, for their support of these projects.

10 I am grateful to Núria Triana Toribio and Mariana Freijomil for our discussions of this group in the context of the previously mentioned Leading Women project (note 9).

11 The eight articles published over 1976 and 1977 include pieces on women in front of the camera, 'La mujer en el cine español: de la represión al destape. La española cuando besa' (Fuentes 1976), 'La mujer en el cine español: la caída del sostén y el alzamiento del tampax' (Fuentes 1977a); and behind it, 'Mujeres detrás de la cámara'

(Fuentes 1977b). An unpublished manuscript by Marta Selva Masoliver and Anna Solà Arguimbau, written in 1985–6, on women in historical 1940s to 1950s cinema, 'Los personajes heroicos femeninos en le cine histórico español (1941–1961)' may be consulted at the Drac Màgic archive and is mentioned by Martin-Márquez (1999, 12).

12 Note that Bartolomé took part in then Podemos leader Pablo Iglesias's interview series in 2020 (Iglesias 2020). Podemos lies politically to the Left of the PSOE.
13 Anonymously, Bartolomé made countless television adverts over many years (see Appendix Interview p. 210).
14 In her autobiography, Molina states she graduated in 1968 and Bartolomé in 1969 (2000, 57); García López states both women graduated in 1969 (2020, 1).
15 Preceding *Thelma and Louise* (Scott 1991) and the Hollywood boom of feminist road movies by a decade and a half, Bartolomé's film does not symbolically punish its female protagonists at its ending, as Ridley Scott's does (Pérez 2013, 133).
16 Lacking any data on alternative gender affiliations, this book today uses the cis categories of 'male' and 'female', though anticipates their future revision should new information emerge.
17 https://cimamujerescineastas.es/informes/, accessed 12 April 2023.
18 See, for example, García López (2021).
19 My answer to this question, in the forms of Chapters 1 and 2, aims to dialogue with studies of feminism across multiple fields, including those that analyse critical associations like the Seminario de Estudios Sociológicos sobre la Mujer (Sociological Studies of Women Seminar), associated with Catholicism and created in 1960, and the Movimiento Democrático Feminista (Democratic Women's Movement), associated with Left-wing politics and formed in 1964, to which, given her politics, Bartolomé's work is closer. I suggest Bartolomé is referring to this latter MDF in her entertaining account of its meetings in Almagro, Madrid, in interview with Andrea Bermejo. She recalls, for example, bringing along sewing materials, so that if the police arrived, they could pretend they were embroidering a shawl for the Virgin of Pilar (2017, 9)!
20 In theatre, the tradition began with playwright Ramón del Valle-Inclán, who developed a deformed, exaggerated aesthetic in his 1920 play *Luces de Bohemia / Bohemian Lights*, which is especially relevant to exaggerated characterisation (see Appendix Interview on Bartolomé's formative years working in youth theatre groups). Luis García Berlanga was a proponent of the tendency in film, and taught the young Bartolomé at Film School. Even though he was among those who subjected her to sexist treatment (see Chapter 1), and despite his misogyny, by the

time of *¡Vámonos, Bárbara!*'s release, he and Bartolomé were reconciled, and she stated that she 'admira al autor valenciano por encima de su misoginia y le califica como el más grande nacional' (admires the Valencian director despite his misogyny and considers him the greatest national director) (Santa Eulalia 1978a). In more recent interviews she names him her 'maestro' (inspiration (the Spanish term 'maestro' is also used for school teacher; I have avoided the gendered 'master' in my translation)) (e.g. Iglesias 2020).

1

Film School shorts: *La noche del doctor Valdés* and *Carmen de Carabenchel*

When a filmmaking career is severely truncated by censorship, we can overlook it, as Spanish film history has largely done with Cecilia Bartolomé, or we can search elsewhere for a director's corpus of works. In *The Cinema of Cecilia Bartolomé: Feminism and Francoism*, this search means adjusting our critical focus away from feature-length films that achieved commercial release. The book therefore devotes these first two chapters to Bartolomé's 1960s Film School work: the current Chapter 1, which focusses on the two shorts, *La noche del doctor Valdés* / *Doctor Valdés's Night* (1964) and *Carmen de Carabenchel* / *Carmen from Carabenchel* (1965), and Chapter 2, which addresses the medium-length film *Margarita y el lobo* / *Margarita and the Wolf*. In Chapter 3, rather than lament Bartolomé's blacklisting, I instead explore some of the places where we can find her work over the nine years when she could not direct, like her unfilmed scripts.

Paying attention to Film School work is not, in itself, unconventional. However, as Sonia García López argues, this widening of focus to include a director's early Film School work usually occurs retrospectively, through the lens of prior knowledge of a director's subsequent career in the industry. This methodology is therefore inherently conservative, as it tends to reinforce a pre-constituted approach to a consolidated director's work by looking back at student work for early signs of a later authorial signature. In Spanish cinema, as García López shows, such an auteurist approach has characterised the retrospective examination of the early Film School work of subsequently revered male auteurs like Luis García Berlanga, Víctor Erice or Basilio Martín Patino (2021, 1–2). These first chapters aim to avoid this approach, even though it is the case that Bartolomé did go on to release some, if only a modest number, of features. This chapter will examine first the particular nature of Spain's Film School, which existed for most of the dictatorship, 1947 to 1976, before homing in on the gendered experience of female students like Bartolomé. It will read extant archive material held at the Filmoteca Española to capture Film School teachers' and fellow students' responses to the work. This affords us some sense of the contemporary reception of the work – limited, of course, to this group of experts. (In Chapters 4–7, which address commercially released work, I use press reviews in a similar way, though, again, this access to audience reception is also largely limited to professional journalists.) I proceed to survey Bartolomé's extant work at the School, before a close reading of two shorts; I also deploy a close reading methodology for the analysis of the medium-, feature- and television work later in this book.

I argue that these short films' response to Francoism, from the perspective of Bartolomé's feminism, is just as insightful as contemporary dissident work that did succeed in reaching Spanish commercial or international festival screens. For instance, religious and sexual oppression underscore both *La noche* and Luis Buñuel's near-contemporaneous *Viridiana* (1961), a film Bartolomé saw at the School as students had access to work that did not make it to commercial screens (Anon. 1978b). Both Buñuel's film and Bartolomé's short feature the visit, and likely entrapment, of a young niece in the oppressive home of a mysterious uncle. A further link is that while Buñuel's lead actor, Silvia Pinal, is Mexican, she plays a Spanish nun (with improbably bleach-blonde hair); Bartolomé's Coral Pellicer, meanwhile, is Spanish, but her outsider status is indicated in the narrative by her coming back to Spain from Mexico, where she had been living. This short was failed by the School, however, perhaps on grounds of its quality, and years later Bartolomé would modestly suggest she thought it weak, especially its ending (Calpena 2022, 4). *Carmen*, the most extraordinary of all her shorts, was failed for political reasons: it broke extraordinary new ground in Spanish cinema in its treatment of the taboo subjects of contraception and abortion. While the latter is alluded to in contemporary Spanish films like Fernando Fernán Gómez's *El mundo sigue / Life Goes On* (1963), briefly released though quickly censored through limited distribution (Faulkner 2017, 832), Bartolomé's tragi-comic musical *Carmen* is the standout treatment of the subject of abortion in the whole period.

Film School

Originally named the Instituto de Investigaciones y Experiencias Cinematográficas, the Film School was set up under dictatorship so that Spain would have a training venue on a par with European models, like Italy's Centro Sperimentale di Cinematografia in Rome, and France's Institut des Hautes Études Cinématographiques in Paris. Prior to its existence, the only means to enter the Spanish film industry as a director was through lengthy apprenticeships in other film roles, and the connections these brought. This was an informal and contact-dependent means of access that continued alongside the existence of the School. For women directors, this meant only an actor of the status of Ana Mariscal could move into direction (see Introduction). However, the School did not change this situation drastically. For, of the 481 students that graduated, only two women did so in film direction: Cecilia Bartolomé and Josefina Molina.

As part of a draft of modest measures aimed at a controlled and limited modernisation known as the 'apertura' (opening up), introduced by the Francoist 'technocrat' ministers of the 1960s, in 1962 the School was renamed the Escuela Oficial de Cinematografía (see Faulkner 2006, 16–17). Entrance was highly competitive (Bartolomé recalls an acceptance rate of around 10 per cent) and fees were reasonably low, though students (including Bartolomé) often repeated a year. This was allowed up to three times for each year, and was frequent, as standards were so high. The cost of multiple repetition may explain why the student body tended to be drawn – as was the case for Bartolomé – from wealthy, middle-class families. With low tuition fees the operational School's costs were therefore largely borne by the Francoist state. And these costs were extremely high: the fortunate students selected for entrance could film their assessment work on expensive 16 mm and 35 mm stock, and with access to professional-standard studios and equipment. Another privilege, as we have seen regarding the case of *Viridiana*, was that students were also able to enjoy private viewings of films banned to the wider public.[1]

The School, like the dictatorship itself, evolved over its thirty years of existence – three quarters of the period of that dictatorship – under seven different directors – all men. Lucio Blanco Mallada describes three periods: enthusiasm; consolidation; crisis (2016). Summarising all three periods, García López is measured in describing the School as offering 'un espacio de cierta permisividad' (a space for certain permissiveness) (2021, 313); the more colourful description of it as a 'nido de rojos' (nest of Communists) pertains only to its final period of crisis (Rodríguez Merchán 2007, 15). This association with anti-Francoism means that an interesting critical doxa has emerged in auteurist studies of male directors whose careers span dictatorship and democracy: the Film School allowed individual artistic expression and political dissent that directors then developed in democracy after the fall of the regime.

When the question of Film School work and the development of a subsequent directorial career is reframed through the question of gender, however, a different picture emerges. Inequality of access in terms of gender is consistent with wider information about gender, education and work in Franco's Spain. Over the years the School was open, some forty of the 481 graduates were women, a figure of 8 per cent. Gender distribution of teaching staff was six women to 154 men, barely 4 per cent (Odriozola 2020). These figures are not surprising, though it is striking that they did not improve more markedly in the 1960s and 1970s. Women's participation in undergraduate university study increased significantly in this period, as the social perception of women studying at university became widely accepted among Spanish middle classes (Longhurst 1999, 114; Flecha 1991), but subsequent access to professional training, like Film School, or to the workplace itself, clearly remained extremely difficult.

Notable, too, is that admission to the distinct pathways offered at the School was unbalanced. Even if the original 1947 legislation, which stated that women could only be admitted to study acting, wardrobe and make-up, was overturned as soon as 1948, its legacy endured. As we have seen, just two women graduated in directing in the entire history of the School. Behind this figure may lie not only prejudice based on gender, but even nationality too. Sonia García López's interview work has uncovered that American Kathryn Waldo was told she could not study directing, as it would not be tolerated that the first woman to graduate in this discipline at the School should be foreign (2021, 320–1). She was eventually able to graduate in Production instead.

Given our retrospective knowledge of the treatment of *Margarita*, one of the cruellest cases of censorship in the entire history of the School, and, indeed, in the entire history of censorship in Spain (García López 2022, 92), it is difficult not to backlight Bartolomé's entire experience over eight years with this information. But the censorship case was partly a question of unlucky timing, as, unfortunately for Bartolomé, Juan Julio Baena became School Director in her last year as a student. A former member of the Communist Party, and acclaimed cinematographer whose photography became synonymous with modernist aesthetics in Spain, Baena switched his political allegiance to the regime. And the switch coincided with the precise moment that he occupied a position of power. He thus introduced the process of sending final-year Film School work, like Bartolomé's, to the state censors, who, of course, completely rejected her utterly irreverent final-year *Margarita* ('prohibición total' (total prohibition) the Junta de Censura y Apreciación de Películas (Censorship and Appreciation of Cinema Board) states in the letter to Baena of 23 June 1970 (Calpena 2022, 10)). It is surely this experience with Baena that lies behind Bartolomé's reflections a decade later, 'curiosamente, el machismo entre intelectuales es más terrorífico que en otros medios' (funnily enough, machismo among intellectuals is more terrifying than it is in other places) (Padura 1978). She mentions 'intelectuales' in the plural as the Film School documentation, accessible today at the Filmoteca Española, suggests other teachers also placed obstacles in her way. Again, in the interviews that accompanied the release of *¡Vámonos, Bárbara!* she finally gets her say, and names gender bias at the Film School, or, in her words, her obstruction by named teaching staff José Luis Borau, Miguel Picazo and Berlanga 'por ser tía' (for being a woman) (Cleries 1978). Later, as we will see, she softens her views, hailing Berlanga as her principal creative inspiration in interviews. Borau, meanwhile, as we will see, subsequently offered particular support, collaborating on scripts written by Bartolomé in order that his name might be used as a cover to sneak them past the censors, though this was ultimately unsuccessful (see Appendix Interview p. 212 and Chapter 3).

On the one hand, then, there is ample material to furnish a disapproving approach to the problems Bartolomé encountered on the basis of her gender (for Waldo, on the basis of her nationality too). In these Chapters 1 and 2, however, I will attempt to strike a balance, for, on the other hand, the creative collaboration and camaraderie among students, and inspiration and guidance provided by some teaching staff, are significant. In subsequent interviews, Bartolomé has recalled, for example, the supportive friendship with fellow director Josefina Molina ('no nos mangonearon [nuestros] profesores y compañeros porque no los dejamos' (our teachers and classmates didn't boss us about because we wouldn't let them), Vargas 2019). There was also considerable mutual support among those directors whose work was censored. Bartolomé and her classmates Manuel Revuelta, Bernardo Fernández and Manuel Gutiérrez Aragón, for example, fought back against Baena's 'witch hunt',[2] which led to their work being censored. They took legal action against the School on the basis of infringement of intellectual property, though this was ultimately to no avail as they were told no intellectual property law existed in Spain at the time (García López 2022, 100).

Thus, Bartolomé's experience of the School swung between the nurturing and intellectually enriching experiences that are suggested by the noun 'nest' (Rodríguez Merchán 2007, 15), and the hostile machismo of some students and teachers; between the persecution of the 'witch hunt', and the solidarity she shared with fellow students as they attempted, collectively, to confront this. In a 2004 interview, Bartolomé prefers to dwell on the supportive experiences, especially for those students like her on the political Left: 'en plena dictadura [...] la escuela era un pequeño reducto de rojerío donde se intentaba romper con lo que se hacía entonces' (right in the midst of dictatorship [...] the School was a little stronghold of Lefties where we tried to break with what was being done at the time) (Yoldi 2004). I will now test this balance between obstruction and support in the two shorts under discussion, before my close analysis of each.

Bartolomé at Film School

In fact, Bartolomé spent nine years at the School, for, as a determined teenager, she first enrolled for the academic year 1958–59 for acting, as she was too young for the Directing pathway. Doubtless both unimpressed and concerned, her parents insisted she return home to Equatorial Guinea for a year and a half before her entrance, on the Directing pathway, once she had reached the age requirement of twenty-one, for the academic year 1961–62. Over these eight years at the School, she then made, for Year One, the silent three-and-a-half-minute short *La siesta* (1962), then the ten-minute silent documentary short *Cruzada del Rosario* (1963). Bartolomé repeated Year Two three times, submitting *La noche* in 1964, *Carmen* in 1965 and passing with *La brujita / The Little Witch* in 1966. *Plan Jack Zero Tres / Plan Jack Zero Three* failed Year Three in 1967; *Margarita y el lobo* passed in 1969.

Briefly surveying these early pieces, we find in *La siesta* (1962), a brief silent short about a couple in a park and a physical attack by a young man. Cinematography is effectively deployed in the work, as male physical violence is portrayed through the response of the female protagonist that we see through the close-up of her face as she inaudibly cries out. *Cruzada de Rosario* (1963) is also shot outdoors. In this documentary piece, Bartolomé cross-cuts between the officiating clergy and the devotional, at some moments fanatical, crowd. An extreme close-up of the hand of a cleric counting the beads of a rosary shows Bartolomé's eye for detail. Among a group of children in attendance at the event, Bartolomé's camera seeks out one boy in particular who is open-mouthed in wonder. Ten years on, Víctor Erice would also frame such innocent spontaneity in capturing a young Ana Torrent as she is watching James Whale's *Frankenstein* (1931), also open-mouthed in amazement, in *El espíritu de la colmena / The Spirit of the Beehive* (1973).

But Bartolomé's brief first documentary is not limited to church hierarchy and devoted masses, including the young. In her hands this potentially dry, devotional material sings with humour. First, modernity interrupts the medieval ceremony when Bartolomé cuts to a helicopter overhead. This was surely an unplanned event that shows the young director thinking on her feet. Had it been a sound recording, it might have been even funnier, with the woosh of the rotating blades drowning out solemn liturgical proceedings. Mirthful meaning is also conjured through further close-ups. Thinking on her feet and responding to unplanned events again, Bartolomé spots, and captures on film, another open mouth: this time a member of the clergy yawning! The older lady that features at the end of the film may not be bored: instead, her attention is hampered by the fact she has got her own rosary in a knot! Bartolomé seizes on this example of how everyday nuisance interrupts lofty devotion to amusingly irreverent effect.

I will devote lengthier analysis to *La noche* (1964), and *Carmen* (1965) below, as these are the two films for which the Filmoteca Española possesses fullest documentation, though perhaps this documentation is relatively extensive as both works officially failed. With *La brujita* (1966), Bartolomé finally passed Year Two – her last chance to pass so she could move up to Year Three. Gone, in *La brujita*, then, are the class and gender denunciation and smashing of taboos we will explore in *Carmen*. Based on a horror tale ('Sweets to the Sweet', Robert Bloch, 1947), Bartolomé offers instead an introspective study of the vexed experience of heterosexuality, which recalls the near-contemporary feature, *Nueve cartas a Berta / Nine Letters to Berta* (1965), by her successful Film School predecessor Patino. A comparison between the two is also suggested by the casting of Elsa Baeza as the lover in each. In Patino's film, the character does not have a proper name (she is just 'la novia' (girlfriend/fiancée)) and Baeza does not utter a single line; in Bartolomé's hands, while she may play the love interest again, she at least has a name and a voice. And while the suffering and regret of Patino's male protagonist Lorenzo (Emilio Gutiérrez Caba) are conveyed through introspective voiceover, suffering and regret in *La brujita* are channelled through the supernatural powers of the 'little girl-witch' of the title. In Year Three, Bartolomé would again eschew realism through her choice of source text to adapt; here, fellow filmmaker and writer Gonzalo Suárez's Surrealist tale *Plan Jac Zero Tres* (1967). We have the School's failing of this rather uneven attempt to thank for the existence of *Margarita y el lobo* (1969) (Chapter 2). In addition to these six filmed shorts, and one medium-length film, unfortunately undated documentation also reveals the existence of an unfilmed and undated script titled *Juegos de tarde / Afternoon Games*. The trace of this film is now all that can be glimpsed in the archive through the document of teacher comments, one of whom, Carlos Saura, rather tantalisingly observes that it is 'Más personal que "La noche del doctor Valdés". Está bien construído y el tema es interesante. SÍ [apropado para rodar]' (More intimate than 'La noche del doctor Valdés'. Well-constructed and an interesting subject. YES [approved for shooting]. Anon., n.d.).

My lengthier examination of *La noche* and *Carmen* in these pages is based on the existence of documentation, and not on whether a short passed or failed. Indeed, the criteria for failure are not clear: in such a situation it is difficult not to surmise that political and gender issues intruded. If we turn to the director's memories, hardly an objective historical source, of course, she nonetheless strikes a balance, conceding *La noche* was 'weak' but also noting that School assessment criteria were unclear (Calpena 2022, 4). As we will see, failing *Carmen* seems to be a combination of the taboo subject matter and a failure in a duty of care on the part of the School to accommodate Bartolomé's own pregnancy (during production) and childbirth (before post-production). The achievement of passing and graduating with *Margarita y el lobo* was, in any case, something of a pyrrhic victory: as we have seen, when it was sent to the censors it was banned and the director blacklisted.

La noche del doctor Valdés / *Doctor Valdés's Night* (1964)

Filmed during the years when Luis Ponce de León was director of the School, documentation reveals a warm, if not ecstatic, response to the script on the part of teachers: Juan Miguel Lamet and Berlanga judge it 'posible'; Saura, again, 'Una correcta adaptación muy Poe. (Largo como está.)' (An acceptable adaptation, very like Poe. (Even though it is long.)) (García Berlanga, Lamet and Saura 1964). Further documents track details of the production of the short, as well as a number of problems. The details include historically valuable information about the minutiae of the process: shooting permits, budget, work plan, crew, permissions for extensions and requests for more celluloid stock, and exact details of any disruptions like late arrivals on set, rain, or an actor needing time at the hairdressers for continuity of the correct style for the shoot.[3]

Since all incidents had to be recorded, usually by lengthy, handwritten letters, we therefore have a wealth of detail concerning difficulties over the production process, from lack of punctuality and no-shows on set of decorators and actors (there are four letters from Producer Juan José Daza de Castillo, e.g. 1964a), to the withdrawal of actor Coral Pellicer (Daza 1964b), and requests for extensions (Daza 1964c). Bartolomé herself is writing by the 10 March to give an account of traffic and lighting problems, as well an account of how Pellicer – who returned – had banged her head, causing a delay (Bartolomé 1964). An intriguing letter, written one month after the shoot, requests permission to repeat the last shot as 'los nervios del equipo estaban bastante exaltados' (the team was rather agitated) (Flaquer 1964). We do not know if this permission was given or refused, though it remains the case that Bartolomé still recalls her dissatisfaction with the final shot (Calpena 2022, 4). In comparison with the documentation that covers *Carmen*, discussed below, and *Margarita*, discussed in Chapter 2, the files do not suggest that there were any more serious obstacles during this shoot.

La noche fuses different elements of two tales by Edgar Allan Poe (alluded to in Saura's comments). From 'The Fall of the House of Usher' (1839), Bartolomé takes the conceit of a lone traveller visiting the haunted house that Poe was largely responsible for making a mainstay of Gothic fiction. The sickness that infects Poe's original haunted house takes the form, in Bartolomé's adaptation, of uncle Dr Valdés's patients; the invalid aunt also recalls Poe's character Madeline. In the 2022 interview that concerns Bartolomé's dissatisfaction with the ending of the short, she reveals that this was partly attributable to an argument with teacher Borau. Apparently Bartolomé had wanted an ending similar to that of Poe's 'The System of Dr Tarr and Prof. Fether' (1856), whereby the discovery of the doctors' corpses would have revealed that Dr Valdés's patients had usurped the doctors. Borau – again, as Bartolomé recalls – apparently thought this ending 'muy americano y muy manido' (very American and very trite), suggesting an open one instead. There followed an argument between student and teacher: 'Discutimos mucho y al final teníamos pendiente cómo terminar. De ahí ese final absurdo' (We argued a lot and in the end we didn't resolve the question of how it would finish. That's why the end is absurd) (Calpena 2022, 4).

Bartolomé may retrospectively reject the ending, but Ana Calpena has suggested, alternatively, that it indicates Lucía's possibility of escape from her uncle's house (2022, 4). I suggest we might now read Pellicer's enigmatic smile, filmed, we recall, when the production team was rather agitated, as a suitable close to a short that turns around the contrast between the 'light' of both Lucía's name and the modernity of her character, and the 'night' of the film's title, which refers to the shadows of suspicion and fear that lurk in the repression and excessive religiosity of Dr Valdés's house.

With Lucía's arrival in Valdemora by train, the vehicle of modernity that is also tied to cinema's own modernity (the first known footage being *L'Arrivée d'un train en gare de La Ciotat* / *The Arrival of a Train at La Ciotat Station* (Lumière 1896)), Bartolomé begins the film by playing with these contrasts between the light of modernity and possibility, and darkness of tradition and repression. Thus, as Lucía waits for her lift at the station, Bartolomé contrasts the whistling wind that is the soundscape of the sleepy village (shot on location), with the musical motif associated with the character of lively guitar strings. Visually, the conspicuous 'TWA' airline bag that she carries (Trans World Airlines was the major carrier between Spain and the Americas in the period) speaks to a cosmopolitanism that stands out against the tiny village. The women's magazine that is clearly visible tucked under Lucía's arm also points to a modernity that punctures the tedium of the provincial surroundings. The threat of male violence that we have seen in *La siesta* is then evoked by the presence of an unknown, blond man who follows Lucía when she leaves the café, though this threat is dispersed when her lift arrives and the man is named as José (José Manuel Gorospe). In a later sequence, when Lucía is looking for a place to escape what she calls the 'jaula' (cage) of her uncle Dr Valdés's house, she hides in a stairwell. José's presence again, evokes menace. His approach in the stairwell is conveyed by the threatening dark shadow he casts over Lucía; next, and rather inexplicably, they embrace, and only then is he revealed to be a former lover. Yet he is also shown to be weak: he rejects Lucía's embrace, mumbling 'no sé' (I don't know), an acoustic echo of his own name, 'Jo-sé'.

Contrasts of dark and light imbue the portrayal of the haunted house, both the living quarters of the uncle, Dr Valdés, along with his wife or sister, and a patient clinic. There is a maid, Inés, and a group of nuns who seem to run both the clinic and the home. Lucía is thus greeted by Madre Concepción (María Teresa Durán Dressel) and is conducted to the living room, where she encounters her invalid aunt (Kathryn Waldo), Inés, a further nun, named Sor Anunciata in the documentation, as well as José.[4] In shooting this domestic space Bartolomé's camera first takes in the religious models on the mantelpiece in a tracking shot. So far, so gloomy... But then a cut reveals that the assembled group is watching the chirpy American cartoon *Bug's Bunny* (multiple authors, 1961–75) on television!

However, Lucía represents a disruptive modernity far in excess of the presence of a television set and an American children's programme. She disrupts every space: smoking in the living room and unpacking modern clothes and underwear in her bedroom – 'qué bonito' (so pretty) gasps the flustered nun on seeing one dress. In addition, for the audience at least, modernity is conveyed by the cheerful, extra-diegetic guitar musical motif that accompanies her on the soundtrack as she visits the house's chapel. Some unnamed unorthodoxy is also present in her very blood: as Madre Concepción suggests 'Ojalá tus padres los haya perdonado el señor' (Hopefully the Lord has forgiven your parents). The time she had previously spent in Mexico likely suggests that her parents had fled there as Republican exiles of the Spanish Civil War, like so many, including filmmaker Buñuel.

Unnamed sin also clings to the sinister character of masochistic maid Inés, who wears a cilice on her thigh in self-flagellation, refuses tablets to ease a headache and becomes lost in a mystical trance before the icons of the suffering bodies of Mary and Jesus in the chapel. When uncle Dr Valdés (Norberto Arribas), whose implied presence lingers like a threat in the shadowy house, finally arrives, Inés is the object of his first and only words in the whole short. Managing to both indulge himself in a lewd gaze, and shore up his own patriarchal authority by issuing an order, he admonishes her 'esta falda es un poco corta' (that skirt is a little short). Compared to the other female characters – the masochistic maid, invalid aunt and by turns flustered or censorious nuns – Lucía's final enigmatic smile indeed seems to represent the hope of escape (Calpena 2022, 4) (Figure 1.1).

Bartolomé's interests here, then, concern the role of religion, which seems to empower men (the uncle's monopoly on morality) and oppress women (the nun who longs for a pretty dress; Inés's masochism). Her female protagonist is a ray of light in this shadowy

Figure 1.1 Lucía (Coral Pellicer)'s enigmatic smile in *La noche del Dr Valdés* (1964)

night. The development of her character stands on its own merits, but may certainly be viewed retrospectively as a template for the future Margarita of her medium-length work and unfilmed script, or the future Ana, Bárbara, Rita or Susana of her fictional features. Interrupting the actions through the disruptive presence of a television show, and using music as a counterpoint, will be reprised in her next work, *Carmen*, of 1965, and throughout her career.

Carmen de Carabenchel / Carmen from Carabenchel (1965)

Carmen de Carabanchel forms part of what Bartolomé has retrospectively described as a 'ruptura' in the nature of the student work created in the Film School in the mid-1960s. Unlike earlier generations, these students perhaps felt emboldened by the changes inaugurated by the 'apertura' in the country in general, and by the championing and protection of film as an art by Manuel Fraga Iribarne's (Minister of Tourism and Communications) appointment of José María García Escudero as Director General of Cinema over these same years in particular (see Faulkner 2006, 16–18; and Triana Toribio 2003, 68–9, for a gendered critique of his encouragement of the androcentric Nuevo Cine Español, or 'los chicos de

García Escudero' (García Escudero's boys)). Whatever the reason, Bartolomé recalls a shift among the students at the School between the conscious or unconscious self-censorship, and thus dependence on symbolism, of previous work (see Appendix Interview for her example of *La caza / The Hunt* (Saura 1966), p. 212), and that of her own generation, including her own work and Gutiérrez Aragón's. 'Creo que nuestra generación fue la primera que de repente dijo que no le daba la gana autocensurarse y entonces se montó un pifostio estupendo' (I think our generation was the first that suddenly said, no, we don't fancy self-censorship, and all hell broke loose) (Calpena 2022, 5).

The Filmoteca documentation on the film is not complete, consisting of two complaints and three letters. Missing are details of the production process, like shooting permissions; missing too, regrettably, are teachers' comments on the script. The first, undated, document is a complaint by Bartolomé herself concerning the no-show on set of actor Elvira Ponce (1965a). We do not have access to the response but the name does not appear on the short's credits. The second, mutatis mutandis, is a joint letter of complaint by six actors (not including Ponce) regarding the late notice of a change of location for the shoot (Cotoz et al. 1965). Unfortunately undated again is a letter by the proposed producer of the short. This reveals more serious difficulties for Bartolomé as the letter seems to have been written without her knowledge. Written before the shoot, the producer frets that the project will give 'quebradores de cabeza a todo el equipo' (headaches to the whole team) in general; he or she then numbers their concerns: the proposed number of actors; the proposed use of non-Film School personnel (someone, presumably the Director de Estudios (Director of Studies), appears to agree with the letter-writer, for, next to the names Bartolomé proposed, Luisa Muñoz and Antonio Pascual Costalreda, a person wielding a red pen has written 'no', and the protagonists ended up as Film School students Pilar Romero (Carmen) and Fernando Lacaci (Juan)); the excessive length of the script; the insufficient quantity of film stock; and the high number of scenes, in particular. Although the letter concludes by declaring that the film is 'muy importante para mí' (very important for me), this reads like a producer covering his or her own back should there be future problems (Labybam [approximate transcription;

name partly illegible], n.d.). Whatever the case, the producer, as listed in the credits, ended up being Gabriel Ibarra.

In fact, difficulties with her producer might have been the least of Bartolomé's problems. The next two letters, handwritten by Bartolomé on 30 October 1965, belong to a later period when the film had been failed, and she had been told to repeat the year. One-sided as they are, their insights are extraordinary. As I have discussed, critics attribute the Film School's failing of *Carmen* to its taboo subject matter and irreverent approach (e.g. García López 2020, 2). Bartolomé's letters also point to gender discrimination.

The first letter (Bartolomé 1965b) runs to five pages and contains fifteen points, which lay out problems like the delays during the shoot, then more serious issues concerning the post-shoot dubbing and editing of the film. These, according to Bartolomé, were delayed, as both laboratories prioritised other students' work. It is difficult to underestimate the anguish the director must have gone through concerning these delays, for, no wonder she was in a hurry: she was heavily pregnant. According to her, and without access to any information on how her requests were handled, she states that she made a special plea to dub and edit the work early, before her baby was born. She was apparently given an editing date in June, but, on the very day allotted, she says an accident triggered the premature birth of her son. His fragile health, she recounts, meant she could not work on the short till he became stronger. Happily, two months on, this was possible. However, when she then went to the School, she found that no one was present to help: they had gone on holiday. Bartolomé finishes by noting that the present letter is a written record of the explanation she gave to the Jefe de Estudios (Director of Studies) during a meeting the day before in which he had informed her of the 'possible abandonment', i.e. failure, of the short, and consequent need for her to repeat the year. The second letter (Bartolomé 1965c), written on the same day, details her insistence on proper support for her future Film School work.

It is important to note, again, that this 'exchange' is entirely one-sided. What did the Jefe de Estudios say to the young mother of a premature newborn, Bartolomé, on 29 October 1965? Were there responses to the letters we are reading? We do not know. The fact is that *Carmen* – a film made by a pregnant student, whose request to complete it before her delivery was seemingly ignored, and whose attempt to complete it after delivery was also thwarted – was failed by the School and Bartolomé was obliged to repeat the year. If the later treatment of *Margarita y el lobo* is better known, as more spectacular, her experience with *Carmen* seems to be a case of gender discrimination in a prestigious educational establishment of the state.

Yet despite this – it is difficult to suggest because of this – the film itself is extraordinary. Forcefully exposing the consequences of a lack of contraception and abortion in a working-class context, it retains its power today, not least as debates on the subject of termination have continued, or have reopened some sixty years on, the world over.[5] But it is not just the originality and urgency of the material covered in *Carmen* that make it important. As I will argue of Bartolomé's work throughout this book, it is also her handling of form. Redeploying some of the skills on show in the documentary *Cruzada del Rosario*, there are elements of a documentary approach in *Carmen*, especially in the picking-out of telling details (like the marital guidance book flung in the puddle, as we will see). More striking is the development of music as counterpoint. The extra-diegetic musical motif of guitar strings in *La noche* effectively underscored contrasts between niece Lucía and her uncle Dr Valdés's oppressive home. In *Carmen*, the musical intertext is very well-known and specific – Georges Bizet's *Carmen* (1875) – 'Habanera' and 'Aire del toreador' are named in credits – and its impact is striking. Conjured up by the active, perhaps overactive, imaginations of heterosexual French male travel-writers and composers (Bizet's opera is based on Prosper Mérimée's original tales of 1845), Carmen is the exoticised and orientalised archetypal femme fatale, who seduces men and never falls pregnant. Bartolomé reuses the name for the embattled housewife of Madrid's Carabanchel neighbourhood. With four children and a fifth conceived over the course of the film, and without access to legal contraception or abortion, Carmen, burdened by her own fertility, has only two options: avoid conception, or try a dangerous do-it-yourself abortion.

Commencing with a male voiceover that cheerily announces 'Y Carmen y Juan se casaron muy jóvenes, y tuvieron muchos hijos, y fueron muy felices…' (And Carmen and Juan married very young, and had lots of children, and were very happy…), Bartolomé here both recalls the comfortingly familiar lines of a fairy tale, but simultaneously undoes them: her tale does not end with marriage and 'happily ever after', but starts with marriage and problems thereafter. In the credit sequence that immediately follows, she announces the contrast. The extra-diegetic music track is a jaunty version of the aria 'Habanera', but thoughts of being a sultry temptress are far from our heroine's mind: the stills of the image track in the bar here are tightly framed to convey the claustrophobia of her large family (Figure 1.2). The children Carmen and Juan already have fill and spill out of the frame. When the film proper begins, Carmen's present predicament is succinctly presented to the viewer – the burden of so many children – as is the future one, fear of more. The presence of a bare-armed young woman in the bar (Elsa Baeza) triggers undisguised lechery among the men, despite the children being there too; Carmen fears that her husband's desire is stirred and she will run the risk of another pregnancy. The family leave and walk past a funfair – both the fun and the fair contrast ironically with Carmen's predicament. The contrast is even more forcefully made by the deployment of non-diegetic music again here. Carmen is harried, yet the tinny, cheerful singing voice insists on the opposite: 'Somos españoles, y tenemos paz' (We are Spanish, and we have peaceful contentment). An unpeaceful argument between the couple

Figure 1.2 Carmen (Pilar Romero) with a family that exceeds the frame in *Carmen de Carabanchel* (1965)

then triggers Juan's futile attempt to procure contraception at the local pharmacy.

The soundtrack thus offers a counterpoint to Carmen's predicament – both the Francoist propaganda of Spanish peace and the French erotic visions of sexually available, apparently infertile and thus responsibility-free, women. Developing the inclusion of the television cartoon *Bugs Bunny* in *La noche*, Bartolomé also creates counterpoints by including two television programmes within the diegesis of *Carmen*. First, when the family watch television after their lunch, Carmen is confronted with a chaste figure of femininity in *Reina Santa / The Holy Queen* (Gil 1947), precisely as Juan suggests she should have become a nun if she was not willing to bear as many children as his sexual desire dictated. He does then apologise for this comment, but a fifth is soon on the way. Later, the children watch a sequence of a Western in which a group of white frontier men mounted on horseback circle around a darker-skinned woman, causing her to fall to the ground: Carmen too has fallen pregnant.

Further scenes succinctly summarise Carmen's efforts to seek support. As Juan and his male workmates leave the office – we see 'Administrativo Central' on the plaque behind them – his attitude is summarised by the non-diegetic 'Aire de toreador' by Bizet on the soundtrack. Bartolomé's characterisation of Juan is not unsympathetic, however. As we have seen, he does try to buy contraception. His next attempt, buying Carmen a book called *Intimidad conjugal* (Conjugal Intimacy), is met by his wife's furious despair – we have seen her spend the previous days vomiting owing to the new pregnancy. Juan presents the book to her as she hangs washing on the balcony. What is noticeable in the sequence is that their voices are inaudible as they are at a distance; Bartolomé is more interested in the extreme long shot that shows their balcony, and that of multiple others, which conveys that their predicament is repeated many times over in the apartment block (years later Almodóvar would similarly locate the predicament of his embattled housewife, Carmen Maura's Gloria, against a backdrop of multiple similar predicaments, also by pulling to extreme long shot to show her flat as one of many in an apartment block in *¡¿Qué he hecho yo para merecer esto!? / What Have I Done to Deserve This!?*'s Madrid borough, barrio de la Concepción). Next, Bartolomé cuts to an extreme close-up: Carmen has flung the book from the balcony, and it lands in a muddy puddle where one of the children plays with it, as if were the premonition of a new plaything: a future sibling.

Next, like the unhelpful chemist and her husband's marital guidance book, the Church offers no solace to Carmen either. After a ceremony in which the priest extols large families and 'sacrificios heroicos' (heroic sacrifices), Carmen believes her desire to have no more children is being punished by God when one of them is lost: 'es un castigo del cielo' (it's a punishment from God), she despairs. Bizet's 'Habanera', the aria of the childless seductress, returns on the non-diegetic score to provide the musical counterpoint to our Carmen's anguish, then relief, as the boy is found.[6]

Carmen does find some solace in female friends and neighbours. Along with the use of music as ironic counterpoint, Bartolomé's portrayal of this female support is both original and shocking. The director herself was living in a flat adjacent to the Madrid borough when she became pregnant with her first child (whose birth she describes in the Film School letter, as we have seen) and recounts in subsequent interviews the differences between her own experience and those of her working-class housewife neighbours. The difference is all about social class: Bartolomé had access to birth control through a certain doctor used by middle-class women,[7] and was thus delighted with her own pregnancy as she knew she had control of when she had children (Calpena 2022, 6). Her neighbours, however, always fell into despair over their pregnancies. In the stairwells between flats, in the street and at the hairdressers, these women would exchange dangerous, occasionally fatal, do-it-yourself abortion methods. Thus, when Carmen is in the early stages of a new gestation and experiences a hot flush at the hairdresser, her friend Claudia, who is also pregnant, accompanies her outside and suggests a remedy that is as cheap and accessible as it is potentially lethal. In her village, she declares matter-of-factly, the butcher's wife swears by a bucket of hot ammonia. In the following scene, after finishing the washing, we see that Carmen is off to the shop to refill her ammonia bottle. The 'Habanera' returns on the soundtrack, and, in the next scene, the full bottle is on her kitchen table as she prepares the children's afternoon snack. She seems to have second thoughts and pours it away. Next comes the news that Claudia is in hospital, following a failed termination attempt (this is based on the real-life abortion attempt, and consequent hospitalisation, of one of Bartolomé's neighbours at the time (Bermejo 2017, 5)).

At the film's ending, Carmen sexually submits to Juan again – she is resigned, hardly aroused, as she is pregnant already anyway. Bartolomé then cuts to a series of still photographs of the neighbourhood children playing in the muddy puddles of the streets. Her images of them are neither sentimental nor critical; the children are neither cute nor obnoxious. The only toy they possess is a wheelbarrow, so the only game they play is carting each other around in it. The image neatly conveys that they are too poor for toys (though the family does have a television) and that they must make do with what is at hand (like the do-it-yourself terminations); carrying each other in a wheelbarrow, meanwhile, also implies burden.

In *Carmen de Carabanchel*, the tone is matter-of-fact: Juan is not vilified, and the existing children are not monstrous. The spirit is one of getting by and making do, like the support among women as they both look after one another's children and share homemade abortion methods (another suggestion is nettle tea). Both areas of support are interchangeable, of a piece. The short evokes what Parvati Nair would go on to describe as Bartolomé's documentary attention to the 'grain of everyday life' (2021a), which, this book argues in Chapter 5, is a key strand of the director's feminist documentary aesthetic. Her use of ironic musical counterpoint, especially with Bizet's *Carmen*, is also a key manifestation of ironic humour, which, as we will also see in Chapter 2, underpins *Margarita y el lobo*.

Sonia García López's study of Film School work suggests Bartolomé's *La noche del doctor Valdés* and *Carmen de Carabanchel* are typical of pieces by women directors who portray 'el amor romántico y sus fallas' (romantic love and its pitfalls) – in the cases she analyses, this love is always heterosexual. Her study reaches double-edged conclusions. She reveals the quality of the work of other women who, besides Bartolomé and Molina, studied Direction at the School, some of whom we have seen as actors in the shorts: Manuela González-Haba, María Elisa Corona, Ángela Asensio y de Merlo, Teresa Dressel, Elena Lumbreras (in the period before she added 'H' to her forename) and Kathryn Waldo. While on the one hand, García López finds a celebration of female desire in Corona's assessment pieces, on the other, the exploration of heterosexuality from a female point of view in these shorts (she does not mention any of homosexuality) is generally one of 'la expresión de la frustración, el conflicto generacional y, muy a menudo, una profunda melancolía' (the expression of frustration, generational conflict and, very often, profound melancholy) (2021, 323). This sense of a common cause of feminist denunciation, which is shared in all this work, speaks to the creative companionship among these students at the School. But our subsequent knowledge that only Bartolomé and Molina succeeded in graduating in Direction means the potential that these other women's work presented to the Spanish cinema industry was unfulfilled. The future cases of some, like Waldo, who turned to Production, or Lumbreras, who left Spain for Italy owing to the situation (Ledesma 2014; and Missero 2022, 128–30), are known, and beginning to be better known; vital new work like García López's is beginning to uncover other cases.

Film School was bitter-sweet for Bartolomé, then. Sharing anti-Franco, Left-wing politics in the 'nest' has been the focus of a number of studies, as we have seen; new work is revealing feminist companionship too. But Bartolomé and Molina are the exceptions in graduating. This chapter has attempted to strike a balance in addressing Bartolomé's experiences, between inspiration and support, and obstruction and censorship. It has detailed, too, the case of gender prejudice that Bartolomé suffered at the School, especially her experience of lack of support in the post-production of *Carmen*, and then the School's decision to fail the piece. The experience appears to have armed the director with further determination and resolve: she would need to call on both of these and more for *Margarita y el lobo*, as we will see next.

Notes

1 See Appendix Interview, in which Bartolomé recalls that the costs to the state of the Film School were even similar to those of the Medical School.
2 The title of a final-year assessment piece by Antonio Drove, *La caza de brujas / The Witch Hunt* (1967) was to prove prophetic. Drove had successfully graduated with the piece in 1967, but it was subjected to Baena's new procedure of sending the current and three previous years' Film School work to the censors. Quoting it in her article title, García López uses it to summarise Baena's repressive tenure (2022).

3 These documents are all coded PRA/2/1 in the documentation. I have not made separate entries for these in the Bibliography (Film School Documentation).
4 Sor Anunciata is given as Conchita Gómez Conde in the PRA/2/1 documentation; Inés is not listed.
5 For example, the US Supreme Court's overturning of *Roe vs Wade*, 24 June 2022.
6 Ana Asensio (2022) points out that the loss of the child chimes with the highly sentimental treatment of the same experience in the Francoist, pro-natalist *La gran familia / The Great Family* (Palacios), released just three years earlier in 1962. See Faulkner (2006, 36–7), on twenty-nine-year-old Amparo Soler Leal's performance as the improbable mother of fifteen in this film (her oldest child is played by an actor just seven years her junior). Like Carmen, Mercedes conceives a further child – her sixteenth – over the course of Palacios's film, but, while her working-class sister considers a dangerous do-it-yourself abortion, middle-class Mercedes's new child is heralded as being nothing less than the new Messiah. She announces her pregnancy as the family watch a performance of Handel's 'Hallelujah Chorus' on a neighbour's television (2006, 32); the child's paternity musically confirmed throughout the film by the association of that melody with the father Carlos's musical motif (2006, 34).
7 Bartolomé uses the graphic phrase 'el doctor de los coños progres' (Doctor for progressive, liberal cunts) to refer to Dr Hernández, a Communist Party member, who imported diaphragms from the UK but, she stresses, did not conduct illegal abortions (Bermejo 2017, 3).

2

Feminism and Francoism, *Margarita y el lobo*

As in Chapter 1, this chapter reconsiders how we account for the work of a future director while still at Film School, then reviews the School's little-studied archive records to explore Bartolomé's treatment as a student. It therefore analyses the medium-length *Margarita y el lobo / Margarita and the Wolf* (1969) as if it were the completed film Bartolomé intended it to be, and not as an early indication of a later auteurist vision that would be consolidated by a full career working in the industry itself, since censorship prevented her from fulfilling this ambition to extend it to feature-length. (In Chapter 3 I scrutinise the changes made to the medium-length film in the 1974 script for the feature, which was never filmed.)

Margarita would have been a treat for the audiences it was meant to reach. A hybrid musical comedy, it charts its lively, liberal protagonist Margarita's (Julia Peña) journey from marriage to cute, conservative Lorenzo (Juan Antonio Amor) to separation – divorce would not be re-legalised in Spain until 1981, when democracy had returned – and takes wicked aim at the repressive role of both the Franco regime and the Catholic church in women's lives along the way. Although Bartolomé successfully graduated from Film School with this medium-length piece, as we have seen (Chapter 1), School Director Juan Julio Baena intervened to send it to Franco's censors, who promptly banned it and placed Bartolomé on a blacklist that meant she was unable to make her feature début for almost a decade (Chapter 4). In the director's own words in an interview on the occasion of its première at an international film festival, San Sebastián, in 2004:[1]

> Cuando el director de la escuela, José Julio Baena [*sic*: Juan Julio Baena], la presentó a la censura oficial pues, claro, la prohibieron y eso significa quemar los negativos; afortunadamente la salvamos, pero me costó no poder hacer cine hasta muchos años después, hasta que murió Franco. (When the School Director, José Julio Baena [*sic*: Juan Julio Baena], presented it to the official censors, well, of course, they banned it and this meant burning the negatives. Fortunately, we saved them, but it meant I couldn't make films until many years later, after Franco's death.) (Yoldi 2004)[2]

Yet it might not have been so. Fortunately, before Baena's interventions, the owner of the production company X Films, Juan Huarte, had seen the film at a private screening and 'estaba enamorado' (was in love (with it)) (Calpena 2022, 8). In a 2022 interview with Ana Calpena, Bartolomé recounts that the enamoured Huarte managed to smuggle a clandestine copy out of the School should future problems arise (2022, 8). He correctly anticipated that they would. It was also Huarte, along with X Films producer José María González Sinde, who supported Bartolomé's subsequent attempts to make the *Margarita* medium-length film into a feature (see Chapter 3). At the same time, and as Bartolomé revealed in the same 2004 interview with Pili Yoldi at San Sebastián, Huarte, again, and the President of the European branch of Paramount, Christian Ferry, proposed she screen the film in Paris, alongside Agnès Varda's short, *Réponse de femmes: Notre corps, notre sexe / Women Reply: Our Body, Our Sex* (1975). Bartolomé took legal advice, and was told that if she allowed the French screening of the banned film that was the School's property and not hers, it would be illegal and she would not be allowed to return to Spain. With a young family, and having already moved from Africa to Spain, she decided to stay, for by 1969 the return of democracy – given Franco's age and health – seemed imminent (Calpena 2022, 9). We can only turn to the past conditional to consider what might have been had she made a different decision and followed other great Spanish film directors, like Luis Buñuel and Margarita Aleixandre, into exile. Might she have enjoyed a career on a par with the celebrated Varda – who made over sixty films by the time of her death in 2019 – had she gone into exile in France? What might the histories of Spanish and world feminist cinemas have looked like had that been the case?

While these questions lie in the realms of speculation, this chapter pays particular attention to the transnational influences and address of *Margarita* in order to consider what the reception of such a film beyond Spain might have been in the early 1970s.[3] It examines the film, first as an innovative example of literary adaptation in Spanish cinema, which looks back to the 1960s via its cross-border engagement with the French writer Christiane Rochefort's original novel *Les Stances à Sophie / Céline and Marriage*, first published in 1963.[4] This creative relationship established between Bartolomé and Rochefort, the French feminist activist and writer, would have enhanced, one imagines, audience appreciation of the film at the Paris screening that never took place. Second, this chapter argues that the film also looks forward to cross-cultural developments in international feminism in the 1970s, with which Bartolomé might have directly engaged had she released the film in France. For example, by linking Margarita's character arc shift from innocence to knowledge to the figure of 'Caperucita' (Little Red Riding Hood), of the eponymous fairy tale, and by associating 'el lobo feroz' (the big, bad wolf) of 'Los tres cerditos' (The Three Little Pigs) tale with terrifying masculinity and repressive state patriarchy, Bartolomé not only condemns Francoism – as I propose in this chapter title's purposeful attachment of the opposing concepts 'feminism' and 'Francoism' to the film title's nouns 'Margarita' and 'the wolf'. I also argue that this feminist exploration of terrifying masculinity in the form of the wolf anticipates British writer Angela Carter's engagement with fairy tales in the collection of short stories *The Bloody Chamber and Other Stories*, first published in 1979.

Bartolomé's *Margarita y el lobo* at Film School: 'va a haber muchos, muchos líos... Es una locura' (there are going to be absolutely loads of problems... It's madness)

We begin, though, in Spain. When final-year student Bartolomé was planning the film in autumn 1968, she was given the contradictory feedback that the script should be reduced by a quarter, yet it simultaneously contained too little dialogue (Proharam 1968). The documentation then shows that a series of teachers, who had themselves previously directed films that were critical of the Franco regime, obstructed her progress. For Julio Diamante, the script was 'malito' (a little weak) (1968), but for José Luis García Sánchez, 'muy adecuado' (very appropriate) – though the latter found the planned camera work 'totalmente inadecuada' (totally inadequate) (1968). In a premonition of future censorship, a further, unfortunately undated and anonymous document with official School letter-head states *Margarita* should not be authorised as it stands, picking out the scene of the University student demonstration as particularly problematic 'por los peligros que encierra' (for the dangers it contains), and, again, the unfinished nature of the script (Anon. 1968a); in a handwritten note the situation is summarised in the colloquial comments directed to a 'Julio' (presumably Diamante): 'va a haber muchos, muchos líos... Es una locura' (there are going to be absolutely loads of problems [...] It's madness) (Anon. 1968b).

Bartolomé's responses are not recorded, but by 7 December the project had been accepted by Baena, on the condition that the script should be reduced by a quarter, and that she should meet with teachers 'Ramos' (presumably José María), 'Borau' (José Luis) and 'Diamante' (Julio) 'que le harán algunas indicaciones' (who will give you some instructions) (Baena 1968a); but by 13 December Baena writes again to admonish her for failing to show up to the meeting (Baena 1968b)! The minutes available in the documentation confirm a meeting finally took place on 20 December, when the project was confirmed (Anon. 1968c), though Baena is writing again – on Boxing Day, no less! – to warn Bartolomé that the shoot required too many locations (the standard length of shoot was ten days) (Baena 1968c). Further obstacles over the following two months included a scolding for Bartolomé arriving late to a meeting (Anon. 1969a); a recommendation that the shoot be suspended as it threatened to go over the standard seventy-thousand-peseta budget (Jacoste and Cunillés 1969); further undisclosed 'reservas' (reservations) expressed in late January (Anon. 1969b); and Head of Production Alberto Ochoa's attempt to quit the project (Ochoa 1969). Little wonder that on completion Bartolomé herself writes to Baena twice. In the first letter she understandably cannot resist pointing out that 'los malos augurios' (the bad omens) were unfounded and that the film – 'que según expertos de producción era irrealizable' (which, according to production experts, was unfilmable) – was finished (Bartolomé 1969a). The second contains an official complaint that she was not provided with a script for dubbing (Bartolomé 1969b, 2) and notes on record 'la negligencia de un alumno' (a student's negligence) and – who can blame her for pointing this out too? – 'la incapacidad de esta escuela de someter [a dicho alumno], como me sometió a mí, a una disciplina académica' (the inability of this School to discipline [this student] in academic matters, as I have been disciplined) (Bartolomé 1969b, 2).

After all this came state censorship. Here, Bartolomé was a victim of bad timing, for, as we have seen, sending School work to the censors (even though the films might never be publicly screened) was an initiative of Baena, the former Communist Party member who turned fervent Francoist when he took over in the academic year of 1968–69. His transfer of political allegiance from one side to the other is particularly extraordinary given his previous work as a cinematographer in dissident productions. Film Archives documentation also includes Bartolomé's own statement (1968) that her final year assessment piece was postponed by a year owing to delays occasioned by the relocation of the School site itself: this perhaps explains the inclusion of all three dates 1967, 1968 and 1969 in the opening credits of *Margarita*. But even if these delays had not occurred, Baena would have caught her out, for his repressive interventions were retrospective: he sent work from the previous three academic years to the censors.[5]

From Christiane Rochefort to Cecilia Bartolomé

With a twin focus on literary adaptation and transnationality, this chapter argues for a *Margarita* that reaches beyond national debates about cinematic realism, and reaches out to contemporary international developments in feminism. With the exception of Josexto Cerdán and Marina Díaz's volume of 2001, scholarly attention towards the director's work has only very slowly followed her public recovery, which gathered pace after the San Sebastián screening of *Margarita* in 2004, and has continued since thanks to the awareness-raising activities of festivals and collectives like CIMA since (see Introduction, note 17). In the mid-2010s, two articles appeared. In a survey of female directors in Spain, Silvia Guillamón Carrasco hailed *Margarita* as 'la primera película feminista del cine español'

(Spain's first feminist film) (2015, 289). This is a phrase I have also used elsewhere (Faulkner 2022a), while noting that it must always be placed in quotation marks,[6] not least because there are a number of contenders: first, there are the films that expound 'feminist discourse' discussed by Susan Martin-Márquez (1999) and others (see Introduction); second, other Film School work (García López 2021); as well as, third, alternative films from Bartolomé's own filmography.[7] Next, in 2016, Sonia García Sahagún analysed music in *Margarita* to argue that it offered 'una revolución estética en el cine español' (an aesthetic revolution in Spanish cinema), rejecting realism for a 'una mirada completamente nueva' (completely new gaze) (2016, 77). More recently, Sonia García López's work on this film (2023), along with her studies of Film School pieces by both women and men (2020; 2021; 2022), importantly place *Margarita* in the wider contexts of the Film School. In summary, García Sahagún's 2016 affirmation that *Margarita* 'es ya hoy considerado como un epítome de feminismo y modernidad dentro del cine español' (is today considered the epitome of feminism and modernity in Spanish cinema) (2016, 75) may still be premature, but such recognition is certainly an aspiration for Bartolomé scholarship.

This chapter also argues that *Margarita* reveals a feminist director ahead of her time, but seeks to reframe these questions within wider transnational contexts. It analyses the film as an adaptation of Rochefort's novel for the first time to demonstrate that this aesthetic process of intermedial transfer is also an ideological adaptation of developments in 1960s French feminism, including both Rochefort's portrayal of female subjectivity and her use of comedy, to a Spanish context. Looking to the future, Bartolomé's development of questions of female subjectivity on film, feminism and comedy, and her original riff on the fairy tale (not found in Rochefort), also anticipate insights into these questions developed in wider feminist theory in the 1970s. As previously suggested, this Chapter thus allows itself to speculate about a future as an exile from Spain that Bartolomé did not choose when she refused the Paramount offer. Had she chosen that future life, her own work might have explicitly engaged with the developments in feminism that *Margarita* nonetheless seems to anticipate. These include British film scholar Laura Mulvey's 1975 investigation of the male gaze, 'Visual Pleasure and Narrative Cinema', which Bartolomé's portrayal of Margarita's alternative, active female gaze seems to predict; French writer Hélène Cixous's 1975 manifesto for 'écriture feminine', 'Le rire de la Méduse' (1975),[8] which, again, Bartolomé's engagement with comedy seems to anticipate; or, as mentioned, and most extensively, British author Angela Carter's insights into the fairy tale in her 1979 short stories (1996). In part, this chapter aims retrospectively and creatively to imagine these missed encounters.

Bartolomé's choice of source text for *Margarita*, the contemporary French feminist novel *Céline and Marriage*, which looks to colloquial language and humour to deliver its critique of patriarchy, immediately distances her work from the intra-national approach of most literary adaptations in Spanish cinema in the 1960s. These included adaptations of contemporary popular theatre (e.g. *La ciudad no es para mí / The City's Not For Me*, Lazaga 1965, based on Lozano), a tendency that has received limited critical attention; and adaptations of twentieth-century Spanish prose writers (e.g. *La tía Tula / Aunt Tula*, Picazo 1964, based on Unamuno), to which critics have paid more attention. Eschewing, then, a national literary tradition to which Bartolomé perhaps felt less connection owing to her early life outside Spain in Africa (though peninsular school curricula were followed in the colonies, see Appendix Interview p. 217), it was no doubt logical for the director to look beyond national borders. Rochefort's novel, which her then husband José Luis Alcaine suggested she consider (Tejada 2020), provided both creative feminist inspiration and the stimulating aesthetic challenges of cinematic adaptation. Writing from today's vantage point of knowing the future choices Bartolomé would make, which are always underpinned by her commitment to popular cultural forms that were accessible to audiences, we may affirm that the attraction of *Céline and Marriage* lay in part in its straightforward readability, achieved by colloquial language and literary realism, and thus its popularity.[9] When we add to this popularity Rochefort's ethical commitment to feminism and aesthetic preference for satirical humour, it is not difficult to see the appeal to the young Bartolomé. *Margarita* and the director's filmography as a whole also fuse accessibility, commitment and humour.[10] Moving from 1960s France to 1960s Spain, however, it is important to note that if literary critic Diana Holmes picks out 'anger' as critical to an understanding of Rochefort (1996, 248) – anger at patriarchy, anger at the bourgeoisie – to these we must add, for Bartolomé, anger at the Catholic church and anger at the Franco regime.

Bearing this significant difference in context in my mind, we may examine some of the cinematic solutions Bartolomé finds to adaptation, which, I argue, seed her own creativity in *Margarita*. Principal among these is her rendering of what Margaret-Anne Hutton named Rochefort's 'double voice' (1998, 61), the first-person narrative of the naïve, contemporary protagonist Céline, which is contrasted with that of the knowing, retrospective narrator Céline – the multiple shifts between these two in the text unmarked by either description or punctuation. Take, for example, the opening pages, which must have been the hook for Bartolomé, and for whom finding 'le machin déjà tout constitué' (things already seem to have been set in stone) must have been particularly relevant to her own experience of returning to Franco's 1960s Spain as a young woman. 'Ce qu'il y a avec nous autres pauvres filles' (The problem us poor other girls have), begins Rochefort:

> c'est qu'on n'est pas instruites. On arrive là-dedans, sans véritable information. On trouve le machin déjà tout constitué, en apparence solide comme du roc, il paraît que ç'a toujours été comme ça, que ça continuera jusqu'à la fin des temps, et il n'y a pas de raison que ça change. (is that we're not educated. We arrive, without real information. We find that the machine is already all made, seemingly as solid as a rock, as if it has always been like that, and that it will continue like that till the end of time, and there's no reason for it to change.) (1963, 7)

Yet this knowing, interpretative tone is abandoned in the next vignette, which begins with husband-to-be Philippe's complaints about Céline's appearance, sleeping arrangements and reading. Rochefort intersperses these with Céline's description of Philippe's physical attractions '1 mètre 82, blond, yeux pervenche, nez adorable, bouche volontaire, front vaste et intelligent, etc' (1 metre 82, blond, blue eyes, adorable nose, determined mouth, wide, intelligent brow, etc.) (1963, 8) – the insertion of that 'etc' indicates the future exasperation with his irritating prattle.

Bartolomé's cinematic strategies to convey this double voice through her couple – renamed, as we have seen, Margarita and Lorenzo – are various. First, the intertwining of present and past in the flashback structure of the film conveys doubleness: it begins with marital separation, then cuts to the events that lead to it. As such, the viewer cannot read Margarita and Lorenzo's meeting, courtship, wedding and married life as a singular, direct narrative, but must interpret them at least doubly as overlain with the forthcoming separation. Further, I interpret Bartolomé's significant and entirely original addition of nine musical numbers to this film – so many that they allow for its generic demarcation as a musical – as a second strategy to convey Rochefort's doubling. We are often confronted with jarring and amusing disjunctures between image and soundtracks, like those we have already noted in *La noche del Dr Valdés* and especially *Carmen de Carabanchel* (Chapter 2). Third, Bartolomé extends an invitation to the spectator to view critically the events of the couple's life, and compare past and present, by inserting introductory sections to the five parts of the film, in which the protagonist breaks the fourth wall and reads abridged versions of Rochefort's novel direct to camera. Through framing in medium shot and the presence of the written text, the character Margarita is thus associated both with the religious authority of the priest, who is also framed in medium shot in the credit sequence, and the secular authority of a television newsreader, who is always found in medium shot. In these interpolations, the combination of this implied religious and secular authority and the content of the text read aloud is often highly humorous. Actor Peña can scarcely stifle a giggle as she solemnly pronounces in Part Four that friendship between bored bourgeois housewives 'es el mejor camino para el lesbianismo' (is the best way to lesbianism) (or, as Rochefort has it, 'c'est le mariage que doit rendre lesbienne' (it's marriage that must make you a lesbian) (1963, 138)) – problematically, homosexuality seems to be played for laughs here by both Rochefort and Bartolomé.

In the opening sequences of *Margarita* we may observe these three strategies of doubling in action. Like the switch between the opening vignettes of *Céline and Marriage* examined above, Bartolomé uses flashback to move from the present of Margarita's world-weariness ('mi vida es cosa mía' (my life is my own business)) to the giggling innocence of her meeting Lorenzo when she jumps into his car during the student riots (about which Film School teachers, we recall, warned, and which the censors, of course, banned). However,

Bartolomé, from the outset, further layers Rochefort's doubleness by adding to the French writer's targets both the Catholic Church in Spain and the dictatorship. Thus, visually, the priest's lofty position and symbols of authority, like the crucifix and bible, contrast with Margarita's on-trend 1960s mini skirt (Figure 2.1). Linguistically, Bartolomé slyly undoes the pomposity of the priest's retort to Margarita's 'mi vida… es cosa mía' (my life is my own business), when he says 'cosa suya y de Dios' (your business, and God's), by having him then lengthily leaf through his sacred text to find the number of the correct entry for the separation document! We are also invited to note Margarita's identification with the fight for democracy when Bartolomé chooses to cut from Lorenzo's subsequent description of his future wife to his parents, to the students cries of '¡Libertad!' (Freedom!) and their brandishing of banners that demand 'democracia' (democracy): Margarita, too, will stand for freedom and democracy.

The extra-diegetic music that accompanies these scenes further encourages the doubleness of Rochefort's novel in an entirely original way. In the opening credit sequence we hear Lalo Schifrin's theme to *Mission: Impossible*, broadcast on North American television from 1966 to 1973, and broadcast in dubbed version in Spain as Bartolomé planned *Margarita*. The theme is still highly recognisable owing to the subsequent Tom Cruise films (from the first, in 1996, to the eighth announced for release in 2025). In an interview in 2016, Bartolomé described the inclusion of the theme as a

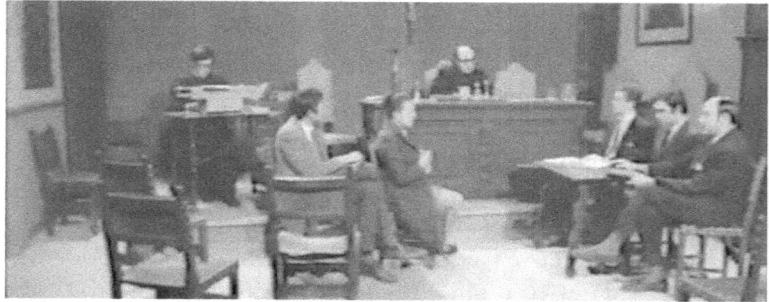

Figure 2.1 Marital separation in Franco's Spain. Margarita (Julia Peña), centre, in *Margarita y el lobo* (1969). Photograph courtesy of the Filmoteca Española

joke about marital separation 'para asemejar [...] la imposibilidad de la mujer para hacer este tipo de cosas' (to draw a comparison with the impossibility of women doing this sort of thing) (García Sahagún 2016, 80, n. 21). The joke still works. At the start of the film, when we first hear Schifrin's theme, 'impossibility' is an intra-diegetic reference to marital separation; when Bartolomé repeats the theme at the close of the film, 'impossibility' becomes also an extra-diegetic reference to making the film *Margarita* itself. Next comes Bartolomé's second reference (after the title) to fairy tale. She includes a popular song, the version of 'Who's Afraid of the Big Bad Wolf?' composed by Frank Churchill for the cartoon *The Three Little Pigs* (Gillett 1933) (García Sahagún 2016, 80). Its childish cheerfulness is undercut by the image of a downcast Margarita in the film; its jolly notes also belie the original tale's encoding of terrifying male sexuality and violence in the figure of the wolf.

After the couple meets at the riots, we then see them embrace in a bedroom, but Bartolomé continues to insist that the audience adopt a critical perspective: she will not let us get too comfortable as she accompanies this scene with urgent extra-diegetic drumbeats. (Further embraces portrayed in the film include those where the couple have stripped to their underwear – today these images may be tame, but in Franco's Spain of 1969, they were, of course, scandalous.) Bartolomé then cuts to the first interpolation for Part One, in which Margarita reads an abridged version of the opening of the novel cited above. 'Lo que pasa con nosotras es que no estamos instruidas...' (The problem us girls have is that we're not educated...) are words that are especially resonant in a Spanish context, where female education is a particular concern of Spanish feminism. The increases in female access to higher education (discussed in Chapter 2), limited as they were to the middle classes, meant these concerns were still relevant to Bartolomé's 1969.

The second interpolation, Part Two, returns to this theme of female education and Bartolomé uses it both to replicate, in film, Rochefort's 'double voice', and explore the contradictions of this historical period in Spain. After the implied question in the interpolation 'No sé qué hacer conmigo' (I don't know what to do with myself), Bartolomé cuts to Lorenzo, who, of course, has the answers. The director's handling of film form here is particularly deft, both landing critical blows on patriarchy, and being fresh and funny. In this sequence it is now Lorenzo who strikes the pose of authority (that was first adopted by the priest in the opening sequence), but here in a domestic setting: he is captured in long-medium shot, centre frame, hands in pockets, and paternalistically explaining 'Te lo digo por tu bien' (I'm telling you for your own good). Bartolomé even slyly places a poster of Leonardo da Vinci's *Mona Lisa* (1503) behind him: after Pygmalion, the male artist par excellence to be celebrated across the centuries for pinning down and defining mysterious womanhood. Bartolomé repeats the footage of Lorenzo's striding towards the reclining Margarita seven times – for seven deadly sins. His words of advice to Margarita change with each repetition, though the footage is the same, as the words are added at the dubbing stage. Bartolomé is thus able to include seven of Lorenzo's complaints, including Margarita wearing laddered tights, not knowing how to sew on a zip, and his criticism for 'perder el tiempo llenándote la cabeza de libros de los que no retienes ni una palabra' (wasting time filling your head with books about which you don't remember a single word) (all of this comes from Rochefort 1963, 8). Margarita's presence is spliced in by high-angle shots of her looking up, each of the seven times a little closer, and ends with a zoom to her face as she asks 'pero […], ¿qué es una vida normal?' (but, what is a normal life?) (also from Rochefort 1963, 10). This time Bartolomé replies, with a cut to Noticiarios y Documentales (commonly shortened to 'NO-DO') footage of working-class women, who are too busy with agricultural, nursing, and secretarial work to indulge in such philosophical musings. This Left-wing political critique is a welcome break from the rather claustrophobic focus on the wealthy bourgeoisie and housewives' ennui of Rochefort's original.

The film proceeds in this innovative, multi-media mode, in which Bartolomé the reader picks out key moments of Rochefort's text, and Bartolomé the innovative adapter recreates them in the film medium, and Bartolomé the citizen of a still repressive, patriarchal dictatorship adds further layers of critique. For example, the metaphor for a wife's experience of marriage as having her mouth taped up is Rochefort's: 'Ce qu'il faut quand on est amoureux c'est non seulement des boules quiès dans les oreilles mais du sparadrap sur la bouche' (when you fall in love you don't just need earplugs but a plaster over your mouth too) (1963, 16). This, in Bartolomé's hands, becomes the lyrics for a musical adaptation of a further fairy tale about the dangers of adult, male sexuality for girls. 'Caperucita' (Little Red Riding Hood), sings Margarita, 'si te enamoras, no cierres solo los oídos, ¡también la boca, con esparadrapo!' (if you fall in love, don't just block up your ears, tape up your mouth with a plaster too!)

A further example of Bartolomé's irreverent and original adaptive strategy concerns the construction of the bourgeois family and the role of the mother-in-law. In Rochefort's hands, the portrait focusses on consumerism, with a hilarious treatment of Céline's quest for lined curtains (1963, 55–9). In Bartolomé's, the characterisation of the mother-in-law is an opportunity to contrast Margarita's modernity, in particular her allegiance to feminism and democracy, with the traditional, Catholic Spain of outdated Francoism. This contrast is present from the outset with the mother-in-law's po-faced description of Margarita as 'vulgar, como siempre' (vulgar, as always) after the separation, which is met by her former daughter-in-law's disinhibited laughter. Guillamón Carrasco offers a close reading of the flashback that concerns Margarita and Lorenzo's early marriage, when the newlyweds are contrasted with Lorenzo's parents. The flashback is a musical number of 'Amarraditos' (Hooked Up) which fuses a reference to traditional marital ties with a contemporary wink at the audience, who know that the singer María Dolores Pradera herself separated from her partner Fernando Fernán Gómez in 1957 (García Sahagún 2016, 81). The two couples, incongruously, and thus amusingly, sing the song as they walk and dance through the old centre of Madrid, with references to tradition provided by the mother-in-law's mantilla, the Habsburg architecture and cross-cuts to a newsreel report about Holy Week. 'Así', Guillamón Carrasco explains, 'la noción burguesa tradicional de la pareja aparece cuestionada en todas sus formas y expresiones, abogando por una emancipación (más que esperada) y exponiendo una apuesta por la autonomía de las mujeres en todos los aspectos de su vida' (Thus, all forms and representations of the traditional bourgeois notion of the couple are questioned, in favour of (longed for) emancipation and a bid for women's freedom in all aspects of their lives) (2015, 291).

A further flashback, which draws on the novel, but develops it in a formally sophisticated and conceptually enriching way, is the similarly uproarious Part Three, which is devoted to adultery. In the original novel Rochefort uses the highly hackneyed scenario of bourgeois Céline's affair with Italian Fabrizio while on holiday (she is not entirely successful in sending up the clichés of this scenario by juxtaposing stereotypical romantic and colloquial language (1963, 179–83), as Holmes claims (1996, 257)). Of course, Film School student Bartolomé did not have a budget for international travel for her shoot, but the choice to replace Fabrizio with university student Andrés works. The *mise en scène* of Andrés's student rooms allows her to include a poster for a film which is itself the poster child for Spain's version of worldwide 1950s–1960s New Cinemas movements, the 'Nuevo Cine Español' (New Spanish Cinema): *Nueve cartas a Berta / Nine Letters to Berta* (Patino 1965). A homage to cinematic modernity in Spain, the presence of this poster also reminds the viewer of the contrast between Bartolomé and Patino's treatments of female characters: Bartolomé's portrays the feminist emancipation of Margarita; Patino's, the entrapment of his young protagonists, especially the previously discussed unnamed Spanish girlfriend.[11] Indeed, Margarita's relationship with Andrés fails as he is only after sex, so Margarita returns to her husband with a frank 'No soy una maquinica de joder y no te he elegido a tí por eso, ya que mi marido lo hace mejor' (Look, I'm not a little fucking machine and I've not chosen you for that, because my husband does it better). In the Gumer Fuentes interview from where I take this dialogue, Bartolomé quips that she thought the censors might have liked the fact that Margarita ditches 'progre' (progressive, liberal) lover Andrés for right-wing husband Lorenzo, calling it, tongue-in-cheek, 'una actitud tradicional y hermosa' (a beautiful, traditional attitude) (1978, 14)! Who can blame her for having such fun with the censors come 1978, with the dictator dead, the constitution signed, and her first feature, *¡Vámonos, Bárbara!*, now safely released?

While making *Margarita*, she and the creative team of Film School students were having great fun too. The uproarious musical number in this section, 'Credo…', sung by Margarita and Andrés while they are still together, is a tour de force that juxtaposes many of the contradictions of the period:

> Credo, credo en la bondad humana, en el amor y en los comentarios de televisión, en la libertad de expresión y en el nuevo cine español.

Credo, credo en la democracia orgánica y en la reforma agraria, en la vida eterna y en las revistas de izquierda. Credo, credo en la paz y en la ONU, en la igualdad de oportunidad, en el mundo libre occidental y en la santísima trinidad. Credo, credo en el plan de desarrollo y en la purísima virginidad. (Credo: I believe in human goodness, love and TV commentaries; in freedom of expression and the New Spanish Cinema. Credo: I believe in organic democracy, agrarian reform, life ever after and Left-wing magazines. Credo: I believe in peace and the UN, equality of opportunity, the free world in the West and the Holy Trinity. Credo: I believe in the Development Plan and holy virginity.)

Worth singling out is 'la libertad de expresión... y en el nuevo cine español' (freedom of expression and the New Spanish Cinema). This line neatly fuses complaints about censorship of that freedom under dictatorship – though unfortunately also anticipates the future banning of the film we are actually seeing – with references to the Catholic church. For all the supposed modernisation of Vatican II in the period, the values of this institution, as Bartolomé shows here, still contrasted risibly with modernity.

Further narrative events that concern the breakdown of the marriage in the film follow the novel closely, like the sequence of Lorenzo's oyster-eating (Rochefort 1963, 19); his belittling of Margarita's painting hobby by inviting an art critic to review her pictures (in a nice touch Rochefort's 'j'étais brûlante de honte' (I was burning up with shame) (Rochefort 1963, 158) becomes an actual fire in which Margarita burns her work); and especially her disgust at masculine arrogance when the couple's friend Alejandro kills his wife, Natalia, who is Margarita's best friend and her implied lesbian lover, by speeding in his car (Rochefort 1963, 149). (As we will see, Bartolomé significantly changes, and improves, the role of Natalia in the script for the unfilmed feature (Chapter 3).) The ending of the film is again brilliantly inventive. In the novel, Rochefort offers Céline's letter to Philippe in which she announces she is leaving him (Rochefort 1963, 210–11). In the film, this becomes a musical tango number, which, far from celebrating the romantic love we may expect from this form, is instead a hymn to freedom. 'Enfin. Seule' are the famous last words of the novel (Rochefort 1963, 214), which, in the film, 'al fin sola' (at last, alone) are repeated twice. First, they appear as part of the song, followed by a cheeky and informal '¡yupi!' (yippee!) from Margarita. That '¡yupi!' marks

Figure 2.2 The film crew, including Cecilia Bartolomé (centre) in *Margarita y el lobo* (1969). Photograph courtesy of the Filmoteca Española

the end of the fiction, as the second time we hear the words 'al fin sola', we can also see the members of the production crew behind the actor. The camera then draws back, we see more of the crew, including director Bartolomé herself, and we also then hear her say '¡corten!' (cut!), before the camera draws back further again. Thus, while Rochefort self-referentially explores language in her literary creation (for example, the conceit of the 'dictionnaire Célino-Philippien' (Célino-Philippien dictionary) (Rochefort 1963, 184)), Bartolomé also insists her viewers are actively engaged by reminding them that they are watching a work of fiction. This is especially marked here at the film's close, when the camera draws further back still to reveal more of the crew, as well as the proscenium arch, which is indicated by two curtains that frame the set (Figure 2.2), and visually echoes the image of the production team among the still frames with which the film opens.

From Cecilia Bartolomé to Angela Carter

Margarita is, therefore, an acerbic portrait of late Francoism, and a critical text in the development of Spanish feminism. Bartolomé's handling of literary adaptation, whereby she moves from Rochefort's novel to film via Spanish cultural references and multiple international musical sources, deserves also to be acknowledged as a highly original contribution to literary adaptations in Spanish cinema.

Threaded throughout the film, and this chapter, is also Bartolomé's transnational address, which reaches from contemporary French feminist fiction, to Hollywood television series and cartoons, from the self-referentiality of the 1950s–1960s New Cinemas across the globe, to the 1960s British pop band The Beatles ('All You Need is Love' 1967), from German Romantic composer Felix Mendelssohn ('Wedding March' 1842) to Argentine tango. To these catholic intertexts I would like finally to add another that is anticipatory.

With no evidence of influence between the two to my knowledge, it is nonetheless intriguing that British novelist Angela Carter, born in London in 1940, and Spanish filmmaker Bartolomé, born in the same year in Alicante, should both turn to the fairy tale, and should both offer feminist reworkings in their respective media. Bartolomé, in 1969, deploys the wolf for two principal purposes. First, as I have indicated with my title to this chapter, the terrifying masculinist violence that the animal represents in the Grimms' tales (1812) is a perfect metaphor for Francoism, a regime which, for all its supposed opening up in the 1960s, was forged from the illegal violence of the Civil War, and was ideologically underpinned by patriarchy. Indeed, so perfect is the metaphor that Carlos Saura reuses it four years later in *Ana y los lobos / Ana and the Wolves*. Bartolomé uses 'wolf' in the singular to represent Francoism and connect with 'el lobo feroz' ('the big, bad wolf') of the fairy tale. Saura uses wolves in the plural to represent the three brothers who stand for Family, Church and Military; his female character Ana ends up raped, scalped and slaughtered and thus, despite being played by North American actor Geraldine Chaplin, she stands for a Spain ravished by the regime.[12] 'Little Red Riding Hood' would be picked up by directors Luis Revenga and Aitor Gorocelaya later in the Transition to democracy, and would again be used to stress Left-wing politics as indicated by their clever, untranslatable title *Caperucita y roja / Little Red (Communist) Riding Hood* (1977); even though the dictator was dead, this film was still held up by censorship.

Bartolomé's second purpose in reclaiming the roles of Little Red Riding Hood and the wolf of the fairy tales – and here she looks forward to Carter – is to enrich her portrait of Margarita's emancipation. I suggest that this enrichment is explained in part by her strategies as an adapter of Rochefort to render the double voice. The older and wiser Margarita of the separation scene is played by the same actor, Peña, with no physical differences, and the younger, naïve Margarita is played by Peña too. Linking the first Margarita so clearly to Caperucita (Little Red Riding Hood), who represents initial innocence, then allowing her to develop as Margarita, who has subsequently acquired knowledge, is a smart way of conveying the doubleness of the character, even when the physical appearance of the actor remains the same.

Film School production documents reveal that Bartolomé's original title for the film was *Ana y el lobo feroz / Ana and the Big, Bad Wolf* (Proharam 1968) (the Christian name Ana must have appealed to Saura). Much, I suggest, is gained from the change to *Margarita y el lobo*. Changing 'lobo feroz' (big bad wolf) to 'lobo' is effective: 'lobo' still recalls the 'lobo feroz' of the fairy tale, but is more widely suggestive. (The effect is not unlike the use of the widely evocative 'guerra' (war), rather than the specifically denunciative Spanish 'guerra civil' (Civil War), in, for example, Juan Antonio Bardem's *Muerte de un ciclista / Death of a Cyclist* (1955), or Saura's *La caza / The Hunt* (1966), even though the removal of the adjective 'civil' was an imposition by censorship.) In any case, the link to fairy tale is also introduced by the female name by the acoustic repetition between the '-rita' of Margarita and '-cita' of Caperucita. Margarita is also the director's own middle name, but I do not think the intention of its use in the title is to invite an autobiographical reading, as others suggest (García Sahagún 2016, 81). In a recent interview (Vargas 2019), Bartolomé has also spoken of the influence of the great exiled Spanish female director, Margarita Aleixandre, on the film, though does not explicitly state that the title is a direct homage to her.[13] A convincing further explanation for both the changes, from 'Ana' to 'Margarita', and from 'lobo feroz' to 'lobo' is, in fact, literary. Both names occur in the Ninth Day and Seventh Story of Boccaccio's *Decameron* (1351–53),[14] which draws on the tradition of moral exemplars that are also among the origins of the modern fairy tale. Thus, in the Italian tale, the disobedient wife, Margarita, is punished for failing to pay heed to her husband, who dreams she will be savaged by a wolf: she ignores him and is attacked by the animal. Bartolomé, as we have seen, has great fun in rescuing this disobedient medieval Margarita from patriarchal punishment in her characterisation of the spirited, liberal Margarita, performed by Peña, who ends the film free of husbands and wolves. However, Bartolomé sets her character in a context of the fairy tales that would have been widely known to her intended audiences, rather than the Boccaccio tale that might not have been accessible to all.[15]

Thus, besides the title of the film – in both its first and second iterations – the fairy tale reference is also introduced through music. In the credit sequence, which portrays the marital separation, the wolf of the fairy tale appears, as we have seen, in the theme tune of *The Three Little Pigs*. During this sequence, then, at least three literary sources are therefore at play: the bible, centre stage in the first moving image of the film as the priest's fingers hover over the text as if typing; Rochefort's novel, declared in the intertitle; and the fairy tale, announced through the music score. *Margarita* nimbly moves from the proscriptions concerning female comportment that the Franco regime took from the biblical text, through Rochefort's feminist denunciation of bourgeois marriage, to the secular and age-old threats to innocence contained in Charles Perrault's (1697) and Grimms' tales. As Guillamón Carrasco notes, while there is an apparent confrontation between Caperucita (Little Red Riding Hood) and Margarita with regards the movement from innocence to knowledge, and from being a victim to overcoming aggression, the protagonist is in fact 'una mujer que es a la vez una y otra, que está, al mismo tiempo dentro y fuera de la ideología' (a woman who is both one and the other [...] both inside and outside of ideology) (2015, 290). To this I would add that the film also brilliantly stresses that this is a process. Margarita and the student band do not perform a finished version of their song 'Caperucita' ('Little Red Riding Hood'), but riff and experiment in its construction: thus womanhood is being-in-process.

Carter, influenced by psychoanalysis, and her experience translating Perrault's tales from the French, would take the fairy tale in a new direction to focus explicitly on female sexuality. In 'The Company of Wolves', for example, she overturns Perrault's fusion of a cautionary tale about the danger of wolves to travellers, and female weakness and punishment in being gobbled up, by presenting a girl who is active, desiring and knowing. At the famous moment of the tale when the wolf states 'All the better to eat you with', Carter's line, in its feminist affirmation, its recourse to humour, and its skewering of patriarchal tradition, might have been uttered by

Bartolomé's Margarita, ten years before: 'The girl burst out laughing; she knew she was nobody's meat' (1996, 219).

Notes

1. In interview in 1978 with Gumer Fuentes, film reviewer of *Vindicación Feminista*, Bartolomé notes *Margarita* was screened in cineclubs and private feminist cinemas up to this point (1978, 14). Sonia García López reports it was previously shown in 1987 at the III Muestra de cine realizado por mujeres (Ateneo Feminista de Madrid) and in 1998 by the Filmoteca Española (2023, 9).
2. I have argued elsewhere that these words are remarkable for their resignation, pragmatism and stoicism (Faulkner 2022b, 285).
3. The Subtitling Project that accompanies this book (see Introduction) also attempted to replicate that early 1970s Paris screening that never took place. On 25 and 26 March 2023 it premièred a version of *Margarita* with English subtitles, alongside subtitled versions of *Carmen de Carabanchel* and *¡Vámonos, Bárbara!*, at the Manchester HOME cinema in the UK, as part of the twenty-ninth ¡Viva! Festival of Spanish and Latin American Cinema. See Introduction, note 9.
4. The Spanish version of this text appeared in a translation by Josefina Martínez Alinari with Losada in 1967. With the original French title, Rochefort provocatively refers to a sexist French medical school ditty about prostitutes. This provocation is lost in the descriptive Spanish title *Céline y el matrimonio* / *Céline and Marriage*. Bartolomé explains in a 2020 interview with Isabel Tejada for the Museo Nacional Centro de Arte Reina Sofía series that her husband gave her the book in French, and she also read it in Spanish, from where it is logical she drew the parts of the text that appear in the film (Tejada 2020). I use my own English translation of the Spanish title here as the published English text, *Cats Don't Care for Money*, would not have been known to Bartolomé. The translations from the French are also my own.
5. It was the directors who trained at the Film School in the early-to-mid 1960s that enjoyed good timing. Given García Escudero's reforms, a lucky few were commissioned to make their first feature-length films on the basis of their assessment pieces by producers keen to receive government subsidies, for films deemed 'Special Interest' by the regime could be assigned up to 50 per cent of production costs. This led to the contradiction in this period that the Francoist state funded its own anti-Franco art cinema movement, the 'Nuevo Cine Español' (New Spanish

Cinema). The contradiction is explained in part by the cultural geopolitics of late Francoism: art cinema was encouraged so Spain could present this supposedly 'modern' cinematic version of itself at international film festivals. See Faulkner (2006, 17–20). The appointment of pro-Francoist Baena as Director was therefore an about-turn, in Núria Triana Toribio's words, an attempt to 'dismantle the School from the inside' (conversation with the author in 2023).

6   I would like to thank the anonymous readers of the journal *Feminist Media Studies* for their role in my refining of this argument.

7   For example, *La noche del Dr Valdés* (1964) and *Carmen de Carabanchel* (1965), whose feminist content I analyse in Chapter 1. There is an especially strong case to be made for *¡Vámonos, Bárbara!* (1978), as it was feature-length, commercially released, and this was how Bartolomé herself presented the film in marketing on its release (see Parrondo Coppel 2001, 74; and Chapter 4). *Vindicación Feminista* film reviewer Gumer Fuentes hailed it as 'probablemente sea la primera película de carácter feminista realizada por una mujer española' (probably the first feminist film made by a Spanish woman) on 1 May 1978 (14); it would then go on to become the first of the acclaimed 'feminist trilogy' for Spanish film historiography (see Introduction).

8   On the development of comedy in Spanish feminist cinema, see Barbara Zecchi's 'La comedia como estrategia feminista: la recuperación de la risa' (2013), which covers films from the 1990s and 2000s, and thus unfortunately does not consider Bartolomé's pioneering work in feminism and humour in *Margarita*, which continues, this book argues, throughout her work.

9   On realism, Diana Holmes clarifies 'despite a tendency to identify French feminism solely with *écriture féminine* […] many French women writers have continued to use the medium of narrative realism to critique and challenge patriarchal culture' (1996, 246). On popularity, see Holmes (1996, 297, n. 1), and Margaret-Anne Hutton, who states six hundred thousand copies were sold (1998, 60), though these figures only relate to France.

10 Cerdán and Díaz have these three slightly differently as 'didactic vocation, rigour or ethical commitment and complexity' (2001, 16–17).

11 The compilation film element of *Margarita* anticipates Patino's work in this area in the 1970s, e.g. in *Canciones para después de una guerra / Songs for after a War* (1971; released 1976).

12 That this film passed censorship is partly explained by the influence of its producer Elías Querejeta.

13 Aleixandre directed three films alongside Rafael Torrecilla before both left Spain for exile in Cuba. Her career intertwines with Bartolomé's

work again in 2005, as Aleixandre was the production manager of *Operación ogro* / *Operation Ogre* (Pontecorvo 1979), a film explored in the television documentary 'El comienzo del fin' (see Chapter 7). Sonia García López also explores the influence of Czech filmmaker Věra Chytilová's 1966 film *Daisies* (1966) on Bartolomé, pointing out that 'Daisy' is a translation of 'Margarita' (2023, 12, n. 4).

14 My many thanks to Manuel Cuesta for suggesting the relevance of this to me.

15 In order to maintain all these references for an English reader and audience, I translate the title as *Margarita and the Wolf*; these references are lost in García López's *Daisy and the Big Bad Wolf* (2023).

3

The unfilmed scripts: *Qué tal Margarita... pero bien* and *La linda Casilda*

As we know, from 1969 until the *¡Vámonos, Bárbara! / Bárbara, Let's Go!* commission came in 1976, Cecilia Bartolomé was placed on the dictatorship blacklist that prevented her from directing. We will never know how many of her projects were therefore lost to film history at this time. The consistency of focus on feminocentric comedy that links *Margarita y el lobo / Margarita and the Wolf* of 1969 to *¡Vámonos, Bárbara!* of 1978 gives grounds for conjecture that the lost work may have fallen broadly into this generic area. Beyond conjecture, we at least have the material trace of no doubt a tiny part of this lost work in the film scripts deposited in Madrid's National Library from this period: *Qué tal Margarita... pero bien / What's Up Margarita...? Not Bad* (1974) and *La linda Casilda / The Beautiful Casilda* (1976).[1] Their existence in this archive is not thanks to a benevolent act of custodianship on the part of the dying dictatorship, however; it was simply a pre-existing legal requirement that scripts presented to the Ministry of Culture for filming permissions, whether these are granted or not, must also be submitted to be stored at this deposit library.[2]

This chapter thus differs from the others, which analyse filmed audiovisual work, Film School documentation or press reports and interviews, to cast light on production processes and reception tendencies. Focussing on unfilmed scripts, it will instead analyse the written word of the script; the only evidence concerning reception is that these scripts were censored by the regime as neither was granted permission to be filmed.

Recent developments in film historiography provide a scholarly context for this endeavour. In a ground-breaking volume of 2008, Dan North argued for the urgent inclusion of what he termed the 'unfinished' in film history: 'a screenplay that was never filmed, a shoot that was shut down prior to completion, even an idea for a story that was mooted and discarded at the back-of-an-envelope stage' (2008, 1). His description of the urgency of this task for British cinema is clearly applicable to other cases. If we replace 'British' and 'Britain' with 'Spanish' and 'Spain' in the following sentence the argument still stands – perhaps even more urgently so, considering that Francoist censorship was far more punitive:

> The British film industry can be notoriously brittle, and its productions prone to abandonment, neglect or pre-productive implosion, so it would seem that the study of only those films which made it to the screen and found an audience gives an inaccurate picture of the ideas and concerns in circulation amongst Britain's film-making communities. (2008, 2)

While North's wide-ranging Introduction makes the point that the 'unfinished' casts light on questions of the British industry (2008, 13) – even as his own first example of an unfinished film in fact concerns a popular Hollywood star and movie (Marilyn Monroe and *Something's Got to Give* (2008, 1–2)) – the chapters of the volume then concern British film auteurs. In a similar way that a Film Studies analysis of the auteur borrows from Literary Studies of the author, so an analysis of the 'unfinished' work of a director's career borrows from the life-and-works approach of literary biographers. Thus, just as the unpublished manuscripts of a writer, who comes to attention on the basis of published work, may be examined in order to gain a fuller picture of that writer's creative trajectory, so film scholars pay attention to the unmade projects of prominent figures to produce a more complete picture of their art, for example Orson Welles and Alfred Hitchcock.

Maintaining a focus on Anglophone cinema, in 2017 Peter Kunze coined the wider term 'Unproduction Studies',[3] to bring together this earlier Film Studies approach with a Production Studies one. While the main body of Kunze's article focusses on auteur Stanley Kubrick with similarly famous figures of the music and theatre worlds Andrew Lloyd Webber and Tom Stoppard, his wider argument is that an Unproduction Studies approach 'privileges the marginalized and suppressed histories to better understand the everyday realities of industrial logics, patterns and decision making' (2017, 19).

In the case of Bartolomé's unfilmed scripts, however, I suggest that there is little to discover in the way of 'industrial logics, patterns and decision making': she was simply the victim of immutable political censorship in these years and unable to direct until the dictator was dead. Thus, while James Fenwick's more recent work on Unproduction Studies and the American film industry yields new insights (2021), and the suggestively metaphorical 'Shadow Cinema' of his co-edited volume with Kieran Foster and David Eldridge may add 'shade and complexity to our established interpretation and knowledge' (Fenwick et al. 2021, 6), in the case of the Francoist censorship we seem to reach a critical dead end. The even more recent feminist reformulation of Unproduction Studies is more productive.[4]

Observing that a history of produced work will only ever be 'a history of survivors' (2022a, 3), Allyson Nadia Field draws on Giuliana Bruno's *Streetwalking on a Ruined Map* (1993), discussed in my Introduction, to call for 'speculation as a key method' for 'work that challenges the empirical, leans into the unverifiable, engages the absent, and trains a lens on the unseeable' (2022a, 1). Moving from methodology to outcomes, Alix Beeston and Stefan Solomon are suggestively sceptical over 'completeness' as a goal for such work (2023). In 2008, North was optimistic about the possibility of 'totality' that the inclusion of unfinished work promised: 'British cinema [...] can only be viewed in its *totality* if we expand the picture' (2008, 16; emphasis added). Beeston and Solomon's forthcoming edited volume shares Unproduction Studies scholars' aim to 'recover projects and practices marginalized by film industries', but do not argue that such recovery will provide completeness. Instead, they newly call for an examination of 'how feminist filmmakers have cultivated incompleteness as an aesthetic strategy' (book description, 2023).

This chapter argues for the inclusion of Bartolomé's unfilmed scripts by deploying Field's methodology of 'speculation' or 'what if' (2022b, 1). 'Incompleteness' was hardly an aesthetic strategy for the director when she was enduring censorship. However, I will conclude by suggesting that the ways Bartolomé has articulated the consequent incompleteness of her career in later life in interviews may be considered such an 'aesthetic strategy'. In the overall

Conclusion of this monograph I will return to 'incompleteness' in connection to wider histories of Spanish cinema.

Qué tal Margarita... pero bien (1974)

Deposited in 1974, some five years after the completion of *Margarita y el lobo*, the script *Qué tal Margarita...* is signed by Bartolomé, her brother, fellow director and former Film School teacher José Luis Borau, and Julia Peña, the actor who had played Margarita in the medium-length film, also at Film School. Modifying the title, using multiple authors and including Borau among these as a kind of insurance against troublemaking were all strategies to get round the censors. They all failed. Beyond the existence of the script itself, we know from interview that Bartolomé intended to transform medium-length *Margarita y el lobo* into a feature-length film, and had secured the support of X Films (Chapter 2). Given Peña's presence as co-author of the script for the feature, we might also reasonably conjecture that she intended to take up the protagonist role as Margarita once again. Other than these details, though, we are in the realm of speculation: what if *Qué tal Margarita...* had been approved? What film might this script have yielded?

So accomplished was *Margarita*, it is not surprising to find that in the 1974 script much of the earlier film is retained. The basic plot, from the Christiane Rochefort novel, concerning Margarita and Lorenzo's courtship, marriage and separation (though not necessarily in that order) remains. Speculative analysis of the unfilmed script also suggests that this longer film would have reconfirmed the auteurist traits of Bartolomé's extant filmed work; though rather than a limited exercise in reconfirmation I strive here to remain speculatively open to the unexpected. As I am dealing with a text accessible only to those scholars who can access the Madrid National Library (and, if not Madrid residents, this means those scholars who are able to travel and have access to grants to support this too) I will include some description of the text by analysing it broadly in the sequence that its plot unfolds and by including long quotes. I will connect the text, where relevant, to tendencies identified elsewhere in this volume, while also stressing new directions.

Bartolomé's twin creative commitments to denouncing Francoism and claiming feminism, the main focus of analysis of this volume, are also tightly interwoven in this piece, which was written when the dictator was still alive. *Qué tal Margarita...* extends the brief but important scenes of student demonstrations against the dictatorship that we saw in *Margarita*. In both extant works, one medium-length and the other unfilmed, these demonstrations are the setting for Margarita and Lorenzo to meet. The moment is similar to the meeting of Elena (Fiorella Florentina) and José (José Sacristán) in José Luis Garci's later *Asignatura Pendiente / Unfinished Business* (1977); the differences between these two films speak volumes of Bartolomé's feminism. In Garci's, Elena and José also meet (or meet again) in the context of street demonstrations, but Elena abandons the possibility of political mobilisation for the romantic cliché: now in early middle age, the couple heat up the cold leftovers of their youthful affair (Faulkner 2013, 146–52). And whereas José's legal career takes off as the affair peters out, Elena loses, apparently forever, the earlier moment for political mobilisation that she sacrificed. In Bartolomé's hands, as we know (*Margarita*) and may speculate (*Qué tal Margarita...*), Margarita is capable of both pursuing a romantic affair and remaining politically active after meeting Lorenzo at the demonstrations. And the unfolding of the story rewards her: when the romantic relationship ends in *Asignatura pendiente*, Elena is left with nothing; Margarita, in contrast, retains her independence and the possibility of working.

Nonetheless, a more mature Bartolomé, or one hardened by the censorship of *Margarita*, introduces a note of caution into the optimistic ending of the earlier medium-length film. That 1969 version offers a feminist happy ending as Margarita joyfully exclaims 'al fin sola' (at last, alone) twice, before Bartolomé self-referentially draws the camera back to reveal the set and the shooting team, including herself (Chapter 2). The second time around, the self-referentiality is not an aesthetic end in itself, but is deployed to sound a note of caution. The 1974 script ends now with Margarita uttering the words 'quiero estar sola' (I want to be alone). Further script directions are worth quoting in full:

> Pero no está sola. Es una actriz y está rodando. Los otros actores y el equipo van apareciendo, igual que el plató donde está el decorado. Se

> ha cortado el rodaje y todos charlan. Alguien dice a la actriz 'menos mal que tú no eres así, como la película'. La actriz se encoge de hombros y contesta 'no, yo aún no me he casado...' (But she is not alone. She is an actor and she is filming. The other actors and the film crew gradually shade into view, as does the set where the decorations are. Filming has stopped and everyone is chatting. Someone says to the actor 'at least you're not like that, like in the film'. The actor shrugs her shoulders and answers 'no, I haven't got married yet...')
> (Bartolomé et al. 1974, 221–2)

This more cautionary tone is hardly surprising from a director placed on a blacklist, whose youthful career aspirations, in ascendance during the writing and shooting of *Margarita*, had been dashed. We may thus similarly speculate about increased caution in the further sequences *Qué tal Margarita...* adds to its intertwined denouncing of Francoism and claiming of feminism. Shrewdly, given the expansion in University numbers, and in particular the increase in female students over the 1960s and 1970s, Bartolomé expands the screen time devoted to Margarita's student days in the 1974 script. Thus, as well as covering student demonstrations, the new script also explores further rule-breaking to denounce repression and claim freedom. We might speculate that the Bartolomé / Peña duo would have had fun in the performance of the scene, described in the script, in which a nun admonishes Margarita for wearing trousers as the actor sings 'Yo soy libre' (I'm free) in a sound bridge from the previous scene (Bartolomé et al. 1974, 17). A later sequence, where Margarita and Lorenzo share a mattress in the student halls of residence, to the shock of the other girls, might have provoked much mirth again. When Margarita is admonished and leaves the halls, there follows a new sequence of musical improvisation. This time, rather than earplugs and Elastoplast, Margarita turns to the Buddhist three wise monkeys to lament: 'El mono me ha dicho, no mires, no veas, tapa tus orejas, no debes hablar' (The monkey said to me, don't look, don't see, cover up your ears, you shouldn't talk) (Bartolomé et al. 1974, 41).

Bartolomé also extends the student scenes to develop the literary intertextuality that we have previously seen in the earlier film. The scenes concerning Margarita's involvement in student drama must have been intended knowingly to critique Lorenzo's vacuous conservatism. Margarita was to be part of a performance of an unnamed Lope de Vega play. Lorenzo's ignorance of the text was to be conveyed by his clapping at the wrong time – no doubt amusingly so. When he subsequently complains to Margarita about the student drama director, whom one might imagine would have been an on-trend 'progre' (progressive liberal) like Andrés in the earlier film, he asks: 'Pero bueno... ¿este chico se ha creído que va a hacer la revolución con Lope de Vega...?' (For goodness sake... does this chap believe he's going to bring about a revolution with Lope de Vega?) (Bartolomé et al. 1974). Here Bartolomé seems to be simultaneously raising the possibility of revolution through the student play, and dashing it through Lorenzo's response.

Beyond the plays of the Spanish Golden Age, a further book is introduced in the context of Margarita's student days. Simone de Beauvoir's *The Second Sex*, first published in the original French, *Le Deuxième Sexe*, in 1949, was published in Spanish translation as *El segundo sexo* in Buenos Aires in 1954. Only clandestine copies circulated in Spain under dictatorship. Such a book did indeed trigger the 'revolution' Lorenzo sarcastically mentions in connection with the performance of the student play, or, more specifically, it significantly contributed to activating Second Wave feminism. Had *Qué tal Margarita..* been filmed, this, to my knowledge, would have been the first appearance of de Beauvoir's book as a physical artefact in Spanish cinema, and who knows how many new readers it might have inspired?[5] In Bartolomé's hands, though, the inclusion of this book would have been far from dourly didactic. The script gives the details that *El segundo sexo* was to be bought by Lorenzo as a present for Margarita ... so far so good. But then we learn that the gift is offered just as an attempt to seduce her! Surely the *esperpento* would have been Bartolomé's mode here, with the potentially earnest reference to international feminism approached through the grotesque exaggeration of a lover's lechery.

When a serious work of feminist theory can be used in such a comic way in the script, we can be certain that Bartolomé's humour in *Qué tal Margarita...* would have been as wry and dark as ever. Feminism and Francoism, or women's rights and the dictatorship's repression of them through legislation underpinned by conservative Catholicism, intermingle in the script as it moves on to portray Margarita and Lorenzo's marriage, following her time as a student. If marriage, here, as in *Margarita*, is shown to be an institution that removes women's rights and voice, it is logical that the script should show that Margarita's agency is removed from the very moment of its announcement. In fact, at an event at his work, Lorenzo simply announces the forthcoming marriage without even consulting Margarita! Her response is to the point, fusing maternal wisdom with crude maternal advice 'Es que mi madre, que era una mujer muy inteligente, la pobre... solía decir... "Te casaste, la cagaste"' (It's that my mother, who was a very intelligent woman, the poor thing... used to say... 'You got married, you screwed it up') (Bartolomé et al. 1974, 55). Less directly vulgar, and more indirectly playful, is the script's description of what is to occur after the couple argue over the announcement. During a reconciliatory embrace, we learn that 'Margarita mira a la cámara por encima del hombro de Lorenzo y hace un guiño de complicidad al espectador' (Margarita looks at the camera over Lorenzo's shoulder and knowingly winks at the spectator) (Bartolomé et al. 1974, 61). Tantalising as it is that we do not have this scene filmed, we can nonetheless see how teasing Bartolomé would have been with the cinematography here, breaking the fourth wall and eliciting the complicity of the viewer.

This direct address to camera may reveal the influence of contemporary feminist counter-cinema, in ascendance in these years, as is well known, in both writing about film and filmmaking itself, on Bartolomé. The overlaps between Bartolomé, born in 1940, and her near-contemporary Cuban Sara Gómez (b. 1942, d. 1974), for example – who worked in the comparatively supportive context of the New Latin American Cinema – indicate these widely shared concerns in the period.[6] Gómez's only feature before her untimely death, *De cierta manera / One Way or Another* (1974; released 1977) blurs fiction and documentary by having characters directly address the camera and thereby break the illusionistic spell in the manner of Brechtian aesthetics in theatre.[7] The parallel with Bartolomé's planned treatment of Peña's Margarita on screen is suggestive. The difference with Bartolomé's work – as far as the script alone can reveal – is the genre of comedy and tone of disarming humour. On the one hand, Bartolomé's breaking of the fourth wall suggests Brechtian anti-illusionism and thus, like classic approaches to the *verfremdungseffekt* (distancing effect), this prevents proximity between audience and character; on the other, in Bartolomé's hands a proximity, even a cheeky collusion, between audience and filmmaker, is also hinted at. Indeed, the look to camera may even remind viewers today of Phoebe Waller-Bridge's multi-award-winning fusion of comedy and feminism in the British television series *Fleabag* (2016–19).

Further sequences of married life in *Qué tal Margarita...* develop Bartolomé's filmmaker-film-viewer collusion. Where Bartolomé's original contribution to self-referentiality in contemporary feminist cinema may have lain is in her insistence on comedy. For example, the potentially clichéd scenario of Lorenzo teaching Margarita to drive is played for laughs. The inclusion of lines like Lorenzo's admonition of Margarita, '¡No te vayas tanto a la izquierda!' (Don't veer over to the left [political Left] so much!), indicate continued comic originality and winking complicity with a viewer able to decipher political wordplay.

The sequence of the wedding and subsequent scenes of marital life in *Qué tal Margarita...* largely match and enhance those of *Margarita*. Bartolomé also wisely retains the effective playful music of the earlier film, including, for example, 'Amarraditos' to refer to Margarita and Lorenzo's marriage, or 'Credo' for Margarita and Andrés's affair (both specified in the script) (see my discussion of both in Chapter 2). If we wonder whether the fairy tale intertext of *Margarita* remains, given the removal of 'wolf' from the new title, the addition of a further musical number suggests it would. Following the tragic death of Natalia and its impact on Margarita, Lorenzo sings the following number to his wife: 'Es un mundo de lobos, y el lobo tengo que ser si quiero sobrevivir... Solo te pido que seas mi mujer. ¡No es mucho pedir!' (It's a world of wolves, and I have to be a wolf if I want to survive... I only ask that you be my wife [woman]. It's not asking a lot!) (Bartolomé et al. 1974, 197).

Margarita also contained tragedy: Natalia's manslaughter by the dangerous driving of her husband Alejandro, which derives from Rochefort's original novel. *Qué tal Margarita...* appears to change this and develop it in a far more interesting and original direction. While in the 1969 film, Margarita and Lorenzo, and Natalia and Alejandro were two leisured, young and childless couples, in the 1974 script Margarita only meets Natalia when she is already pregnant. Bartolomé appears to include a flashback within a flashback as, next in the sequence of the script, Margarita then meets Alejandro's new wife Piluca (1974, 147). Only then do flashbacks reveal details of Margarita's close relationship with Natalia. There are many more scenes that illustrate the friendship between these two women in *Qué tal Margarita...* than in the earlier, medium-length film; they thus look forward to the full treatment we see of female friendship in key 1970s feminist texts like Agnès Varda's *L'une chante, l'autre pas / One Sings, the Other Doesn't* (1977). In *Qué tal Margarita...* the scenes include the birth of Natalia and Alejandro's conventionally named son Alejandrito (he takes the diminutive form of his father's name, as is still traditional in Spain), though we may speculate that the lengthy physical event of childbirth itself likely occurred off-screen. They also include Natalia's experience of post-natal 'nervios' (nerves), which would surely have been explored on screen (1974, 147). A catch-all, euphemistic term for what today we would name poor mental health, the mention of 'nervios' (nerves) after the birth clearly indicates that Natalia was suffering from post-natal depression. Had the script been filmed, this would have been another first on Spanish screens. And the case of Natalia's post-natal depression could not be more severe. The new mother leaves baby Alejandrito with Margarita. The script is busy, first with details of Margarita and Lorenzo's argument about having children that is provoked by the presence of the child (Bartolomé et al. 1974, 169); and second, it ominously reveals that Natalia has rented a cheap guest house for a week. There she dies by suicide (1974, 169). The final scenes of the planned film are, then, much occupied with Margarita's intermingled grief over her friend's death, and fury over how the men around her handle it. Newly widowed husband Alejandro inaccurately dismisses Natalia's actions as 'un rapto de locura' (fit of madness). He and his friend Lorenzo proceed to cover up the inconvenience of the suicide. Certainly, we know in advance how well Alejandro will recover from the tragedy, because the sequences concerning these events are preceded by the future one of him together with his new wife.

Thus *Qué tal Margarita...* would have both cleverly developed and innovatively extended *Margarita*. It would have expanded the sequences concerning student life, a smart move given how familiar university life would have been to ever wider audiences, particularly the women whose access to higher education had soared in these decades. It would have added to the playful use of music of the

1969 film, and evidence in the script allows us reasonably to speculate that the new film would have added new depths to the humour of the first. Revealing Bartolomé's awareness of, and inspiration by, the self-referentiality of contemporary feminist counter-cinema, it would have increased the earlier film's self-referentiality by breaking the fourth wall mid-film. The complicity with the viewer would also have been enhanced by the new ending, which would have connected fictional character Margarita with the actor Peña. Where an unfilmed script is based on a previous, extant, film, and when a director has a preceding and succeeding oeuvre that develops her individual auteurist signature, a difficulty of the speculative approach advocated by Field is that it is difficult not to read the unknown material as a reconfirmation of the known. The exploration of post-natal depression and maternal suicide in *Qué tal Margarita...*, while consistent with the director's overall feminism, nonetheless indicates that the new film would have explored new directions, both for Bartolomé as a director and for Spanish cinema as a whole.

La linda Casilda (1976)

The encounter with the 1976 script, *La linda Casilda*, must necessarily be far more speculative, however. Written with Concha Romero, with whom Bartolomé would also go on to collaborate on the script of *¡Vámonos Bárbara!*, the only trace of this project, to my knowledge, is the script, and a brief reference in a press interview years later.[8] And while the *Qué tal Margarita...* script included some indications of film form, like diegetic music and the self-referential address to the camera, beyond its generic demarcation as a Western set in Córdoba, Andalusia (Bartolomé and Romero 1976, 23), the *La linda Casilda* script only offers the plot.[9]

The themes that unite *Margarita / Qué tal Margarita..., La linda Casilda* and *¡Vámonos Bárbara!* are the failure of marriage in a context when divorce was illegal and the repression of women's rights through legal mechanisms like the permiso marital (marital permission). Had circumstances been different, these four films – two unfilmed and two filmed – might then have made up a loose quartet within Bartolomé's work.

The development of the portrait of the husband in this 'quartet', of which only the first and last parts are filmed, speaks to Bartolomé's approach at different moments. Lorenzo of the *Margarita* films is based on Rochefort's dashing but dull Philippe: Bartolomé, like the novelist, satirises his aspirational pretensions, his political Conservatism and social conservatism. Carlos, meanwhile, of *¡Vámonos, Bárbara!*, is absent. As we will see (Chapter 4), like the repressive state, and, indeed, God, he is both invisible and powerful: we never see him, yet he can close Ana's bank account and exercise the 'permiso marital' that the repressive legal system assigns him. Without any indication of his audiovisual representation, the husband in *La linda Casilda*, Diego, appears simply to be a stereotype of Andalusian machismo. Casilda and Diego's wedding night is described as 'más bien una violación' (more like a rape) (Bartolomé and Romero 1976, 23), the husband dresses his wife like a doll (1976, 28) and Casilda's sexual dissatisfaction is attributed to him: 'ni siquiera sabe que existe una cosa llamada orgasmo femenino' (he doesn't even know that such a thing as a female orgasm exists) (1976, 29). This does not stop him, of course, from engaging in adulterous affairs – to which Casilda responds by having an extra-marital encounter of her own.

If the treatment of machista Diego on the page is one-dimensional, more interest turns around denouncing Casilda's lack of education and the lack of support she receives from female family relatives. When she turns to her mother and grandmother to understand her own sexuality 'sale de la entrevista más confusa que cuando llegó' (she emerges from the interview more confused than when she arrived). It is tricky to speculate how Bartolomé would have handled the seemingly grotesque detail of the interview when her grandmother shows her the piece of lace, yellowed with age, with which she apparently covered her own thighs during congress with the grandfather (Bartolomé and Romero 1976, 30–2). While the non-blood relative of her mother-in-law seems to be more supportive of her daughter-in-law, the story appears to end with Casilda's suicide (1976, 78).

While details revealed by this script are limited, we might speculate, then, that *La linda Casilda* would have raised a number of feminist issues. The script suggests the film would have laid bare the consequences of a lack of female education, as even the female support networks provided by blood relatives are wholly inadequate. The issues of female mental health and suicide might also have linked this film's Casilda to *Qué tal Margarita...*'s Natalia. The major focus of the script seems to be female sexuality, however. As Núria Triana Toribio has argued,[10] any feminist study of Spanish film of the 1970s must address the *destape*, contemporary boom of soft porn that anticipated, then took advantage of, the end of censorship in the period. Titillating and trite, such work falsely laid claim to 'modernity' by celebrating post-Franco sexual freedoms. However, the only sexual freedoms being celebrated were those of heterosexual men: celebrations that took place over the partially clothed and unclothed bodies of women actors on screen. In the late 1970s and early 1980s this began, very slowly, to change, with work like the 'feminist trilogy' by Bartolomé, Miró and Molina, which considered female sexuality (*¡Vámonos, Bárbara!* (1978), *Gary Cooper, que estás en los cielos* / *Gary Cooper, Who Art In Heaven* (1980) and *Función de noche* / *Night Performance* (1981), where Molina's female protagonist Lola, like Casilda, also never experiences an orgasm in her marriage); and with Ventura Pons, Pedro Almodóvar and Eloy de la Iglesia's films' exploration of LGBTQ+ desires (such as *Ocaña, retrat intermitent* / *Ocaña, Intermittent Portrait* (1978), *Pepi, Luci, Bom y otras chicas del montón* / *Pepi, Luci, Bom and Other Girls on the Heap* (1980), *La ley deseo* / *Law of Desire* (1987) and *El diputado* / *Confessions of a Congressman* (1978)). Years before this work, the potentially explicit material of Bartolomé's *La linda Casilda* might have brought an otherwise entirely absent condemnation of aggressive male heterosexuality, and claiming of female erotic desire, to the one-dimensional *destape*. But the script was not approved for filming. This speculative, creative reading of the unfilmed script aims to add Bartolomé's anticipation, in the early-mid 1970s, of the exploration of sexuality and desire that has heretofore largely been associated with the post-Franco period (and male directors) from the late 1970s to the 1980s.

Examination of these two scripts reveals the potential, but also the limitations, of Allyson Nadia Field's advocation of 'speculation' as an approach to film history. Where an earlier, filmed version of a subsequent script exists, as in the case of *Margarita* / *Qué tal Margarita...*, it is difficult not to read the second uniquely in the light of the first, thus confirming rather than creating new knowledge. Where nothing exists but the script, speculation may give way to hesitancy, hence the comparative brevity of my comments on *La linda Casilda*. Nonetheless, this chapter has argued that Bartolomé's unfilmed scripts do reveal new dimensions of her work, especially those surrounding female mental health and suicide, in both scripts, and female education and erotic desire, particularly in the second. Even if these perspectives do not depart radically from the overall feminist vision of Bartolomé's work developed in this book, these insights are important. They perhaps enhance the contours of the picture of her work that the filmed pieces paint. But they also bring in entirely new subjects to the national cinema, allowing us to rewrite the history of the *destape* (developed, as we will see, in *¡Vámonos, Bárbara!* (Chapter 4)), and allowing us to align Bartolomé with some of the concerns of feminist cinema internationally.

The dictatorship blacklist meant this work was never filmed. The consequent 'incompleteness' of Bartolomé's career was thus an act of repression. Silenced in this way over the nine years from *Margarita y el lobo* to *¡Vámonos, Bárbara!*, it is perhaps small comfort that in later years, Bartolomé would have a voice, which she has used in numerous interviews and speeches which have appeared in print and in freely accessible internet recordings (see Introduction), to give her version of this period. If this voice may only retrospectively describe, it has done so powerfully; indeed, at times it is difficult for the scholar, in the absence of other sources, not to rely too heavily on it. In Chapter 3, I pointed out the resignation, pragmatism and stoicism with which the director in 2004 retrospectively describes the censoring of *Margarita y el lobo* and the subsequent blacklist years, qualities that contrast sharply with the tendency of lament adopted by contemporary directors when they look back, even when the limitations placed on their careers were far more minor than those placed on Bartolomé (e.g. Miguel Picazo in Faulkner 2006, 101–2). That interview with Bartolomé was conducted on the occasion of the screening of the film at the San Sebastián Film Festival of 2004, and is the first in the growing attention the director has attracted subsequently, and thus in the number of interviews she has conceded (see Introduction). I had first taken the contrast between Bartolomé's and other censored directors' descriptions of Francoist repression to be a difference of character. However, Alix

Beeston and Stefan Solomon's argument that women directors may deploy 'incompleteness' as a feminist strategy is relevant here too. As we will see, Bartolomé, especially at the time of the painfully laboured release of *Después de...* diptych, can be a highly vociferous critic of censorship and neo-censorship in interviews (Chapter 5). But in retrospect, speaking during the 2000s about the 1960s and 1970s, she takes a different approach. Rather than bemoaning censorship, which renders the speaker its victim, she sounds her feminist voice strategically to describe the incompleteness of her career, and thus speaks from a position of power.

Notes

1 A renamed version of *Qué tal Margarita...* also exists as *¿Qué tal Teresa? / What's Up, Teresa...?* (1971) at the Archivo General de la Administración. Changing the characters' names and the script's authors did not succeed in fooling the censors, who also rejected this version.
2 The library of the Catalan Film Archives, in Barcelona, holds a further unfilmed script, dated 1971, and co-signed by Bartolomé and Manuel Gutiérrez Aragón. The lengthy title is: *Historia de Sabigoto, su marido Aurelio, sus primos Félix y Liliosa y Jorge, Monje de Belén, Mártires en la Córdoba de Abderraman II según el memorial de San Eulogio por los cronistas franceses Usuardo y Odilardo / The Story of Sabigoto, her husband Aurelo, her cousins Félix, Liliosa and Jorge, Belén Monk, Martyrs in the Córdoba of Abderraman II, According to the San Eulogio Memorial by the French Chroniclers Usuardo and Odilardo*. Based on the martyrdom of five Christians in ninth-century Muslim Córdoba, the filming of this script would have yielded a sardonic view of the supposed 'convivencia' (peaceful co-existence) between religions in medieval Spain, as it portrays bigoted Christians in contrast with a Muslim population associated with learning, sensuality and tolerance. Bartolomé's contribution, based on what we know of her creative interests elsewhere, is particularly evident in the prologue, which portrays the two French monks' travels through Spain in search of relics. Before they reach Córdoba, they encounter famished monks and an illiterate abbot. Bartolomé's interests in music and humour fuse in the choral commentary provided by the children's song that accompanies these encounters. Irreverently lampooning the veneration of relics, they sing '¡Buscad reliquias muy santas, / huesos mártires, costillas, / atormentados riñones,

/ y venerables cenizas. / También mechones de pelo, / alguna muela bendita, / la oreja de un cura vasco, / y una asesinada tibia!' (Look for holy relics, / martyrs' bones and ribs, / tortured kidneys, / and venerable ashes. / Also clumps of hair, / the odd blessed back tooth, / the ear of a Basque priest, / and a murdered woman whose corpse is still warm!). It goes without saying that the script did not pass censorship, and was never filmed. In 1999, Dolores Devesa and Alicia Potes report that Bartolomé had even signed a contract with Paramount-Europe to make this into a film, to no avail, and it later also re-emerged as a television series script of seven chapters of an hour and a half, this time with José Luis Guarner and José María Gutiérrez as additional scriptwriters (1999, 38 and 39). That television series remained unfilmed too.

3 My thanks to Hilary Owen for pointing out the relevance of Unproduction Studies to the analysis of the curtailed careers of women directors to me.

4 Kunze acknowledges that work in feminist media studies predates 'Unproduction Studies' (2017, 29, n. 20). Fenwick notes that the exclusions of film history are not limited to those denounced by feminism: 'there is a history of unmade films by LGBTQ+ and persons of colour, films that remained unmade because of structural inequalities and industrial gatekeepers' (2021, 12). This point is echoed by Field (2022a, 4), whose twin volumes of *Feminist Media Histories* propose that 'a speculative approach is hospitable to feminist, queer, trans, diasporic, and racially marginalised work, and concerns of other historically excluded identities and positionalities' (2022b, 8).

5 The work of the French author did previously appear in Kathryn Waldo's self-referential Film School short, *Día de rodaje / Day of the Shoot* (1961), in which one of the students reads her essay on Brigitte Bardot (García López 2021, 319). A Film School piece, the short was of course not commercially released.

6 Like Bartolomé and Molina at Francoist Spain's Escuela Oficial de Cinematografía (Official Film School), Gómez was the only woman at Cuba's better-known Instituto Cubano del Arte e Industria Cinematográficos (Cuban Institute of Cinematographic Art and Industry)); she was also a woman of colour, one of only two Black filmmakers to study there in the early years. For a close reading of *One Way or Another* as feminist counter-cinema, see Kuhn (1994, 157–60). For further examples see Kuhn (1994, 163–71).

7 My thanks to Andy Willis for suggesting the influence of contemporary counter-cinema to me here.

8 Bartolomé speaks in 1978 of her plans to film 'Una historia andaluza con una joven protagonista' (An Andalusian story with a young female

protagonist), in her words, 'Hay un mundo irreal con elementos surrealistas. En el fondo el ambiente rural, de los terratenientes, un ambiente social que se le escapa a la protagonista' (An unreal world with surrealist elements. A rural context, that of landowners, a social context that the protagonist doesn't understand) (Masó 1978b).
9 The title of the film may possibly refer to the 1900 Habanera by Josefa Fernández Martín.
10 In correspondence with the author in the context of the 'Invisíveis e insubmissas / Invisibles e indomitas: Leading Women in Portuguese and Spanish Film and Television, 1970–1980' research project (see Faulkner, Owen and Triana Toribio 2021).

4

Putting Bárbara into ¡Vámonos, Bárbara!: Girlhood Studies and 'Spain's first feminist film'

In 1976, some seven years after *Margarita y el lobo / Margarita and the Wolf* (Chapter 2), and following the repeated frustrations of being unable to film owing to her presence on the dictatorship blacklist (Chapter 3), Cecilia Bartolomé was finally commissioned by veteran producer Alfredo Matas to make her first feature. The commission was to make a Spanish version of Martin Scorsese's *Alice Doesn't Live Here Any More* (1974), and was offered to Bartolomé after Manuel Gutiérrez Aragón and Pilar Miró had refused the job (Torres 1992, 130; Martin-Márquez 1999, 151); Gutiérrez Aragón recommended her instead. Film history that is written from the perspective of auteurism might be sceptical about a commission, as the impetus and requirements of the commissioner imply that the individual creativity of the auteur-director is curtailed. Hardened – rather than wounded – by the setbacks of the previous decade, I argue that Bartolomé was not only ready, but in fact perfectly placed to transform such a commission into the film she wanted to make: of her two feature-length fiction films, *¡Vámonos, Bárbara! / Bárbara, Let's Go!* (1978) is the more successful, even though she formed her own production company to make *Lejos de África / Far from Africa* (Chapter 6). This is not to say that she ignored Matas's requirements – she could not jeopardise the precious opportunity to make her début after so many years of waiting (as she acknowledges in a contemporary interview (Hernández Les 1978)) – rather, she met, or, indeed, made a virtue of them.[1] The producer's imposition of his actor wife, Amparo Soler Leal, as the protagonist, Ana, for example, Bartolomé transformed into a particularly effective professional collaboration between the two (see e.g. Padura 1978; Appendix Interview p. 213; Soler Leal also brought to the film her own experience of having separated from her first husband Adolfo Marsillach in 1956).[2] With her co-scriptwriters, Sara de Azcarate and Concha Romero, she was able to rewrite the patriarchal ending of Scorsese's *Alice*, in which the eponymous protagonist settles down with a new, abusive man, into a feminist, emancipatory one: Ana and Bárbara ditch the increasingly terrible new patriarch Iván, and choose the open road, the two of them alone. In her hands, then, the commission became the 'first' feminist film of Spanish film history – a contested claim, as we have seen (Chapter 2).

Subsequently, though still relatively unknown, *¡Vámonos, Bárbara!* has been hailed by select critics as both an important document of the Spanish Transition and 'radical' in its approach to history (Camporesi 2001, 59), and as the first feminist road movie of film history, anticipating the 1990s Hollywood boom that began with *Thelma and Louise* (Scott 1991) by over a decade (Pérez 2008, 216).[3] In the crowded field of celebrated Spanish cinema of the 1970s, like *El espíritu de la colmena / The Spirit of the Beehive* (Erice 1973) and *Cría cuervos / Raise Ravens* (Saura 1976), to name but two, I argue that *¡Vámonos, Bárbara!* deserves recognition alongside them. Not only a key contribution to Spanish culture of the Transition, beyond the national context it also makes a distinctive contribution to the history of feminist cinema and the representation of Girlhood.

The plot apparently turns around wife, mother and interior designer Ana's decision to leave her philandering and abusive husband, Carlos. She takes to the open road, along with her daughter Bárbara (Cristina Álvarez), and, over the summer holidays, visits and revisits significant locations from her childhood, in and around the Catalan coastal resorts of Tarragona, Castell and Aguamar. Carlos is never seen, but he is ever present through his actions (rather like the state itself in the form of the dictator, or, as Bartolomé quipped, a biblical prophet ('por sus obras le conoceréis' (by their deeds you will know them) (Anon. 1978a)).[4] Three years before divorce was re-legalised in Spain in 1981, these actions include the various punishments sanctioned by the Código Civil (Civil Code): closing the couple's joint bank account; seizing property that belonged to his wife before marriage; and attempting to prove his wife's adultery to take custody of their daughter. Ana, however, keeps on the move, encountering multiple models for self-reinvention among diverse groups of female characters. Foremost among these, and previously largely overlooked by critics, is Bárbara: hidden in plain sight in both the title and the narrative. It is Bárbara, for example, who encourages her mother to leave Iván, ensuring the film reaches its all-important ending of the pair on the open road, driving towards an uncertain future, but doing so independently (see Appendix Interview on the particular challenges of making this ending, which were resolved thanks to the supportive interventions of Soler Leal).

While Bartolomé controlled the production of the film, including, especially, the comic genre and tone that animate this plot, the problems began in distribution and exhibition, and here we find the reasons why ¡Vámonos, Bárbara! has not subsequently received the recognition it deserves. Bartolomé's unusual career development perhaps did not equip her with the necessary experience in these areas. At Film School, as we have seen in Chapters 1 and 2, she coped with sexism, yet gained experience in filmmaking; after Film School, again, she coped with blacklisting, yet gained experience in pre-shoot planning, including scriptwriting (Chapter 3), and in shooting, through the publicity commissions from which she made a living. She was thus more than ready to direct her début, both creatively, in making an innovative film, and practically, in being willing to compromise, handle the interventions of the producer, and lead her team. However, the stalling of her career meant she had gained less experience in distribution and exhibition, thus the problems that beset ¡Vámonos, Bárbara! began after the production of the film was complete, and had left her hands. As producer, Matas controlled these; his various mistakes, and Bartolomé's apparent lack of agency to rectify them, explain why the film failed to reach a wide audience, and why it has slipped out of the sight of film history.

First, Matas commissioned a version of the film dubbed into Catalan that was carried out without Bartolomé's knowledge (Cleries 1978), let alone her creative supervision and leadership.[5] Second, he premièred this unauthorised, dubbed version, *Anem-nos-en, Bàrbara!*, in Barcelona – again without the director's knowledge. Indeed, she only travelled to the Catalan capital as a friend told her about the début (Cleries 1978)! This double release strategy of the unauthorised Catalan and authorised Castilian versions in Barcelona first (6 April 1978),[6] then the authorised Castilian one in Madrid second (18 October 1978), may explain Matas's third, and perhaps most regrettable, error: neglecting the film's further distribution, meaning it reached only 147,445 viewers (see Textual Note). This may be because, having received Generalitat (Catalan autonomous government) subsidies for the Catalan version, financially, he could afford the neglect. Perhaps, also, by this point, the relationship between director and producer had broken down. We do not know to which period of their collaboration Manuel Gutiérrez's untranslatable punning recollection of it refers, though it could well be to this final phase: Bartolomé and Matas 'se llevaron a matar' (they were at each other's throats ('matas' means 'you kill'; 'matar', 'to kill')) (Torres 1992, 130). The fact is that for many contemporary viewers in Spain, and for subsequent film history, ¡Vámonos, Bárbara! was lost. It also remains to this day a film that is difficult to interpret, lying in between Bartolomé's successful completion of the commercially driven commission, and Matas's failure subsequently to distribute it commercially.

Being difficult to locate, or in-between, would in fact become a common thread in responses to the film, including the new approach I propose in this chapter. I begin with an assessment of the previously only partially examined press reviews published at the time of the film's release, in which journalists perceived in-betweenness as a weakness. In the particular national context of the Transition, it seemed a film that could not be pinned down; it was unmoored, located somewhere between a Catalan setting, an unauthorised Catalan version and authorised Castilian one. In a wider context, it also could not easily be located between its feminism and its socialism. I proceed in this chapter by analysing scholarly responses, which appeared in the 2000s, and which, conversely, stress precisely this in-betweenness as one of the film's strengths. Scholars identify in-betweenness in Bartolomé's characterisation of the protagonist, and interpret it as an astute response to the Transition, a historical period when Spain itself was in between dictatorship and democracy.[7] The portrait of Ana, a middle-aged woman in the process of marital separation and self-reinvention, represents the nation's current moment of vacillation, uncertainty and error. Her sometimes successful, sometimes bungled, attempts at disentanglement from a past of patriarchal oppression, and her sometimes rewarding, sometimes pathetic, attempts at self-renewal for the future, both shrewdly reflect a nation caught between the legacies of its past and the various options for the future.

My own argument is that this focus on the adult protagonist Ana has led us to miss Bárbara, or only account for her in terms of her role in the family structure, as her mother's daughter. If Ana's character arc moves the narrative forward, just as her driving of the car moves it physically forward, she represents in-betweenness and dislocation through narrative means: making decisions, both sound ones, like leaving abusive Carlos, and silly ones, like choosing an outfit of flimsy underwear when she decides to hang up her twinset and pearls! With a mother on the move, Bárbara, meanwhile, is, rather, a source of constancy, a still at the centre of the narrative, the rock to which the rash Ana who rushes about clings. (In beach scenes with Ana's love interests Quiquet (José Luis Nogueras) and Iván (Iván Tubau), Bárbara stays on a shoreline rock while Ana is literally and figuratively at sea with the different men.) Bárbara's embodiment of in-betweenness and dislocation comes, rather from her age and sexuality: she is an adolescent, and, I suggest, there is evidence in the film of her as queer, though there is no open discussion of her sexuality, so we must look for it obliquely. Played by twelve-year-old Álvarez, a red-headed newcomer to cinema, she was chosen from seventy at audition (Masó 1978b), and was widely admired for her performance by contemporary critics, but, to my knowledge, made only this film. Her red wavy hair may also connect her to Valérie Mairesse of *L'une chante, l'autre pas / One Sings, the Other Doesn't* (Varda 1977), though Bartolomé recalls choosing her as she was simply the best at audition – plus her ginger hair recalls the colour of Soler Leal's (see Appendix Interview). Bartolomé, two of whose own children were slightly younger and slightly older than twelve at the time of the shoot, creates a portrait of the Girl that invigorates the somewhat tired, by 1978, Spanish traditions of the filmic 'cine con niño' (child-focussed cinema), and literary 'chica rara' (unconventional girl). Deploying transnational Girlhood Studies' insights into the Girl's special, destabilising relationship to ideology, especially Clara Bradbury-Rance's work on the adolescent and queer Girl (2016), I demonstrate the primary importance of this supposedly secondary character to the film's shrewd cultural response to the in-betweenness and dislocation of the Spanish Transition.

Between Barcelona and Madrid, feminism and socialism: how contemporary reviewers located and dislocated ¡Vámonos, Bárbara!

It should be noted that contemporary press reviews offer only a selective insight into audience response: only three years since the death of the dictator, the profile of a journalist under Francoism had hardly transformed – a select few of the population who were literate, university-educated, usually urban-based and, till recently, either pro-regime, or adept at writing in a way that made it seem as if they were, and – based on the admittedly problematic analysis of their printed first names only – predominantly male. Nonetheless, the Filmoteca Española's collection of reviews[8] is reasonably wide (twenty-nine articles), and, if not nationwide, at least offers a balance of Barcelona- and Madrid-based publications. On the basis, again, of my analysis of journalists' Christian names where given, which presumes cisgender, it includes the views of eighteen men to seven women (four articles are anonymous), 72 per cent to 28 per cent. The collection offers, then, an important, if slanted, insight into Bartolomé's very first encounter with the viewing public.

In general, contemporary press reception was positive (not one of overall 'desconcierto' (perturbation) (Ibáñez 2001, 26)). Given that the marketing campaign for ¡Vámonos, Bárbara!, presumably attributable to Matas, was to present it as 'Spain's first feminist film',[9] the significance of this positive reception should not be underestimated. As we have seen (Introduction), comedy is a particularly slippery genre and tone to work with, prone as it is to audience misunderstanding, and it is true to say that a number of critics found these aspects disconcerting (Ibáñez 2001, 26) (e.g. Crespo 1978; Viader 1978; Roca-Sastre 1978; Gorina 1978; Marinero 1978; A.-J. 1978). However, other critics spotted that wry humour was Bartolomé's great achievement. José Luis Guarner, for example, writing in *Catalunya Express*, salutes ¡Vámonos, Bárbara! as possibly the most promising début of 1978, avoiding, as it does, 'la solemnidad estetizante y romántica de Agnès Varda [...] para cultivar el desenfado, cuando no el descaro' (the aestheticising and romantic solemnity of Agnès Varda [...] in favour of a disinhibited, if not damn right cheeky, style), hiding its complexity behind an apparent simplicity, and offering both an 'espíritu observador' (observing spirit) and a 'sana mala uva' (healthy dose of annoyance) (1978). Diego Galán (well-known as a future defender of Pedro Almodóvar's brand of humour) is also enthusiastic (1978). *Avui*'s Enric Ripoll-Freixes picks out Bartolomé's skilful handling of a scenario that in other hands 'hauria caigut en el tòpic' (would have fallen into cliché), and, as I do in this chapter, singles out Bárbara: 'Quina troballa, la nena, com a personatge i interpret!' (what a find, the girl, as a character and an actor!) (1978). Ángeles Masó, meanwhile, wittily repurposes the 'tercera vía'[10] strapline ('cine de autor para mayorías' [auteur cinema for mainstream audiences]) to describe the film as 'cine feminista para mayorías' (feminist cinema for mainstream audiences) (writing in *La vanguardia* 1978b). Mary G. Santa Eulalia (1978a) salutes Bartolomé: 'con ella viene el feminismo' (with her feminism is on its way). In anticipation of the Madrid début she also reports that in Barcelona 'el público ha sido sensible a la óptica' (the audience has been sensitive to the approach) (1978b). This is a tantalising glimpse of audience response, but is only anecdotal; see also Bartolomé's reference to sitting in the cinema at the première of the film and hearing two older women say 'Aixó es veritat, esto es cierto' (that's true, that's how it is) (Ordóñez 1978).

It may be noted, however, that a number of reviewers, while positive, all opt for a similar formulation of back-handed praise about the film's feminism, along the lines of it being a good film *despite*, not *because*, it is feminist. Journalists soothe what they must have perceived as potentially hostile filmgoers with assurances that the film was not pamphleteering (Guarner 1978; Ruiz de Villalobos 1978; Cleries 1978), or an attack on men (Aguilar 1978). One 'M. A.-J.', of the former regime's newspaper *Arriba*, even applauds both the 'renuncia al panfleto' (avoidance of a pamphleteering approach) and 'al episodio lesbiano' (the lesbian episode); such an 'episode', for this reviewer, apparently, 'parecía inevitable' (seemed inevitable) (1978)! The marketing strategy therefore meant that the director had to handle almost every press interviewer asking her whether she was feminist, whether the film was feminist and what she understood feminism to mean (making feminist cinema means 'tocaré problemas de mujeres, porque los vivo, porque han sido dados de lado y creo que conviene abordarlos' (I will deal with women's problems because I live them, because they have been side-lined and

I think we need to address them) is a representative example (Santa Eulalia 1978a)).

Within this overall positive response, however, there were two areas of exception, both of which turn around a negative perception of Bartolomé's work as dislocated, or in-between. First is the previously unexamined question of ¡Vámonos, Bárbara! falling in between the unauthorised Catalan, and authorised Castilian versions. Matas may have collected his subsidy, but the unauthorised Catalan version, *Anem-nos-en, Bàrbara!*, meant Bartolomé attracted criticism for dubbing decisions in which she was not involved.[11] There are queries around whether the film is part of the Catalan linguistic 'normalisation project', or whether the Catalan version is conceived simply for commercial ends (Ruiz de Villalobos 1978). In interview, Bartolomé reveals she had originally wanted to make a multi-lingual film – in Castilian, Catalan and English, in accordance with the languages spoken in the film's settings – but the producer refused. According to (Alicante-born) Bartolomé, (Barcelona-born) Matas told her that her own use of the Catalan language was 'too Valencian', and thus unsuitable for the requirements of the restored Catalan government, the Generalitat (Cleries 1978). Presumably he had a plan that he did not disclose to Bartolomé to dub the film into the 'required' Catalan – after the shoot, and without Bartolomé – for the subsidy. For a policy designed to promote linguistic diversity, it is therefore somewhat ironic that Bartolomé's contribution was rejected by Matas... for being too linguistically diverse! The director herself criticises in interview the 'polished' Catalan version, and its use of inauthentic terms (Cleries 1978). Frustratingly, precisely these same faults are pointed out by other reviewers, who of course implicitly attribute them to her: 'el lenguaje utilizado resulta las más de las veces fingido o cuanto menos chocante' (the language used, when it's not forced, is jarring), complains Jordi Viader, 'y ello es tanto más grave en cuanto el filme pretende ser [...] una comedia de costumbres' (and this is even more serious as the film aims to be [...] a comedy of manners) (1978). It is clear that *Anem-nos-en, Bàrbara!*, owing to post-production decisions beyond Bartolomé's control, had become a punchbag for critics to land blows on the new linguistic normalisation policy in general: 'doblar films al catalán', criticises Alejandro Gorina, 'haciendo que todos hablen como académicos de la lengua [...] no es como para echar campanas al vuelo acerca de la normalización de un cine en esta lengua' (dubbing films into Catalan, making everyone speak like members of the language academy [...] doesn't exactly make you feel like celebrating the normalisation policy of cinema in this language) (1978).

For some reviewers, then, *¡Vámonos, Bárbara!* itself is lost in-between Barcelona and Madrid, or linguistic policy questions that are particular to Spain in these years of the signing of the Constitution and establishment of the 'Estado de autonomías' (State of Autonomous Communities) in 1978. Elsewhere, the film falls in between wider international debates between feminism and socialism, which were particularly acute in these years. Kathleen Vernon quotes at length the sarcastic hostility of one R. Santiago, critic of *Punto y coma* (2002; 2011). This new, Barcelona-based fortnightly culture magazine was edited by Anna Comas i Mariné, and its stated aim was to 'aportar algo nuevo, al poder actuar en una línea de total independencia dentro del terreno cultural, respetando todas las tendencias existentes en el mismo' (bring something new, by being able to act with complete freedom within the cultural context, respecting all the tendencies that exist within it) (Anon. 1977). For Santiago, 'apartar algo nuevo' seems to have meant, first, bringing out the tired argument that a wealthy housewife cannot represent women's problems in general, let alone the nation's. (In fact, the first time we see Ana she is at her workplace, the design studio – bizarrely multiple reviewers also mistakenly describe her as a housewife.) Bartolomé, in other published interviews, is careful to counter this argument and justifies presenting the world that she herself knows, and that fitted the actor chosen for her (Aznarez 1978). Second, the reviewer attacks the film's supposed maniqueism in its presentation of gender roles, obscuring 'El problema real de la mujer española' (The real problem of Spanish women) – to which this reviewer feels he or she has apparently reliable access, 'El problema, **Cecilia**, ya no se puede presentar bajo la vertiente de que todos los hombres son malitos' (The problem, **Cecilia**, can no longer be presented under the idea that all men are jerks), the reviewer complains. But it is with this sentence that Santiago goes in for the kill:

> El problema, **Cecilia**, está, intuimos, en cambiar esta podrida sociedad que oprime a niños y a hombres, a niñas y a mujeres, por otra que posea un orden político-social-económico diferente que modifique

las relaciones humanas, en todos sus sentidos. (The problem, **Cecilia**, we intuit, lies in the need to change this rotten society that oppresses boys and men, girls and women, for one with a different political-social-economic order that transforms human relations in all senses of the word.) (Santiago 1978; translation Vernon 2002, 122 n. 6; the aggressive use of bold is in the original)

This response to ¡*Vámonos, Bárbara!* illustrates how Bartolomé was caught in the crossfire of the Spanish Left in these years. 'Algunos grupos feministas' (Some feminist groups) criticised the film for being too mainstream, as it makes 'muchas concesiones' (many concessions) (Aguilar 1978); others mention its dismissal by 'lenguas viperinas' (viper tongues) (Fiestas 1978). As Vernon summarises, 'Both the content and highly personal tone of *Punto y coma* journalist Santiago's critique hark back to a long-standing quarrel.' Drawing on Anny Brooksbank Jones's work, she explains:

> From the 1960s on, women militants engaged in 'doble militancia' (characterized by a dual emphasis on feminist and revolutionary political goals), were dogged by charges that their fight to promote women's issues was harming the cause by distracting attention from the more immediate sociopolitical priorities. Such conflicts were never resolved [...] and would also contribute to the increasing fragmentation within the Spanish women's movement in the '70s. (2002, 102)

¡*Vámonos, Bárbara!*, and indeed, I would argue, Bartolomé's whole career, its perception and its reception in Spain, were caught in between this 'supuesto conflicto entre revolución socialista y liberación femenina' (supposed conflict between Socialist revolution and female liberation) (Vernon 2011, 148).

'Destiempado' (Time out of joint) take one: Ana and the Transition to democracy

If many contemporary critics found the film's in-betweenness a weakness – linguistically, between Catalan and Castilian, politically, between feminism and socialism – it is precisely this in-betweenness that subsequent scholars have seen as the film's strength. Several readings focus on Ana to argue for her character arc as a brilliant portrait of an evolving Spain of the Transition. Eva Parrondo Coppel interprets the opening scene as a rebirth, in which Ana emerges from a goldfish tank (2001, 34) – the water and the vessel recalling amniotic fluid and the womb – and thereby avoids the 'muerte subjetiva' (subjective death) indicated by her self-description, at over forty years of age, as a 'mujer acabada' (woman for whom life is over) (2001, 35). The film narrative then journeys 'hacia la libertad' (towards freedom) (Parrondo Coppel's title) – of Ana and of Spain. The point, of course, is that preposition 'hacia'.

In a comparison of *¡Vámonos, Bárbara!* with the two other remarkable films of the Transition's 'feminist trilogy', *Gary Cooper, que estás en los cielos / Gary Cooper, Who Art in Heaven* (Miró 1980) and *Función de noche / Night Performance* (Molina 1981), Vernon nuances 'hacia' to focus on the dislocation implied, for both protagonist and country, of being in-between or out-of-place in time: 'destiempado' (2011) (which I translate as 'time out of joint': see the Shakespeare reference discussed below). As Ana's bed-ridden, belligerent and chain-smoking mother puts it to her: 'el país, patas arriba; hasta tú te estás contagiando' (the country's turned upside down; even you are getting infected); a point her simpering sister echoes: 'tú, o no llegas, o te pasas' (you either don't make it, or you go too far).

Valeria Camporesi, taking the mother's words as her chapter title, offers a suggestive reading of this in-betweenness that stresses the unfinished nature of the Transition, one that proposes not only reading the film against this historical context, but also reading the historical context against the film, a dialogue in which the two 'se iluminan recíprocamente' (reciprocally illuminate one another) (2001, 54). Thus, rather than interpret the opening as the rather solemn 'rebirth' of Ana/Spain, Camporesi is sensitive to the tone of this scene. The film opens with Ana finishing having sex next to the goldfish tank – part of the décor of the design studio where she works. Soler Leal's performance here is crucial: 'cuando vemos a Ana/Soler Leal dar las gracias a su casual compañero sexual, con una actitud relajada y distante, el tono de la película está marcada' (when we see Ana/Soler Leal thank her casual sexual partner in a relaxed and distant way, the tone of the film is set) (2001, 55). Indeed, when we learn that this was sex outside marriage for Ana for the first time, we might retrospectively have expected sentimental romanticism and erotic spectacle, especially given the similarity of the scene with the standard treatment of seduction in a similar sequence of Joseph Losey's *Eva / Eve* (1962). Not in Bartolomé's hands. The scene, first, is de-eroticised: beginning right at the end of the act, there is none of the suggestive foreplay on which Spanish cinema, both under censorship and during the soft-porn *destape* and beyond, endlessly relied and relies for audience titillation.[12] But neither is there ponderous reflection on breaking her marriage vow of fidelity for the first time. To the chagrin of the critics who disliked the 'pequeños episodios sin el correspondiente aval de profundización psicológica' (brief episodes lacking the corresponding endorsement of psychological depth) (Crespo 1978; see also Marinero's critique of 'superficiality' 1978) Bartolomé, and her protagonist Ana, are women in a hurry.

Thus Ana and the film set off on multiple journeys (Parrondo Coppel counts nine (2001, 35)) and encounter multiple different models of femininity for her potentially to emulate in her reinvention. This, for Camporesi, is Ana's 'apropriación progresiva de conciencia de sí' (gradual acquisition of self-awareness), just as it is for the country. The first model is found in the uproarious portrait of her elderly aunt, tía Remedios (Josefina Tapias), who lives alone in contentment, and seems mainly to survive on her priest brother's home-made raw morcilla and red wine. A kind of solitary female Noah with her animals, she lives in her tumble-down farm, complete with unused wooden ploughs, located in among the ugly skyscrapers that house the visitors to Tarragona of Spain's recent tourist boom. Lest the characterisation runs the risk of fond sentimentality, however, Bartolomé is sure to include contradiction. Despite her own contented solitude, tía Remedios advises Ana to return to her husband; then, far from being a 'remedio' (cure) for Ana's problems, she betrays her niece by telephoning Carlos and revealing her whereabouts so he can collect his child, and possibly errant wife, too.

The next model for reinvention is provided by Ana's old school friend, Paula (Julieta Serrano), a woman who is also content outside the institution of marriage. She is separated, has a daughter too, runs a tourist shop in Castell and has a younger boyfriend with whom she enjoys frequent alcohol- and drug-fuelled socialising. Paula, though, is a walking stereotype – a hippy on the make with her tourist shop – but, given the film's comic tone, this is the point. Like tía Remedios, she is also flawed: when a storm breaks while her daughter is out camping in the open air, she is not concerned; she is to be found, rather, stoned and in bed with her toy boy.

To these individual characters Bartolomé adds brilliant collective portraits. The riotous scene of the group of older ladies on the bus was inspired by a similar episode that the director claims she in fact witnessed (Ordóñez 1978, 13; Hernández Les 1978); her representation of it was then exaggerated via *esperpento* (Aznarez 1978). After lifetimes of endless pregnancies in a country where contraception was illegal (see Chapter 1's analysis of Bartolomé's earlier exploration of this in *Carmen de Carabanchel / Carmen of Carabanchel*), the women quarrel with the crude, sexist bus driver, and end up chasing him from the bus! (Contemporary reviewers who sought serious psychological depth in their feminist cinema hated it, like Jordi Viader, who strangely described it as a sequence of 'science fiction' (1978).)

Next comes the group of Ana's old school friends, the whingeing housewives who enjoy sunbathing on the beach while complaining about their husbands (including graphic details such as the pain of having sex with a descended uterus).[13] Finally, Bartolomé includes the group of retired English lady tourists, for whom Iván is the tour guide. Significantly, these women, travelling on holiday alone, without men, are much happier than the other groups. They also enjoy a particular connection with Bárbara, who, given they do not share a language, intuits their independence. In the interview conducted by Núria Triana Toribio and the author included in this volume (see Appendix Interview), Bartolomé reveals that this group of women were retired performers of Barcelona's Paralelo club, whom she found thanks to the efforts of Matas's brilliant casting director. Not only did these women correspond physically to the foreign look of the time that Bartolomé sought, the performers' own previous, independent careers also match the film's study of female independence.

For Camporesi, the crucial point is that Ana does not follow any of these individual or collective options for reinvention. Bartolomé conveys her resistance to Ana settling on any option by having the character be continually on the move in the narrative, and also through film form. For example, Bartolomé cross-cuts between Ana and Paula, then the housewives on the beach, showing that Ana aligns herself with neither. She also uses long takes with a similar effect. Ana shares the frame, for example, in the choral scenes with the housewives, or the English tourists, but she only shares the frame with, and does not settle within, each group. If we read the film in the context of the Transition we might note it 'abre gradualmente una serie de ventanas sobre un mundo plural, a la vez radicalmente nuevo y singularmente antiguo' (gradually opens up a series of windows onto a plural world, one that is simultaneously both radically new, and singularly old) (Camporesi 2001, 59), but if we read the Transition against the film we note each window throws light on the 'límites y potencialidades del discurso politico de la Transición' (limits and potentials of the political discourse of the Transition) (Camporesi 2001, 60), thereby offering 'una mirada radical acerca de la historia en general, y de la relación entre ésta y la materialidad de la existencia de los individuos' (a radical view on history in general, and on the relationship between this history and the material conditions in which individuals live) (Camporesi 2001, 59).

Camporesi, however, misses a window, or model of female independence, whose obviousness seems to have obviated it from critical view: the Girl, Bárbara. And Ana's choices depend on Bárbara. For example, when Ana believes she is choosing the model of Paula's bohemian life by beginning a relationship with Paula's friend Iván, Bárbara sees immediately that she is in fact returning to the model of the 'mujer acabada'. Iván will be the new Carlos, becoming increasingly sexist and homophobic the further away he gets from the holiday coast, and the closer he gets to Barcelona. It is Bárbara who points out the similarity, 'otra vez igual' (here we go again), prompting Ana to act, and the film thereby achieves its feminist open ending thanks to the Girl. Thus, while Soler Leal's Ana apparently drives the narrative, just as she does the car, this chapter suggests we refocus from primary to secondary character to put overlooked Bárbara back into the frame. Ana may be in-between past and present through her actions in the narrative. Bárbara, an adolescent, queer Girl is always and already in-between, a figure that is therefore even more suited to exploring the in-betweenness of the Transition.

Girlhood Studies and Spanish culture

With the launch of the Berghahn journal in 2008, Girlhood Studies established itself as an interdisciplinary field that is part of, but distinct from, Feminism and Women's Studies. In the inaugural issue, the editors of *Girlhood Studies: An Interdisciplinary Journal* set out the aim of 'defining and mapping out what Girlhood means, what it encompasses in different interconnected cultures in the twenty-first century' (Mitchell, Reid-Walsh and Kirt 2008, ix). Given the hyper-visibility of the Girl in the present moment, there has been a particular urgency to focus, then, on contemporary Girlhoods. This is especially true in media studies, where the problems and allure of postfeminist 'girl power' have been a particular concern. Fiona Handyside and Kate Taylor-Jones's timely volume, *International Cinema and the Girl: Local Issues, Transnational Contexts* (2016), added new perspectives to scholarship which, the editors point out, had previously tended to focus on first-world, white and Anglophone girls. They also point out that 'the recurring theme in the contemporary media that girls are newly visible does not stand up to historic scrutiny', highlighting, for example, debates about 'the girl' and the figure of the 'flapper' in the 1920s in the UK (2016, 3) – although their edited collection itself largely continues the focus on the contemporary era.[14]

This chapter adds a further, non-Anglophone perspective to this scholarship, but shifts the focus from the twenty-first century by insisting on the importance of the Girl in the 1970s, the decade of the rise of feminism internationally, and also the decade of the end of Francoism in Spain. Rather than looking for girls in earlier periods who provide precedents for contemporary figures, like Rebecca Hains's work on 1930s girl heroes as a precedent for 1990s girl power (2008), this chapter takes a chronological approach. Noting the influence of representations of the Girl in Spanish literature, when she rose to prominence with Carmen Laforet's Andrea of *Nada / Nothing* in 1944 (adapted to film by Edgar Neville in 1947), and likewise the influence of the 'cine con niño' film genre of the 1950s to 1970s, I locate Bárbara within the 1970s, and trace her legacy on Bartolomé's own portraits of Susana and Rita in her 1995 *Lejos de África* (Chapter 6). Beyond Bartolomé's own work, failings in the timely distribution and exhibition of the film mean that its influence on the representation of future Spanish cinematic sisters may still lie in the future.

The contemporary press, as we have seen, rightly hailed both Bartolomé's characterisation of Bárbara, and Álvarez's performance

Putting Bárbara into ¡Vámonos, Bárbara!

as her (Ripoll-Freixes 1978), for avoiding the sentimental portrait of many of the characters of the 'cine con niño', like the youthful Joselito (José Jiménez Fernández) of the 1950s to 1960s. The contemporary press does not connect Bárbara with Spanish art cinema's version of the 'cine con niño', however, perhaps revealing the lesser cultural impact of art cinema inside Spain (if greater impact outside Spain). The previously mentioned *El espíritu de la colmena* and *Cría cuervos* explore the traumatised child as an enigmatic cipher for adult traumas, through Ana Torrent's performances as Ana in both films. 'Emotionally and politically stunted children', like the characters played by Torrent, represented a generation of directors that Marsha Kinder famously named 'The Children of Franco' (1983, 58). Sarah Wright, paying particular attention to the horror genre, shifted interpretations away from the child as a representation of adult concerns, to assign some agency to the child, with her thesis of the 'child witness' (2013, 89–128). While Álvarez's Bárbara could not seem further away from Torrent's Ana with regard to genre – from Erice and Saura's arthouse horror, to Bartolomé's accessible comedy – if we look again, these characters all belong to bourgeois families with enigmatic or stern matriarchs – and all adopt a questioning gaze on their surroundings and choose unconventional paths.

The difference is the question of agency, for Bárbara not only witnesses but also has power. After her mother's admittedly key independent decision about marital separation, Bárbara seems from then on to be the one deciding, and saying '¡Vámonos, mamá!' (Mum, let's go!) She directs her newly separated mother's life by choosing the suggestively circuitous, or 'sideways',[15] road route out of Barcelona and thereby encourages her to return to her pre-marital girlhood in order to reconstruct her post-marital womanhood. She directs her mother's choices of new sexual partners, rejecting, first, Quiquet, then, as we have seen, Iván. She decides that mother and daughter will stay in Aguamar, rather than return to Barcelona. And she chooses the all-important feminist ending of the film – the open road full of possibility and the mother-daughter 'pacto' (pact). Mischievously referencing both explicit contemporary 'pactos' in legislation (like the 'pactos de Moncloa' 1977), and tacit contemporary societal 'pactos' (like the 'pacto del olvido' (pact of forgetting)), Bárbara also cheerfully quips that 'los pactos son para romperlos' (pacts are for breaking).

Choosing an alternative, sideways path outside the family home, choosing or rejecting romantic and sexual partners and choosing an uncertain future of contingent pacts: Bárbara is both the active subject of this powerful verb 'choose', and makes unconventional choices. These also connect her with the important literary precedent, in ascendance in Spanish literature during Bartolomé's own girlhood and formative years: the 'chica rara' (unconventional girl). This is the title of the essay penned by novelist Carmen Martín Gaite in 1986 (and published by Espasa Calpe in 1987), in which she tracks the importance of a figure that first appeared as Andrea in Laforet's *Nada* (1944), and continued in the work of contemporary Spanish women writers like Ana María Matute (her Valba in the 1948 *Los Abel / The Abels*), Dolores Medio (her Lena in the 1952 *Nosotros los Rivero / Us Riveros*) and Martín Gaite herself (her Natalia and Elvira in the 1957 *Entre visillos / Behind the Curtains*). Martín Gaite identifies the ways these girls all share a condition of being 'distinta' (different), 'infrecuente' (unusual), 'inconform[ista]' (non-conformist), or – her preferred adjective – 'rara' (unconventional) (1993). Bárbara shares many of the characteristics of these literary antecedents, which rose to prominence in Spanish literature of the 1940s to 1960s, when, Martín Gaite was to affirm in 1986, most novels by women appeared in Spanish literature ever (1992, 121). Like these literary sisters, Bárbara fulfils the characteristics of being 'rara': she rejects the confines of the home, though the city street of the novels – 'una calle casi siempre idealizada' (an outside space that is almost always idealised) (1992, 113) – becomes the open roads of the Catalan coast in this road movie. Like the 'chicas raras', Bárbara is from a bourgeois family, has few friends of her own age (she is happy to leave behind the ones she has made at the summer camp at the start of the film), and her home in Barcelona, though luxurious rather than shabby, connects her in particular to *Nada*'s Barcelona-based Andrea. It is crucial that it is she who encourages her mother to reject the 'happy ending' of potential remarriage, this time to Iván. Even though these are proxy partnerships for Bárbara, her choices echo the behaviour of the 'chicas raras', whose key manifestation of non-conformity, for Martín Gaite, is rejecting the romantic choices that lead to marriage, as these choices dominated contemporary sentimental literature, the 'novela rosa' (sentimental novel) (1992, 121).

It is tempting to translate, and update, 'rara' with the English adjective 'queer', and thereby reread the literary characters Martín Gaite analyses as not only resisting the societal conformity of romance and marriage, but also exploring, even seeking, non-heterosexual alternatives. However, the literary 'chicas raras' are defined by class and the rejection of proscribed life paths, 'middle-class independently minded girls with aspirations beyond motherhood and marriage' (O'Leary and Ribeiro de Menezes 2008, 27), not necessarily sexuality, thus I have opted for the more neutral adjective 'unconventional' here.[16] Bárbara's queerness is thus a new development in representations of the Girl; I draw attention to her connections with the 1940s to 1960s literary 'chicas raras', but do not assign her queerness to those earlier girls retrospectively.

Also key is Álvarez-as-Bárbara's age of twelve, and thus her representation of adolescence. Bárbara's changing body is briefly highlighted in the scene where she and her mother buy a new bikini top. Ana suggests her chest is barely developed enough for one, but Bárbara, perhaps in a dig at contemporary 'destape' cinema, refuses to go topless. If only referenced in the narrative once, Bárbara's adolescent body, in various states of undress, is nonetheless ever-visible. Ever-visible and thus seemingly everyday and without importance, Girlhood Media Studies perspectives shed light on the significance of the adolescent, however, both physically and mentally. Writing on *Pariah* (Rees 2011), Clara Bradbury-Rance's analysis of the adolescent, queer Girl is illuminating. 'The adolescent state itself', she writes, is 'constructed through prepositions, the teen finds herself *after* childhood (if biology does its job); *before* adulthood (if society does *its* job): if not, then *alongside* both... or neither' (2016, 84–5). Such a state is, then, particularly resonant within the Transition in Spain: *after* Franco; *before* democracy; *alongside* both... or neither. Working with theorists of liminality (David Sibley) and adolescence (Arnold von Gennep, Victor Turner), Sarah Thomas makes the case for the resonance of the adolescent in Transition Spain too, and explores male heterosexual adolescent Juan and female heterosexual adolescent Goyita in her case studies Jaime de Armiñan's *El amor del capitán Brando / Captain Brando's Love* (1974) and *El nido / The Nest* (1980) (Chapter 4, 2019). She does not include *¡Vámonos, Bárbara!* in her study as her focus is on films where children are protagonists (2019, 21). In the next section, I will argue for the significance of Bárbara in the non-narrative textures of ¡Vámonos, Bárbara!, which in fact give her prominence despite her not being the protagonist. As well as adolescence, I will suggest that her queerness adds a further layer to her disrupting presence in the film. Bradbury-Rance, again, suggests queerness amplifies the in-betweenness of adolescence. Drawing on Elizabeth Freeman, who in turn draws on Shakespeare's *Hamlet* (1599–1601), queer adolescents are 'denizens of time out of joint' (2016, 86), an observation which, I will argue, overlaps suggestively with Spanish film historians' identification of the 'destiempado'[17] (time out of joint) of the Transition.

'Destiempado' (Time out of joint) take two: the queer adolescent Girl

Bárbara has an agency and a power in the narrative that suggests we move her from the secondary focus of previous criticism to the primary focus of this chapter. While critics read Ana as a manifestation of the 'destiempado', this is as a function of narrative – she leaves Carlos and the Francoism he represents for an uncertain future that aligns with the uncertainty of the new democracy. She represents 'destiempado', then, despite, rather than because of, her age: a middle-aged woman in her forties she behaves like a child, dressing up in new clothes and experimenting with new sensations like smoking marijuana. The queer adolescent girl, however, embodies, rather than represents, 'destiempado', there is no need for such narrative signposting, both because of her age and her sexuality. In this section I will begin with an analysis of the non-narrative film resources of movement, sight and sound, to draw out Bárbara's in-betweenness, before returning to apparently irrelevant narrative events that also signal these, to conclude that these non-narrative and secondary-narrative elements make up Bartolomé's renewal of the representation of the Girl.

We have seen that Ana is a character who is constantly on the move in the narrative, while Bárbara functions as her centre, her north. Leaving the narrative aside, if we revisit this through an analysis of camera movement, we see that Ana's movement is often captured by a static camera, for instance when she rushes around

Putting Bárbara into ¡Vámonos, Bárbara! 95

packing at tía Remedios's house, drives the car in and out of frame, or moves from background to foreground (as when she meets her old friend Paula, then walks back to the group of housewives) (Figure 4.1). This use of a static camera and long take to capture the movement of characters, or the sometimes frenetic activity of a chorus of characters, has been attributed to the influence of Berlanga, principally by Bartolomé herself.[18]

Within this context I thus find the representation of Bárbara significant, not her physical movement, but her embodiment of movement through the physicality of her own adolescent body. For Bárbara, unlike for Ana, Bartolomé instead often chooses a central location within medium close-ups. This location and camera shot represent Bárbara's role as a hinge: both dependent on, yet independent from, or in-between, two different planes – left and right in the frame, foreground and background in the focus. Take the scene of Ana's return to tía Remedios's Tarragona farm after her first sojourn at Paula's tourist shop and flat in Castell. It takes place at the dining table. Bárbara is located in the centre at the end, flanked by her mother, to her right, and tía Remedios, to her left (Figure 4.2). Ana is flushed with the excitement of her new adventure (and new love interest Iván), and wears a white sundress she has acquired at Paula's shop; she tells tía Remedios that it looks like an old-fashioned petticoat, but her aunt complains it makes her look both sluttish and poor. Here, the film suggests, might be one possible future path for Spain, one that is represented by Ana, following

Figure 4.1 Ana (Amparo Soler Leal), standing, and the housewives in ¡Vámonos, Bárbara! (1978)

Figure 4.2 Bárbara (Cristina Álvarez), the 'hinge' between Ana (Amparo Soler Leal), left, and tía Remedios (Josefina Tapias), right, standing, in ¡Vámonos, Bárbara! (1978)

the example of Paula. To Bárbara's left stands tía Remedios, clad in one of her shapeless dresses and a house apron. Here, then, is the traditional model of womanhood from Spain's past. Apparently, the scene is all about the vociferous argument between mother and aunt. Tía Remedios has betrayed Ana by telephoning Carlos to report her behaviour and organise his collection of their daughter from the house: Ana is not pleased. Obeying the 180-degree rule, the camera cuts between the two arguing women and the silent Bárbara, who looks from left to right as she turns from one woman to the other. We do not share exact point-of-view shots from Bárbara's position, rather the eyeline matches signal we adopt her perspective, switching from mother to great aunt. Rather than the verbose argument, then, the scene is in fact all about Bárbara's representation of in-betweenness within it. She embodies the in-between within her adolescent body, not through wearing modern or traditional clothes. This is complemented by the filmic representation of her position in-between, and connected to, the two medium shots of her relatives, which stresses her position as an in-between 'hinge'.

While 'hinge' was used as a metaphor to describe the decade of the 1950s in Spain as it pivoted from post-war austerity and isolation to capitalist opening up (García Delgado 1995), a process that accelerated over the 1960s, I suggest that this metaphor becomes even more relevant in the 1970s. Franco's death in 1975 was preceded by the final days of dictatorship, during which much of the nation looked forward to democracy with tentative hope, and was succeeded by the first days of democracy, during which much of the nation looked back at dictatorship with nostalgic regret. Adolescent Bárbara, whose very body fuses childhood with adulthood, is the privileged manifestation of such a hinge moment. And her centrality in this scene, in which her body is still, but her head turns from right to left, matching the camera cuts, is its effective representation.

Bartolomé also creates an effect of in-betweenness in *mise en scène* through careful framing of Bárbara in a middle or centre ground. When Ana and Bárbara leave tía Remedios after the argument, Bartolomé places Ana in the foreground in the car, tía Remedios in the background at her Tarragona house, and Bárbara in-between them in middle range. Similarly, once mother and daughter have left Paula's shop and flat in Castell for Aguamar, Bartolomé places Bábara in medium-long shot between Ana and new lover Iván canoodling in the foreground, and the independent English tourists in the background. Again, in the penultimate scene of the film, when Ana sits in the foreground, in the front seat of the car, Bárbara is in middle range on the back seat, while Iván is in deep focus as he walks towards the garage.

Just as Bartolomé uses movement in cinematography, and composition in mise en scène, to represent Bárbara's eloquent in-betweenness, she also attends to sound film's further resources of sight and sound. The genesis of Bárbara's role as her mother's 'lazarilla' (Parrondo Coppel's felicitous description (2001, 35)) may have begun with Bartolomé's creative collaboration with Soler Leal. The director reveals in a contemporary press review that it was the actor's idea to wear glasses (Masó 1978b). From this seed of an idea, Bartolomé grows much of the comedy of the film. The spurious excuse for the mantillas striptease is that Ana is literally somewhat blind without her glasses, and therefore cannot see the tourists in front of whom she accidentally dances and strips. Figuratively, if Ana is blind to the dangers and opportunities before her, Bárbara, her lazarilla, leads her. However, unlike the blind man's guide of the renaissance original (*Lazarillo de Tormes*, 1554), who ends up a disempowered cuckold, Bárbara both guides and leads. Once again, where Bárbara leads, though, is not a specific location, but a dislocation, a sideways meander, or space that is in-between. The film is book-ended by these choices. Bárbara figuratively sees the importance of an indirect route that enables her mother to revisit significant locations of her childhood at the start of the film.[19] At the end, Bárbara sees that new lover Iván is old husband Carlos take two, so mother and daughter instead choose the open road to an uncertain, though independent, future.

The acoustic portrait of Bárbara also suggests the in-betweenness of the 'destiempado'. The legislation that enforced the dubbing of non-Castilian language films into Castilian was passed in 1941, but despite its association, therefore, with dictatorship and censorship, the practice was far too embedded within cultural practice by the 1970s for there to be any change (it continues today). In addition, the recording of direct sound was expensive, so Castilian-language films were also dubbed, well into 1980s (Whittaker and Wright 2017, 5).[20] As we have seen, dubbing would also be put to the service of new democracy and its linguistic policies too, like linguistic normalisation in Catalonia. Expensive direct sound and the use of actors' own voices in the 1970s and 1980s were therefore associated with auteur cinema. For example, Ana Torrent's dubbing of her own voice in *El espíritu* brought significant authenticity to Erice's representation of the child, an aesthetic choice supported by a producer who was the foremost advocate of art cinema in Spain in the period, Elías Querejeta. A commissioned, commercial film, *¡Vámonos, Bárbara!* was dubbed, partly as this was cheaper and common practice, though partly, as we have seen, so that Matas could secure the subsidy for the Catalan version. Only the record for the Castilian version of the film is available at the Spanish Dubbing Database; it reveals that while adult principal actors dubbed themselves (Amparo Soler Leal as Ana; Iván Tubau as Iván; Julieta Serrano as Paula), Cristina Álvarez was dubbed by the adult voice actor Ángela González.[21]

While the process of dubbing, whether from a foreign language or within the same language, might aim at maximum naturalisation and invisibility, an inevitable gap arises between the recording of mouth movement in the image and the dubbed sound added in post-production. If a skilled actor dubs themselves, this gap is narrowed, but it creeps open when dubbing occurs across languages, or – my interest in this chapter – across generations. Sarah Wright notes the 'disorientating' (2013, 44) and 'uncanny' (2013, 45) effects of this gap in her investigation of the common practice in Spain of the dubbing of child stars by adult, female dubbing artists. She argues that in the film narratives, like *Marcelino, pan y vino / The Miracle of Marcelino* (Vajda 1955), in which little boy Pablito Calvo (born in 1948) is dubbed by thirty-year-old woman Matilde Vilariño, the children become 'errant voices, crossing the screen, reminding us of the suppression of the voices of children (and indeed of a nation) during the long years of the Franco regime' (2013, 52).

In *¡Vámonos, Bárbara!*, the dubbing of the teenage, rather than child, Álvarez by adult González is rather one of disorientation and in-betweenness. In the 1960s González had dubbed popular twin child stars Pili and Mili (Pilar and Emilia Bayona Sarriá), thus the sound of this adult woman's voice, a voice that carries the echo of these famous on-screen children, dubbing a teenage girl, in fact complements my thesis of in-betweenness. The Castilian-dubbed version of *¡Vámonos, Bárbara!* – over which, unlike the Catalan version, we presume Bartolomé had some control – complements, then, the portrait I have painted of Bárbara as a 'hinge' between dictatorship past and democratic future. She is portrayed as the 'hinge' between shots in camera-work; she is to be found in the eloquent mid-range of deep focus photography; she is the bearer of the look when her mother is literally short-sighted and figuratively blind; and, finally, she is the carrier of a voice which, if not her own, fuses actual adult articulation with echoes of the girls which that voice had previously dubbed.

¡Qué barbaridad! (How Outrageous!): Bárbara from background to foreground

Having tracked the importance of Bárbara in the non-narrative, aesthetic textures of this film, spatial, visual and aural, I finish by analysing two apparently incidental narrative developments in which she is the protagonist. The first concerns the sub-plot that runs throughout the film of Bárbara's vegetarianism and connection with animals; the second is a single sequence of queer play-acting whose significance, I argue, is greater than the relative brevity of the scene.

As Spain experienced rapid urbanisation from the 1950s to the 1960s, its culture tracked the new and mass experience of the rural/

urban divide. In cinema this led to the comic elderly 'paleto' (country bumpkin) figure, a character from the country who is disorientated in the city, embodied, for example, by Paco Martínez Soria in films like *La ciudad no es para mí* (Lazaga 1965). Like these popular comedies, art films drew from the same inspiration. Carlos Saura's *La caza*, of the same year, for example, made the matching, though opposite, move of portraying the disorientated urban character, the youth Enrique (Emilio Gutiérrez Caba), in rural surroundings. In both popular and art modes, the rural/urban divide may be explored through the preparation of food: Martínez Soria's tío (uncle) Agustín cuts an amusing figure carrying live chickens through the centre of Madrid so he can slaughter them and thus prepare a fresh broth at his son's expensive modern flat. Guriérrez Caba's Enrique, meanwhile, responds to the slaughter of the sheep he sees at the village with nausea; when Luis tells him hunger drove Spaniards to eat rats during and after the Civil War while Enrique eats the paella made with the rabbits the group has hunted, his nausea finds its way into the script 'me estás dando asco' (you're making me want to puke). Bartolomé fuses both these tendencies in *¡Vámonos, Bárbara!*. As an urban youth at tía Remedios's country farm, Bárbara connects with Saura's Enrique; simultaneously, as the film adopts a comic mode, Tapias's performance as the aunt recalls Martínez Soria's as uncle Agustín. While tío Agustín is disorientated in Madrid, the aunt, like the building she inhabits, is disorientated too, surrounded as she is by the tourist flats of Tarragona. There is an explicit reference to *La caza*, though, when Bárbara experiences the same queasiness as Enrique, while he eats rabbit paella, a dish her great aunt also prepares. As she helps tía Remedios skin the rabbit her great aunt will cook, she is not just queasy, she actually runs off and vomits.

Yet, unlike Enrique, Bárbara's response to the skinning of the rabbit is not that of the city-dweller disconnected from the rural practices of food production. The instance is in fact one in a narrative thread from which Bárbara emerges as a constant champion of the rural world, not, like her great aunts and uncles, as a farmer, but, rather, as an animal-lover and vegetarian. Thus Bárbara is afraid of tía Remedios's guard dog, as he is associated with the old world of farming, but enthusiastically takes up her role as a modern female Noah to the male and female chicks she is given as pets. Working in the genre of comedy, it is important to stress that Bárbara's connection with nature is far from solemn and seems, rather, played for jokes, as when the chicks climb on Bárbara's head when mother and daughter sleep in the car, or flap about in the car on their return to Barcelona. Nonetheless, when the death of the male chick predicts the break with Iván, and Bárbara's freeing of the lone female chick represents her and her mother's future of female independence, we note the connection of this apparently irrelevant narrative thread to the main plot.

Bárbara's vegetarianism – a word and phenomenon that was still rare in the 1970s,[22] though gaining in familiarity through internationally famous celebrity vegetarians like Paul McCartney – also appears to be played for laughs. Raw black pudding (morcilla), for example, becomes a shorthand for the rural traditionalism of tía Remedios that sickens Bárbara. However, the scene on the beach with her mother and cousin Quiquet, where Bárbara rejects the morcilla sandwich, merits further attention. Bárbara looks on at her mother flirting with Quiquet with the same disgust with which we see her pick the blood sausage out of her sandwich. There follows a smutty pun on the verb 'bucear' (dive) – something Ana suggestively claims she has learned to do with Quiquet. What is indicated, then, is that the morcilla is a metaphor for her mother's heterosexuality; it is made clearer with Bárbara's outburst to her: 'que te gustan los tíos' (you like men). Ana ditches the potential romantic liaison with Quiquet in favour of reconnecting with her daughter (though she will later pursue Iván), and ditches the morcilla sandwiches in the sea in favour of going to a beach kiosk with Bárbara.

If there is a queer subtext to Bárbara's vegetarianism that emerges here in the words she speaks in anger, queerness becomes even more explicit in the play-acting scene between Bárbara and Andreu at Paula's flat. Children play-acting in cinema may, of course, be dismissed as just play. However, comparing two art films from the poignant contexts of the 1970s Transition, *Cría cuervos*, and the 1990s AIDS crisis, *Estiu 1993 / Summer 1993* (Simón 2017), Rachel Beaney has shown that, rather than a 'mute witness or cipher of victimhood […] playful interactions offer cinematic child protagonists a plethora of ways to speak in the narratives' (2021, 367). In both films, young girls dress up as their deceased mothers to 'speak' and work through their trauma.

Working in the genre of comedy, and working with an adolescent character, the tone and content of the dressing-up, play-acting scene are very different in *¡Vámonos, Bárbara!*. Nonetheless, like her cinematic sisters, the scene allows Bárbara to 'speak' the queerness that is only implied elsewhere in the narrative. It begins with Ana entering Paula's shop and house to find an androgynous young figure clad in white dancing in the gallery – the internal balcony space where Ana herself had explored new liberated identities by dancing with the mantillas and performing the striptease. The figure does not remove any clothes, but her dance movements, as she dances alone, just as her mother had danced alone in the same space, also connote freedom. This white-clad youth has their own hair tucked away and wears a shorter blond, curly wig, which recalls the young male love interest Tadzio of Luchino Visconti's *Death in Venice* (1971).[23] In another echo of the Italian film, the white child figure then sits on the adult Andreu's knee. Andreu, the film's gay character, is somewhat crudely drawn, especially in this scene that may imply paedophilia.[24] Bartolomé's intention, I suggest, is first to focus our attention on Bárbara, her pleasure in dressing up, hiding her hair, dancing and play-acting as a boy, and second to underline Ana's hypocritical response. Ana laughs at her own appearance in the gallery, when she play-acts as a stripper, but is angered at Bárbara's play-acting as a boy with her homosexual friend. The only moment in the film when Ana utters '¡qué barbaridad!' (how outrageous!) is as a joke when Bárbara's chicks escape on the beach – it is a phrase that might have been better used here. For Bárbara, this scene provides a moment in the narrative where she may reveal a non-heterosexual identity. While it is brief in duration (just one minute), its significance lies in the fact that it explicitly explores, through play, dance and a cinephilic reference to Visconti, a queerness that has only been implied by metaphor and the odd angry outburst elsewhere in the narrative.[25]

There is no doubt that the protagonist of *¡Vámonos, Bárbara!*, Soler Leal's Ana, dominates the film – just as Alice (Ellen Burstyn) did in Scorsese's original. Critics have previously noted the feminist significance of Bartolomé's transformation of Scorsese's ending, which restored the patriarchal, heterosexual status quo, into *¡Vámonos, Bárbara!*'s open one of freedom. The significance of Bartolomé transformation of Alice's clearly pre-pubescent eleven-year-old son Tommy, of Scorsese's film, into a twelve-year-old and clearly adolescent daughter Bárbara, however, has heretofore not been noted.

Putting Bárbara into ¡Vámonos, Bárbara!   103

This chapter thus proposes a new reading of ¡*Vámonos, Bárbara!* by adjusting our focus away from protagonist Ana, or by looking askance: at Bárbara. With her portrait, Bartolomé bequeaths to Spanish film history the rich representational possibilities of the adolescent Girl to convey change and transformation. We have seen that the teen Girl shifts from periphery to centre if we look anew at space – beyond the foreground or close-up to the middle; vision – beyond what can immediately be seen, to enhanced perception; and sound – listening to an adult voice that previously dubbed famous cinematic children, and thereby locating teenage Bárbara between the echoes of childhood and the premonition of a future voice of adulthood. When we are alert to these non-narrative textures of the film, we may return to the narrative to see that various sub-plots related to Bárbara may in fact be the film's actual plot. Her function as a 'hinge' between old and new Spains; her environmentalism; and her queer sexuality, which we only glimpse in moments of anger or play, all make up a character who, far from being peripheral, is in fact central to understanding trauma and transformation in Spain's culture of the Transition. Bárbara's previously unexamined function in the narrative as a role model to her own mother is therefore complex. On the one hand, her adolescence and queerness locate her in-between. On the other, her role as a hinge between old and new worlds, along with her feminism, ecologism and queerness, these elements all remain stable, in contrast to Ana's identity-in-flux. Rarely glimpsed on Spanish screens, Bartolomé's queer teen Girl should be placed alongside the cute children of the 'cine con niño', the traumatised children of arthouse cinema, and the unconventional Girl of Spain's literary 'chicas raras', in the legacy it leaves for portraits of the Girl in the future. Since the film sank into obscurity for many years, that legacy may still be to come, though we may look for it in Bartolomé's own work in her next, and final, fiction film, *Lejos de África*'s Susana and Rita (Chapter 6).

Notes

1 Another success is the transformation of the grammatical third-person of Scorsese's title's description of Alice to Bartolomé's colloquial phrase, spoken by the protagonist Ana. In interview on release, the director

reveals she would have liked an adaptation of the phrase 'Más vale lo malo conocido...' (Better the devil you know) as the title, like 'Más vale lo desconocido aunque también sea malo' (Better the devil you don't know, even if it's not great either) (Aznarez 1978). She does not reveal why this changed, but I suggest the final title is successful for its grammatical first person, its use of colloquial language, its implication of movement and urgency and because it places the girl Bárbara centre stage.
2 Bartolomé also recalls working effectively with production manager Marisol Carnicero, for whom this was also her first feature film (Bermejo 2017, 10–11 and Appendix Interview p. 213). For Carnicero's perspective on her career as a production manager, see the interview in Faulkner and Triana Toribio (forthcoming).
3 Pérez notes that Bartolomé's vision is more feminist than Ridley Scott's, as Ana and Bárbara are not 'punished' by the narrative (2013, 132); they drive to an independent, if uncertain, future, rather than the suicide of Scott's film.
4 There is a jokey allusion to this when, in Ana's response to Paula's question about Carlos's floozies, she answers 'las encuentro por todas partes' (I come across them everywhere).
5 The Generalitat, restored in 1977 following Franco's death, pursued a policy of linguistic 'normalisation' to recover the use of the Catalan language that had been prohibited during the dictatorship. Cinema and television were key to this process. The Congrés de Cultura Catalana (1976) and Simposi sobre el Cinema a les Nationalitats (1977) debated Catalan language and cinema, and in the former, after a division over Catalan language use, support for its essential role in Catalan cultural production prevailed (Porter i Moix in Triana Toribio 2003, 171 n. 3). With regards cinema, acts of legislation that formalised subsidies for dubbing films in the Catalan language were passed, following the creation of the Generalitat Departament de Cultura after the first elections to the Catalan parliament in 1980. ¡Vámonos, Bárbara! appears to be a pilot case for a situation that Iván Tubau, himself the actor who plays Iván in the film, and also a writer, retrospectively denounced as follows: 'ha generado que las productoras aprovechan esta oportunidad para obtener dinero oficial, y el resultado es un film concebido en castellano y posteriormente doblado al catalán para acceder a estas subvenciones' (it has meant that producers take advantage of this opportunity to obtain official money, and the result is a film that has been conceived in Castilian and subsequently dubbed into Catalan to access subsidies) (1989, 28).
6 References in the Catalan press in April reveal that the Castilian version was also released in Barcelona on the earlier date.

7 Sarah Thomas also identifies 'the in-between' as a focus for her excellent study of the representation of children in the cinema of the Spanish Transition (2019).
8 In most cases no page numbers are recorded on articles.
9 The first use of this phrase occurred in April 1978, on account of the film's début in Barcelona, by *Catalunya Express* reviewer Monty Padura. Interestingly, within the main body of the article he uses the phrase 'la primera película española, auténticamente feminista' (the first authentically feminist Spanish film), but the title article, possibly his own, or one altered by editorial staff, is 'Primera película catalana y feminista' (first Catalan and feminist film) (Padura 1978). The phrase was then used by Fuentes, writing in *Vindicación Feminista*, in May 1978. *Arriba* reviewer Malen Aznarez used it in July; Vernon is right to note that it is remarkable to see the title 'primera película feminista del cine español' (first feminist film of Spanish cinema) (1978) in this official regime newspaper (2011, 146).
10 This middlebrow tendency in 1970s to 1980s Spanish film, particularly associated with the producer José Luis Dibildos, sought a 'tercera vía' (third way) between highbrow art and lowbrow popular genre cinema of the period (see Faulkner 2013, 6–7 and 81–118).
11 To my knowledge, this Catalan dubbed version is lost: neither the Spanish Film Archives in Madrid nor the Catalan Film Archives in Barcelona possess a copy.
12 All the nudity in the film is de-eroticised, and treated as a joke: this first sex scene, when apparently Matas insisted on the inclusion of the full-frontal nudity of his wife, even though the male partner's naked body is only seen obliquely (see Appendix Interview); Ana's topless shower; and, most ridiculously of all, Ana's accidental striptease with mantillas in front of the tourists. The jokey tone of all these scenes is Bartolomé's wry way of dealing with the frankly embarrassing joke that was the *destape* cinema: she critiques both filmmakers' obsession with including female nudity, and the game they played with the censors, whose own focus on female nudity, of course, in fact partly created the very *destape* cinema it sought to disallow (see Triana Toribio, 'What censorship created', 2003, 95–8). Censorship was still in place, but about to be abolished, as ¡*Vámonos, Bárbara!* was filmed (December 1977), thus Bartolomé intervenes in current debates by mischievously sending up the absurdity of this situation that it created. What most irked the censors was the inclusion of female nudity without narrative justification. To satirise the whole situation Bartolomé ensured that the mantilla striptease was ludicrously unjustified in the narrative (see Appendix Interview).

13 Like the do-it-yourself abortions of *Carmen de Carabanchel*, Bartolomé explains that the conversation among the friends is 'absolutamente real' (absolutely real). In what must have been quite a funny moment in interview, she tells her two male-identified interviewers, who may, or may not, have been unfamiliar with such female-coded spaces, 'no hay más que irse una vez a la peluquería para escuchar las cosas que allí se dicen' (you only have to go to the hairdressers once to hear the things that women tell each other there) (Hernández Les and Gato 1978, 45).

14 As well as the questions of representation that are the focus of Handyside and Taylor Jones and their contributors' chapters (2016), Girlhood Studies focussing on the media also address girls themselves as consumers of images, as in the Audience Studies approach adopted by Danielle Hipkins's 'Girl's Eye View' project (https://agirlseyeview.exeter.ac.uk/en/), as well as girls as agents and authors, present since its inception (see the inclusion of 'the voices of girls themselves', Mitchell, Reid-Walsh and Kirk 2008, vii).

15 I refer here to Kathryn Bond Stockton's suggestive reading of twentieth-century queer children as growing 'sideways' (2009).

16 Jo Labanyi uses 'queer girl' as her translation of 'chica rara' in 2013, but confesses that there is a risk in using 'queer girl' in a non-sexual sense, as this risks weakening the force of the term 'queer' in English (2013, 4).

17 Literally, 'el tiempo está fuera de quicio'.

18 See, for example, Bartolomé in Hernández Les and Gato (1978, 43), where she attributes both the long takes and the *esperpento* to Berlanga's influence on the film.

19 In the original script, mother and daughter were also to visit a village, a scene possibly cut for cost-saving reasons, and a decision perhaps taken by production manager Sol Carnicero.

20 Some films continue to be dubbed in the twenty-first century (Wright 2013, 43).

21 The Castilian version of the film was dubbed by Tecnisón, Madrid, and details of actors and voices are available at www.eldoblaje.com, accessed 26 September 2022. Without records of the dubbing actors for the Catalan version, I have relied on press reviews for the information that Soler Leal dubbed herself in *Anem-nos en, Bàrbara!* (Masó 1978a).

22 Mónica Granell Toledo notes that 'radical ecology' formed part of the influence of May 1968 on Spanish counter-culture, specifically through ex-Secretary General of the Barcelona Vegetarian and Naturist Society Diego Segura's participation in the counter-cultural magazine *Ajoblanco* (2020, 226; 234). The magazine also provided a space for LGTBQ+ readers, referred to as 'gai'/'gay' or 'homosexual' in early

1970s Catalonia/Spain (2020, 236). My thanks to Mariana Freijomil and Núria Triana Toribio for sharing this article with me.
23 My thanks to Peter Buse for suggesting this intertextual reference to me.
24 In a wider reflection on the treatment of male homosexuality and homophobia in the film, Jorge Pérez points out that Bartolomé does break new ground. Her film shows that while wealthy women like Ana may enjoy reinvention and middle-class gay character Andreu has some freedom, working-class men, like Curro, whom Andreu pays for sex, and who has a girlfriend in his village, experience homophobic prejudice, for example from Iván (2008, 220).
25 While Bartolomé transforms Scorsese's Tommy, of *Alice Doesn't Live Here Any More*, into Bárbara, this scene may reveal the influence of a far more interesting character in the American film, the androgynous child Audrey, played by eleven-year-old Jodie Foster.

5

Filming between the jaws of the wolf: documentary and denunciation in the diptych *Después de...*

It may be that we have the unpropitious climate for women directors in 1970s Spain to thank for the very existence of the remarkable documentary diptych, *Después de... primera parte: No se os puede dejar solos / Afterwards... Part One: You Can't Be Left Alone* and *Después de... segunda parte: Atado y bien atado / Afterwards... Part Two: All Tied Down* (co-directed with José Juan Bartolomé 1983), counter-intuitive as this statement may seem. Recalling the genesis of the project, Bartolomé puts a characteristically cheerful spin on this perverse situation. While working on a script for a comedy, she postponed the project in order to address the urgent political situation that was unfolding in the country around her. 'El país estaba pasando por un cambio impresionante' (The country was going through a huge change), she recalls, 'y la auténtica realidad merecía ser contada. Se conocía la opinión de los líderes, pero no la de la gente de la calle' (and the authentic truth deserved to be told. The opinion of the leaders was known, but not that of ordinary people) (quoted in Boyero 1983). The extraordinary films themselves, as well our subsequent knowledge that they predicted the military coup d'état of 23 February 1981 (known as the Tejerazo, after Lietenant-Colonel Antonio Tejero, or 23-F), which quickly failed, are eloquent testimony to that urgency. Nonetheless, we may read between the lines of Bartolomé's statement. Given her experiences of Film School in the 1960s (Chapters 1 and 2), the blacklist and consequent unfilmed projects of the early-mid 1970s (Chapter 3), and then the distribution and exhibition problems of ¡*Vámonos, Bárbara! / Bárbara, Let's Go!* in 1978 (Chapter 4), Bartolomé was no doubt encountering continued difficulties in getting a comedy off the ground. The documentary project, however, did take off – at least as far as the pre-production and production stages were concerned. As we shall see, it was only once the films were deposited for approval at the Ministerio de Cultura (Ministry of Culture) on 17 February 1981, six days before the coup, that the problems began.[1]

For once, therefore, Bartolomé appeared to be in step with contemporary trends in Spanish cinema. Decades of dictatorship had meant that the documentary genre in Spain had been limited to the regime's newsreels, the Noticiarios y Documentales, or NO-DO. These preceded every film screening by law from 1943 to 1981 (they ceased to be obligatory from 1975); thus, prior to the rise in television ownership in the 1960s, they constituted Spaniards' principal encounter with 'news'. The scare quotes here stress what historian Vicente Sánchez Biosca has shown to be the very limited nature of that encounter: the NO-DOs largely avoided current affairs (until the tourist boom of the 1960s), preferring to report rituals, like annually celebrating particular dates, which led to a viewing experience of a 'hermetically sealed, atemporal circle' (2013, 530). Keen to break this atemporal spell, documentary directors of the Transition took advantage of greater creative freedom, especially the supposed end of political censorship in 1977 (it was replaced by a rating system), to author an important group of documentaries.[2] In this potentially propitious climate, Bartolomé, as well as convincing friends to join her and her brother in contributing financially to the production costs, was therefore able to secure the backing of producer Producciones Cinematográficas Ales S.A.[3] and distributor Suevia films (quoted in Fernández-Santos 1983).

We do not know the details of the comedy that Bartolomé put aside to co-direct these documentaries – by the time she was able to make a feature film again, *Lejos de África*, in 1995, she eschewed this genre (Chapter 6) – so it appears to be another project lost to film history. Consolation for this loss may be found, though, in the originality of the *Después de...* films themselves. For far from merely joining a pre-existing group of documentaries, they significantly innovated within it. Press reviewers and subsequent critics have stressed that this innovation lies in Bartolomé's focus on the present moment of the film's shoot from April 1979 to December 1980, with the majority filmed by December 1979 (Fernández-Santos 1983). The documentaries that immediately preceded *Después de...* had used the genre to turn to the past of the Second Republic, Civil War and dictatorship, in an attempt to settle accounts with Francoism (for example the exploration of Francoist poet Leopoldo Panero in *El desencanto / Disenchantment* (Chávarri 1976)). The *Después de...* diptych, in contrast, addresses the urgent present, with Bartolomé suggesting at the time of filming that the work might better be termed a 'film-witness' rather than a documentary (Galindo 1979).

An innovation in the Spanish documentary context of sober reflections on the past, the Bartolomés' films' urgent present is of course not unique in film history, and draws in particular on contemporary militant Latin American documentary. Not only her brother and co-director José Juan, but also her Chilean sound director Bernardo Menz, had just worked on Patricio Guzmán's *La batalla de Chile / The Battle of Chile* (Parts I–III, 1975–79), which uses street interviews and footage to track the months of sociological change that preceded the death of democratically elected President Salvador Allende and military takeover by Augusto Pinochet in 1973. The Bartolomés similarly track sociological change in Spain (especially in Part I), as well as uncannily predicting the military coup, paying particular attention to a speech by General Jaime Milans del Bosch, who would go on to join rebel Tejero. Given our *ex post facto* knowledge of the coup, such sequences may now make us wince. At the end of Part I, an anonymous male Fuerza Nueva (literally: New Force) interviewee at the final Valle de los Caídos sequence darkly predicts a change of course away from democracy (the significance of the Valle de los Caídos is discussed in further detail below). More disturbing is when those within the democratic party system intuit this possibility, even as they reject it as, for example, Santiago Carrillo does during the Partido Socialista Unificado de Cataluña's conference meeting in Part II. Part II ends with the voiceover presciently naming the army as 'la gran incógnita' (the great unknown) of the Transition, then contrasts the expelled pro-democracy military commander Luis Otero's warning that the military was set on a non-democratic path (even though he excludes a coup in the short and medium terms), with Milans del Bosch's call-to-arms speech.

While the focus on this present was therefore an innovation in Spanish documentary, it followed the trends of Latin American cinema here. Important – and dangerous – as this present tense focus was, it is important to be clear that the Bartolomés innovate in the national, rather than in the transnational, cinema in this respect. I will therefore argue that the originality of the contribution lies particularly in the films' deployment of documentary form. To do so, I begin with an account of the comparatively advantageous circumstances in which the shoot took place, then the vexatious circumstances of its curtailed distribution and exhibition. A focus on the press criticism that chronicled the shoot between 1979 and 1981, then the delayed release in 1983, allows me to track the impact of the material, as well as to stress that, once release in 1981 was prevented, any subsequent viewing context, from 1983 to 2023 (my own time of writing) is delayed. We must return to the context of 1979, however, to understand the innovations of the Bartolomés' handling of documentary form, which I group into three areas: the shoot in the street; the importance of editing; and, especially, the deployment of humour. While José Juan's experience in Chile influenced the former, I argue that, in Cecilia's hands, the 'street' is used to develop her a feminist aesthetic of the quotidian, or everyday; decisions in montage, in collaboration with editor Javier Morán, may have been shared by the directorial team. The humour of the films, which an auteurist approach reveals characterises Bartolomé's filmography as a whole, also speaks to her overall creative leadership here.[4]

'Libertad condicional' (conditional freedom): censorship under democracy

The Bartolomés chose 'Libertad condicional' (Conditional Freedom) as the working title of the script as it conveyed the contingency surrounding the present uncertainty of Transition. Democratic freedoms had apparently been restored, yet were simultaneously under threat from: a nostalgic and resurgent Spanish Right in the neo-Francoist party Fuerza Nueva; a Basque terrorism buoyed by the role of its own violence in hastening the demise of the dictatorship with the assassination of Francoist Government President Admiral Carrero Blanco (also see Chapter 7); other autonomous groups inspired by the Basque model; and further fury and violence triggered by demonstrations and street riots, against a backdrop of economic depression, unemployment and a lack of attention to women's rights. Unfortunately, the 'conditionality' contained in the phrase also fits the future fate of the films: the team was free to shoot them, but not release them.

Subsequent frustration at their censorship should not overshadow the advantageous circumstances of the shoot, however. First, the story of the switch from working on the comedy to these documentaries, with which I opened this chapter, reveals Bartolomé's ability to be responsive to circumstance at this point of her career. Secondly, technological innovations in film made the shoot possible. Just as the Impressionists could only paint outside once portable easels and paints had been invented, so filmmakers could only leave the studio and shoot outside, or, as here, on the street, once the comparatively light, hand-held Arriflex CP 16R camera, and portable Nagra recorder for sound, became widely available and affordable.[5] The existence of these two pieces of equipment meant that the Bartolomés could keep their shooting team small at just four members and, therefore, both flexible and cheap. The team was: Bartolomé; her brother José Juan in co-direction, whose voice we occasionally hear as he asks the interviewees the questions (this presence of his voice brings intelligibility, as well as self-reflexively reminding audiences of the presence of the filmmakers); José Luis Alcaine (also Bartolomé's then husband), who was responsible for the camera; and Bernardo Sanz, for sound (Sanz's Nagra recorder is also occasionally visible, in another self-reflexive touch). Post-shoot, Morán was the film's editor, and editing took place in sequence. This shooting team of four could therefore adopt a flexible modus operandi, often spending hours in conversation with interviewees before and after recording the material Bartolomé pinpointed as significant. The sequences that portray youth culture, with the 'hijos del agobio' (overwhelmed youth) (Part I), for example, are an edited version of the many hours they spent with the group. With so little kit, the team could also be nimble. In the particularly tense sequence of the street altercation between the unemployed agricultural workers and the priest (Part I), for example, Bartolomé and crew had packed up and were moving away, but were swiftly able to set up again and record this spontaneous confrontation (see also Appendix Interview).

A third advantage of the shoot was what today we may see as the relatively relaxed approach to interviewees' consent. The

Bartolomés explained (Anon. 1981) that 'las escenas rodadas han contado [...] con el permiso de quienes las protagonizaron' (the permission of the protagonists was secured for the filmed scenes), a statement that perhaps contains some ambiguity over whether all interviewees were 'protagonists' who gave their consent, and surely cannot include members of the large crowds filmed. One wonders if they are referring here to those interviewees who held leadership positions and are named through subtitles in the film, such as Felipe González and Jordi Pujol, to name the two figures who would be familiar to subsequent audiences as they went on to dominate Spanish politics as Presidents of the Partido Socialista Obrero Español (PSOE; Spanish Socialist Party) and Convergència Democràtica de Catalunya (Catalan Nationalist Party), respectively. However, one might conjecture that consent may have been more loosely defined for the many anonymous street interviewees. Part II, for example, includes a Basque woman who is clearly uncomfortable with the filmmakers' line of questioning regarding support for ETA (Euskadi Ta Askatasun, armed Basque pro-independence and far-Left terrorist group), and she reluctantly offers the statement 'no quisiera yo hablar' (I didn't want to talk) to the camera. At the end of the film, at the Villalar Comuneros demonstration, an older man quips with regards participation '¿Esto va a salir? ¡Así me meten en la cárcel!' (Is this going to come out? They'll put me in jail for it!), but does then add 'al fin y al cabo, decimos la verdad' (at the end of the day, we're telling the truth). Had the shoot taken place within a tight legal framework of formal consent and the right of participants to review, edit and withdraw material before broadcast, these films could surely not have been made with such flexibility and freedom.

However, the legal wrangling, which would concern the whole film, not certain contributions, would come later. The post-production fate of *Después de…*, like the better-known case of Pilar Miró's *El crimen de Cuenca* / *The Cuenca Crime* (1980) (see Díez Puertas 2012), is testimony to the fraught fight to recover creative freedoms after such a long period of repression in Spain. The dictatorship may have been over, but a kind of muscle memory of its restrictive machinations remained. Deposited at the Ministerio de Cultura just six days before the coup, the Bartolomés' films fell victim to the political censorship Cecilia had known ever since Film

School. On the flimsy excuse that they contained too much archival footage, the Junta de valoración técnica (Technical Evaluation Board) awarded no subsidy and the Ministerio then threatened to sequester the films, despite the fact that they had not been released.[6] Bartolomé summarises the situation as the continuation of old Francoist censorship under the new and more sophisticated guise of 'sanciones económicas y amenazas legales' (economic sanctions and legal threats) (quoted in Bedoya, 1982). In this context, the distributor Suevia got cold feet. The screenings at the San Sebastián then Barcelona film festivals were merely 'symbolic',[7] meaning the company gained dubbing licences in exchange for the supposed releases, then abandoned the films to their fate (Bartolomé quoted in Fernández-Santos, 1983). In 1983, Bartolomé was still holding out hope for distribution via European television (Parra 1983), but eventually it was the intervention of Miró herself as PSOE Director General of Cinema from 1982 to 1985 that released the films from legal limbo and allowed the Groucho cinema in Madrid to step forward and screen them, for one week, from 7 to 13 November 1983.

But February 1981 to November 1983 were thirty-two very long months in the history of twentieth-century Spain. In particular, the immediacy of the film's critique of the UCD (Unión de Centro Democrático, Union of the Democratic Centre Party), and the urgency of its uncanny prediction of the coup, had evaporated by 1983. The UCD had disappeared from the political landscape, peace had followed the failed coup and the PSOE was in power, having won landslide elections under the banner of 'cambio' (change) in 1982. The damage was done: in Luis Fernández Colorado's regretful summary of the situation, *Después de...* had become 'algo más próximo a un objeto de museo que a la obra dinámica e impulsiva que había pretendido ser originalmente' (something closer to a museum object, rather than the dynamic, impulsive work it had originally aimed to be) (2001, 65).

Mirror, mirror, on the wall... press response

Press clippings archived at the Filmoteca Española tell us both about the films themselves, but also about the Spain in which reviews were written. They contain the story of the directors' own positioning in interview vis-à-vis their potential audience and critics; of reviewers' often highly political responses; and of a Spanish press that was itself experiencing uncertainty over its own role and authority during these years of Transition. The three pieces contained in the archive that were published in 1979 that report on the shoot are representative. The sarcastic piece by Fernando Montejano published in August in the Francoist *El Alcázar* betrays the anxieties of those on the Right who had enjoyed authority for decades and now saw this under threat. The journalist's words in fact echo the portrayal of the Right explored in the films themselves. While in the main section we find a seemingly neutral description of some of the sequences of the film, Montejano's whole piece is coloured in advance by a preface that looks forward to a future in which he would accuse the Bartolomés of lying: 'Seguramente después, cuando me sienta en la butaca a ver *Después de Franco* [sic] no será lo que ahora me están dicen que está siendo […] honesta [e] imparcial' (I'm sure that afterwards, when I sit down in the seat at the cinema to watch *Después de Franco* [sic] it won't be what they are telling me that it is now […] honest [and] impartial) (1979). In this tense and hostile context, Bartolomé uses an interview published in September in the also regime-supporting *ABC* to allay fears by stressing that the films do not adopt a political stance, but portray 'sociological' (not political) change (Galindo 1979). However, the slightly later third 1979 report published in October in the sympathetic *Mundo Diario* includes details of the directors' experience that the shoot 'obliga a estar siempre con la escopeta cargada' (made it essential that we always had a shotgun loaded) (Anon. 1979), an unnerving figure of speech given the violence to come, and which the films themselves portray.

Press reports published between the films' completion and deposit at the Ministerio de Cultura in February 1981, and their final release in Madrid's Groucho cinema in November 1983, chart both the chequered distribution history of these films in the singular and the limits of post-Franco creative freedoms in general. Writing in Spain's newspaper of democracy, *El País* (founded in 1976), in May 1981, veteran film critic of the Left, Diego Galán trusts in their imminent release and celebrates them as part of Spain's 'cinematografía adulta' (adult filmmaking), which can now reveal 'la imagen [de España] que los medios oficiales han ocultado' (the image [of Spain] that the official media has hidden). But his trust in the freedoms of democracy is misplaced.[8] By June of the same year, the Bartolomés themselves write a piece for *Madrid Abierto* in which they refer to *Después de...* as a 'mirror' that the Ministerio de Cultura wanted to 'break' as it did not like the reflection of Spain that they saw in it (1981).

On the occasions of the two single screenings of *Después de...* in San Sebastián and Barcelona, journalists were able to focus on the films' content and draw out, in particular, the question of balance. Fernández Colorado tracks the response of Mikel Insausti, writing in the Basque daily *Egin*, who queries the films' excessive focus on extremists, the omission of Galicia in the coverage of Spain's new 'autonomías' (autonomous communities) and the Bartolomés' incomplete analysis of Euskadi (1981, quoted in Fernández Colorado 2001, 71 n. 6). Barcelona-based *La Vanguardia*, meanwhile, reports viewers' responses, which are similar: the films contain too much focus on Fuerza Nueva, omit the case of Galicia and offer incomplete analysis of Catalonia (Anon. 1981).[9]

The following year, with the films still held up, *El País* published a report that attempted to provide balance. It quotes Bartolomé in an interview in which she excoriates the new regime of neo-censorship, whose machinations, she claims, are more complex than the Francoist censorship she knows so well, as they include withholding financial support and legal threats. It then quotes a representative of the UCD, named as the 'Director General of Books and Film', Matías Vallés, who defends his (in fact inaccurate) judgement that the films contained too much archive material to receive any financial support through subsidy (Bedoya 1982).

Once the *Después de...* films are finally released in the Groucho cinema – and thus only to Madrid audiences who can catch them over one single week – reviewers are less guarded. Veteran journalist and cineaste (most famously co-scriptwriter of Víctor Erice's *El espíritu de la colmena / The Spirit of the Beehive* (1973)), Ángel Fernández-Santos uses his platform as chief *El País* film reviewer to denounce the neo-Francoist censorship to which the films fell victim. In the same newspaper, Galán, again, both echoes his colleague's criticisms and hails the innovation of the films' content. In the archive consulted, Galán is the first to note what we have seen subsequent criticism would go on to stress: while previous 1970s documentaries focus on the past, the *Después de...* films are the first to address the present (ironically transformed into the recent past for 1983 audiences owing to the début delay): 'es la primera entrega de urgencia de una realidad que no por más cercana es menos compleja' ([the diptych] is the first urgent episode to portray a reality that is no less complex for being close) (1983). This innovation is also stressed by *Pueblo*'s Isabel Vaquero (one of the two female journalists whose writing is present in the Filmoteca archive, according to a cisgender criterion of analysing first names), with these films 'se inicia una nueva etapa en la historia de los documentales españoles' (a new phase has begun in the history of Spanish documentaries) (1983).

However, these were the opinions of film specialists. Elsewhere the *Después de...* diptych was attacked by extreme Left and extreme Right. According to Fernández Colorado, Left-wing militant journalists accused the films of 'acerarse al pensamiento joseantoniono' (being close to fascist thought)[10] (2001, 69). The Right-wing press, meanwhile, railed against the exact opposite. Pedro Crespo's angry review published in 1983 in *ABC* echoes Montejano's 1979 sarcastic report, and in fact expresses on paper the opinions spoken by the extreme Right on screen. Whereas Montejano's piece was based on misunderstanding in anticipation, Crespo's turns around misunderstanding after the fact. It insists that the films seek to cause 'la revolución violenta' (violent revolution), rather than, as the Bartolomés intended, portray the path by which the country ran the risk of arriving at it. The military coup, which the films predict, was a very real moment when such bloodshed may have occurred; but this event goes unmentioned. Crespo attacks the films instead for 'Su denuncia – al Ejército, a los franquistas –, sus diatribas, sus manipulaciones' (Its denunciation of the Army, of Francoists; its diatribes; its manipulations), furiously contrasting, for example, 'Los niños más guapos [...] en la fiesta del PCE, y contra ellos y sus seráficos padres [...], los falangistas y fuerzanovistas, presentados [...] como unos bárbaros sedientos de sangre' (The cutest children [...] in the PCE [Partido Comunista Español, Spanish Communist Party] festivities, and, against them and their serene parents [...], the Falangists and members of Fuerza Nueva, presented as [...] blood-thirsty barbarians). The effect on the author is the precise opposite of his claim that the work 'aburre más que irrita' (bores rather than irritates me); the depth of his outrage also conveys the precise opposite of his final claim that the works are now 'obsoleta' (obsolete) (1983).

Regrettably, it seems that Crespo's parting shot may have been the most accurate part of the review. For, notwithstanding the sympathetic press's celebration of the films' originality and importance, their distribution history following the Groucho screenings is one of 'obsolescence'; only recent digital availability and public recognition of Bartolomé (see Introduction), modest though these have been, have led to anything like a recovery. This chapter, therefore, aims to play its part in making the work more accessible to Anglophone readerships and audiences by publishing criticism in English. In the next section, I argue why the films should be rescued from obsolescence for their prescient thematic content. I then analyse their innovative use of form, especially in the three principal areas of the quotidian, editing and humour, to argue for their urgent inclusion in histories of the documentary genre, in both Spanish, and world – especially feminist – cinema histories.

A 'distant mirror'

It may have become a commonplace of cultural commentary to argue for the importance of past texts that particularly speak to a present moment of consumption, or texts that offer a 'distant mirror', in Barbara Tuchman's famous description of the connections between the medieval period and the present day (1978). However, when a text never reaches its intended contemporary audience owing to censorship, finding such connections is a necessity. The commentator may lament the loss of that intended, auratic, encounter, or attend to the specificities of actual encounters. I choose the second route to suggest that the press responses to the screening of the films in 1983 are just as much a reflection of the footage shot between 1979 and 1981, as they are a reflection of the wider hopes and fears of a Spain of 1983, entering the period of PSOE's government. As we have seen, the selection of press reviews available does suggest political polarisation: the Left-sympathising press queries the portrait of, and screen time afforded to, Fuerza Nueva; the Right expresses anxiety over its own loss of authority. Positive reviews by film critics, meanwhile, celebrated the overcoming of the censorship that all believed hampered Spanish creativity throughout the dictatorship.

I would suggest that subsequent criticism, with this chapter included, likewise alights on aspects of *Después de...* that are particularly meaningful at their times of writing. The celebration of the centenary of the existence of film as the seventh art in 1996 provided a context for the reconsideration of Bartolomé in Josetxo Cerdán and Marina Díaz's edited volume, *El encanto de la lógica* (The Enchantment of Logic), which I have frequently cited in these pages. This volume is the fifth of a series entitled 'Los olvidados' (The Forgotten)[11] cineastes of Spain, which began in 1996 itself. With the tense political polarisation of the early 1980s somewhat dissipated, Cerdán and Díaz's mission, in 2001, to rescue the director from being 'olvidado' leads to analysis of both the form and content of Bartolomé's work, which I echo twenty years on. In the same year, Marta Selva i Masoliver, in another 2001 volume, the first in Spain on documentary (Català, Cerdán and Torreiro), stressed how important the films are both to understand Spain of the Transition and Spain of the time of writing, a point also made in Elena Blázquez Carretero's 2014 article, in a volume titled 'El futuro del pasado' (The Future of the Past), or in Parvati Nair's sensitive introduction to the screening of the films as part of 'Espacio Femenino: Pioneras' Instituto Cervantes online season in 2021.

As Selva i Masoliver contends,

> La diversidad de las situaciones registradas, el distinto grado de representatividad de cada uno de los episodios históricos a los que se hace referencia permiten acercarnos a *Después de...* como si tratara de un fresco del que solo nosotros y nosotras podemos y temenos que extraer finalmente su significado. (The diversity of the situations registered, the distinct degree of representativity of each one of the historical episodes that are referred to, allow us to approach *Después de...* as if it were a fresco, of which only we, as male or female viewers, can, in the final analysis, extract meaning.) (2001, 274)

Some may find their own 'meaning' in the films' portrait of the Spanish Left, poised as the PSOE was between 1979 and 1981 for its electoral landslide of 1982. For others, it may lie in their portrait of the tensions between centre and autonomies: ETA may have laid down its arms, but tensions are still keenly felt in Spain today. Others may link Fuerza Nueva to today's far-Right populist party Vox (Prieto 2018). This chapter finds the particular 'meaning' of the films in the declared emphasis of this book on questions of Francoism and feminism. I will explore these elements in what I suggest are the films' three principal innovations in documentary form in the following three sections.

The word on the street: Bartolomé's feminist aesthetic of the quotidian

Después de... confirms Bartolomé, here in directorial collaboration with her brother José Juan, as one of Spain's primary cineastes of the quotidian. In order to place this statement in context, I will first examine the history of documentary cinema prior to 1979, before suggesting that this aspect of her film craft enables her specifically to engage with, and explore her own creative vision of, feminism. As we have seen, *Después de...* seemed to be in step with a group of documentaries that were made following Franco's death in Spain, enough so to secure the backing of a producer and distributor. Like these contemporary documentaries, the films shared an aim aesthetically and ideologically to break from the regime's NO-DO. However, while, as we have seen, predecessors sought to engage with events of the past in order to break with the ahistoricity of the official newsreels, *Después de...* does so through a focus on the present. It has been frequently noted that this engagement is inspired by José Juan Bartolomé and Bernardo Menz's recent documentary work with Chilean Patricio Guzmán (who had also previously attended Film School, like the Bartolomés, in Madrid). That the Bartolomés were not the first to bring the relevance of Latin American militant documentary filmmaking to bear on a Spanish context has not. Bartolomé's near contemporary at Film School, Helena Lumbreras, who, as we have seen (Chapter 1), abandoned Spain to develop her career abroad rather than endure repression, as our director did, also authored low-budget documentaries that focussed on Spain's present. Lumbreras appears to be omitted from discussions of 1970s Spanish documentary like those of editors Josep María Catalá, Josetxo Cerdán and Casimiro Torreiro's first volume on the subject (2001). This may be because she worked underground, outside the mainstream of commercial distribution – as noted by Cerdán in later work (e.g. 2013). But Lumbreras is surely relevant to the genesis of Bartolomé's documentary practice, even though Bartolomé sought mainstream distribution. Working when the regime was still in power, Lumbreras's aims, in collaboration with her partner Mariano Lisa, both of whom worked together in the Collective 'Colectivo Cine de Clase', are nonetheless relevant to Bartolomé: 'Spanish clandestine filmmakers believed that it was not sufficient to combat Francoist ideology through films that echoed the matter-of-fact, realist style of the state's main instrument of propaganda, the NO-DO, rather, it was necessary to alter the form and style of the "official" filmic discourse in order to counter its message' (Ledesma 2014, 277). If Lumbreras deploys intermediality to engineer disjunctures in film form that shock, awaken and engage audiences – at one point, in *El campo para el hombre / Field for Men* (1973), she does this by actually flinging paint at the screen – Bartolomé opts for engagement with the quotidian, combined with editing and humour, to shake audiences out of the hypnosis of the viewing experience of the NO-DO. The quotidian aesthetic of street interviews was clearly inspired by Guzmán, but Bartolomé's distinctive documentary voice of the quotidian is also inspired by the way her compatriot Lumbreras adapted Latin American documentary techniques to an anti-Franco Spanish context. For both women directors, their search for an anti-Franco, anti-NO-DO, aesthetic was also interwoven with their commitment to a feminist one.

The following comment by Bartolomé, made shortly after the release of *¡Vámonos, Bárbara!* in 1978, and in reference to that film, in fact sheds light on the genesis of this aesthetic of the quotidian, or street interviewing and filming, in *Después de...*, which she shot shortly afterwards:

> El mundo que te rodea habitualmente es más importante en tu vida de lo que se piensa: el cartero, el señor de la esquina, la amiga que te encuentras al cabo de los años, forman también parte de tu existencia y es, además, algo muy relacionado con lo español, en donde la comunicación a nivel de la calle todavía no se ha perdido del todo. (The world that surrounds you everyday is more important in your life than you might think: the postman, the chap on the street corner, the female friend that you bump into after years, they all make up part of your life too and, what's more, this is something that is very

related to Spanishness, in Spain talking to one another in the street hasn't yet been completely lost.) (Hernández Les and Gato 1978, 45)

The quote reveals just what an ear Bartolomé has for picking up on the significance of what might be said in an informal context; note too that every context she mentions here is a 'street' one. Her reference to a particularly 'Spanish' 'talking in the street' speaks to the country's wider informal 'street' culture, which is usually lost in the literal translation of 'calle' to 'street', and includes, for example, chatting in the hairdressers or in the stairwells and landings of blocks of flats. I have thus used formulations like the 'quotidian' and the 'everyday' in my translation of 'calle' to convey this wider sense. (As we have seen, conversations at the hairdressers are vital to the development of *Carmen de Carabanchel / Carmen of Carabanchel* (Chapter 1) and *¡Vámonos, Bárbara!* (Chapter 4).) This chapter contends that Bartolomé's distinctively feminist documentary practice melds the anti-Francoism and anti-NO-DO stance of Lumbreras, with the street interviewing and filming techniques of Guzmán, along with her own particular responsiveness to what she sees as a 'Spanish' 'street' culture – informal, everyday, conversational or quotidian. (I use inverted commas around the adjective Spanish here to stress that this is Bartolomé's view – she of course spent her childhood in Africa – rather than essentialising this as a national stereotype.) It is in this particular blend that we may find Bartolomé's originality in feminist documentary. Beyond Spain, interviewing techniques had already been widely used to give women a voice;[12] Bartolome's innovation is the shift in focus from an often interior, domestic context, to an exterior, but also everyday one.

It should be noted that not all the interviews or events of *Después de...* are shot on the 'street', or in an informal environment. The inclusion of interviews with specific contemporary leaders,[13] who are usually filmed inside,[14] in medium shot and long take, and who even have their names and titles announced on the screen by subtitle, serves two purposes. First, it anchors the viewer in the contemporary context – especially necessary for delayed, transnational viewings today, where the parade of multiple events can be overwhelming – and second, these interviews in fact throw the anonymous 'street' encounters that occur before and after them into relief. The films' voiceover serves these ends too. Added against

Filming between the jaws of the wolf 123

Bartolomé's will in order to make the material more intelligible, this need for explanation has increased for viewers over time. In addition, the voiceover, the disembodied male voice of supposed authority, which is so redolent of the male commentating voice of the NO-DOs, in fact serves as a counterpoint to the 'word on the street', which is captured through spontaneous interviews with anonymous members of different crowds or groupings. An obvious example of the disjuncture is the description of Spain in voice-over as an 'ejemplo de transición pacífica…' (example of peaceful transition) to images of street violence.

It is the case that in their films the directors seek a balance, and seek to give a voice to various sides of the political spectrum. This balance, as we have seen, therefore attracted criticism from all sides of that spectrum, as the film was seen as too ambiguous and open. However, there is a world of difference between an interview with an anonymous interviewee whose anti-Francoist voice has not been heard for forty years, and one with an interviewee who may be anonymous, but whose Francoist views have dominated over the same period. Interviewing the former, in the films, often leads to stunning new revelations, as the interviewees reach for what seems like a new lexicon to describe their experiences. Interviews with the latter, by contrast, rely on familiar Francoist rhetorical clichés that reveal immobilism and a nostalgia for the past.

Take the examples of the older women who are interviewed at key moments of Part I. The film begins with an intertitle in yellow (intertitles in yellow were added to both Parts to explain that the films were completed before the failed military coup of 23 February 1981), then an intertitle in white (which is part of the original final copy of the film) in which the Bartolomés thank participants. There follows a sequence by two members of the Colectivo de Cine de Madrid that sets the agenda both for the films, and for post-Franco Spanish media more widely, by querying the distinction between 'información' (information) and 'contra-información' (counter-information). The cut that follows the words 'los contra-informadores eran ellos' (the counter-informants were them) to an archive NO-DO in which an elderly Franco is glimpsed at the 1972 opening ceremony for the Atazar Dam, could scarcely make the point about propaganda more clearly. Next we cut to the film's first anonymous interviewee, a first in a series of spirited older ladies, who condemns the dictator for he 'ha dejado a muchos hijos sin padre, y a muchas mujeres sin marido' (has left many children fatherless, and many women without a husband). Her words ring in our ears as we cut to footage of his lying in state, then the official interment of his remains at the Valle de los Caídos, as a young Prince Juan Carlos (today Spain's disgraced and exiled 'Rey emérito' (emeritus King)) oversees the ceremony. To these images the title of the film and the credits roll.

The pre-credit sequence in which the Colectivo de Cine Madrid questions the divide between 'información' and 'contra-información' is an instruction for us to open our minds to what we are about to see. Bartolomé moves next to film the first extended outdoor event, a picnic at the Casa de Campo to follow the previously illegal Workers' Day, 1 May, after the Left-wing rallies we see in the streets of Madrid. In these first outdoor interviews of the film, it is, again, two older ladies who make shocking revelations about their treatment and life experiences having been on the 'wrong side' under dictatorship. The first recalls, in a disarmingly matter-of-fact tone, that one of her children died of hunger at two years old while her husband spent eight years in jail, and that she was forced onto the street to beg to feed her other four. The second, though more upset than the first, is still able to delve back in time to remember and share her arrest by the authorities, which meant that her five children were left alone at home unsupervised. Many other men and women are interviewed in the sequence, but Bartolomé cuts back to the first woman. Particularly memorable is her question '¿Os cuento más?' (Shall I go on?) (Figure 5.1). What other stories does this older woman have, the viewer wonders, like the one we have just heard of losing a toddler to hunger?

With balance in mind, the team next films a matching open-air event, but this time one that has enjoyed four decades of not just legality, but celebration: the annual 18 July celebration (the Civil War broke out on that date in 1936), here hosted in its 1979 edition by the neo-Francoist party Fuerza Nueva. The interviewees are similarly anonymous and free to express their views, but their words echo dictatorship propaganda, rather than shock with their originality, like the Casa de Campo stories. A young woman, sporting a badge that commemorates the outbreak of the Civil War with the number 18 on her breast, looks happy, but uses a shockingly violent

Filming between the jaws of the wolf 125

Figure 5.1 Anonymous older lady at the 1 May 1979 Workers Day: '¿Os cuento más?' (Shall I go on?). In *Después de... primera parte: No se os puede dejar solos* (1983)

figure of speech to articulate her disapproval of democratic politicians (the UCD President Adolfo Suárez in particular) by suggesting the need to 'aplastarles como culebras' (grind them into the ground like snakes). An older woman, apparently the snake-slaying girl's grandmother, who claims herself to be national president of the Carlist Women's Section, 'Las Margaritas', takes on the first-person plural, so familiar in populist speechmaking, to declare '¡jamás acataremos la monarquía liberal y capitalista!' (we will never comply with the liberal and capitalist monarchy!).

Just as the Bartolomés contrast the newly legal 1 May rally, with the annually celebrated 18 July one, so too they juxtapose two graveyards, one on the Left, which was previously unmarked, and one on the Right, which is very much marked. The location and nature of the first are announced by intertitle as 'La Barranca, Logroño, Fosas communes de republicanos fusilados por los "nacionales"' (mass graves of Republicans shot by the 'Nationalists'); the second by 'Camposanto Mártires (Cemetery of the Martyrs), Paracuellos de Járama'. The Bartolomés open the sequence at the first location by filming a Republican flag that has been precariously tied to an electricity pylon. Among the interviewees in this sequence, an older lady shockingly describes the lack of proper burial received by the slain Republicans, which included her husband. The corpses were left exposed in a hole in the ground, she states, in a voice weakened by age,[15] but strengthened by the urgency of her tale, where, she pointedly adds, the rabbits could eat them. She describes her own young son filling the hole with stones to prevent this. A Republican flag tied to a makeshift flagpole, an older lady's broken voice telling the tale of abject degradation in the treatment of the dead, the description of stones instead of gravestones, and the monument erected by relatives that has been graffitied: such is this unofficial graveyard. It could not contrast more eloquently with Paracuellos de Járama. Here the 'martyrs' for the Francoist cause lie in 'holy ground' ('campo santo'), their well-kept gravestones engraved, and their relatives able to mourn their 'fallen', while supporters sing Francoist anthems.

Just as there is a symmetry between the women interviewees of 1 May and 18 July, and between the widows of La Barranca, Logroño, and Paracuellos de Járama, so there is a symmetry too between the opening words of an older lady on the Left, who rails against the dictator who left orphans and widows in his wake, and the closing words of an older lady of the Right, the Fuerza Nueva. Some controversy surrounds the inclusion of this interviewee in the film, and Bartolomé has recounted in interview her doubts over the woman's mental stability, though also recalls the woman's absolute insistence that her voice be included (see Appendix Interview). At this point at the end of Part I, the Bartolomés are shooting on 20 November 1979, the occasion of the fourth anniversary of the Caudillo's death, at the Valle de los Caídos (Valley of the Fallen), the grotesque fascist structure on the outskirts of Madrid built by Republican prisoners (the dictator's mortal remains were transferred to a family mausoleum in 2019 amid much controversy), a sequence that includes the arrival of the dictator's widow, Carmen Polo. In a state of considerable rage, the anonymous older lady shouts a vicious diatribe direct to camera, calling for nothing short of another Civil War. In doing so, she repeats the violent, Catholic rhetoric that had been so frequently used over the dictatorship years that she has internalised it as her own. The Bartolomés film her in a close-up shot that largely blocks out all others, just as the extremist Francoist rhetoric she repeats allows for no other views or positions. Her final lines, also the final lines of Part I, give a good sense of her fury: 'Sabemos que temenos que pasar este baño de sangre pero el sagrado corazón de Jesús nos ayudará' (We know that we have to endure this blood bath, but the sacred heart of Jesus will be our aid).

What is clear, then, is that a wealth of lexical and rhetorical differences lies between anonymous interviewees whose voices have never been heard, and those interviewees who, though they may be anonymous, appear familiar, owing to their recycling of Francoist rhetoric. Readers may object that my selection of examples, all of which contrast women on the Left and Right, may portray balance in terms of politics, but not in terms of gender. Of course, the Bartolomés included interviews with a multitude of anonymous men, young and old, too. They also appear at the 1 May, 18 July and 20 November celebrations, as members of town councils, as small business owners, as priests and as members of grass-roots Christian groups; they are included among those interviewed in the streets protesting for and against abortion, among disaffected youth, the urban and the rural unemployed (Part I), as well as being members of Spain's autonomous communities, especially Catalonia, the Basque Country, Castile and Andalusia (Part II). My justification for citing female interviewees is that the inclusion of anonymous female voices of the Left, and especially those of older ladies on the Left, is so original.

Part of the organisational structure of both films is the inclusion of headings and subheadings. Mid-way through Part I the heading is 'El descontento o los límites de la reforma' (Discontent, or the Limits of Reform), the first subheading for which is 'Malestar en las mujeres' (Unease Among Women), followed by 'El paro juvenil' (Youth Unemployment), 'El campo protesta' (The Countryside Protests), 'Los pequeños empresarios se sublevan' (Small Business-Owners Revolt) 'Los obreros se sienten defraudados' (Workers Feel Deceived) and 'La otra cara del descontento' (The Other Side of Discontentment) – this last the title of the sequence shot at the Valle de los Caídos, just discussed. While one of the many remarkable features of these documentaries as a whole is their prescience, not least with regards the military coup, it is nonetheless striking that the issues covered in this 'Mujeres' section still remain current: they might almost be found in media coverage today. Abortion may have been legalised in 1986, for example, but it remains highly contested in Spain and elsewhere in the West today. Feminist lawyer and future PSOE minister Cristina Alberdi's comments on the legal definition of abuse and rape remain current at the time of writing too, some forty years on, with the media today following the vexed passage of the consent bill, known as 'sí es sí' (only yes means yes), through parliament.[16] In the rest of the 'Mujeres' section, the success of the street interviews, or the aesthetic of the quotidian, is considerable. The series of street interviews with anonymous women – and some men – yield frank views about birth control and abortion in 1970s Spain. Emotions run so high that one older lady actually forgets how many children she has in justifying it – six, then five. A subject that had only been glimpsed in publicly distributed fiction – with Bartolomé's own *Carmen de Carabanchel* locked behind Film School doors, references were limited to texts like the novel and film *El mundo sigue / Life Goes On* by Juan Antonio de Zunzuengui (1960) and Fernando Fernán Gómez (1963) respectively – abortion is explored here through a panoply of views of women and men, young and old, on the street and at a rally.[17] For the intended viewers of 1979, but still for those of 1983, here was the shock of the new: a matter-of-fact discussion of what had been taboo.

Bartolomé's feminism in *Después de...* can clearly be located in the originality and urgency of the issues discussed in the section marked 'Mujeres', but, critically, it is not limited to this section. Fencing off one section and labelling it thus wrong-foots the viewer: in fact both films are about both women and men, just as men's voices are included in the 'Mujeres' section. What unites them is Bartolomé's feminist aesthetic. As I have argued, this aesthetic lies in Bartolomé's adaptation of the technique of interviewing and filming in the street to her own ends. José Juan's contribution to co-directorship, drawn from his previous work with Guzmán, is this street interviewing technique; I detect Cecilia's leadership of the co-direction in the way she adapts this technique for her own purposes. These purposes are seeking out the quotidian, often focussed on women, or capturing 'the grain of the everyday', as Parvati Nair nicely has it (2021a).

In her aesthetic of the quotidian, I therefore see Bartolomé's feminist intervention as three-fold. Expanding and validating the presence of those who have never previously been seen or heard on the historical record is a political move, as it is in Guzmán's *La batalla de Chile*, but in Bartolomé's documentaries I reframe it as also a feminist one. This move is not limited to the women's issues and voices explored in the Part I 'Mujeres' section, which might readily be understood as feminist in its thematic focus. In fact, her adaptation of documentary cinema's interviewing and filming on the street as an aesthetic of the quotidian, refashioned to suit what for her is a particularly 'Spanish' 'comunicación en la calle' (talking in the 'street'), governs the whole of both films.

As Annette Kuhn notes, oral history has been an 'instrumental' methodology for feminism, 'inserting groups hitherto largely "hidden from history" – women and the working class in particular – into the mainstream of historical discourse' (1994, 147). This is true of *Después de...*, though these documentaries also give a voice to a wider panoply of groups, which enables them to be compared and contrasted through editing, as we will see. Rather than her use of oral history in itself, I am interested here in locating Bartolomé's feminism in exactly how she uses it, or the nature of her practice of oral history. The only interviewer voice that is audible asking questions in the films may be her brother's, but recent quantitative research on women directors in documentary interviewing teams reveals that the presence of women interviewers tends to yield interviews that are more intimate and personal, so much so that Lisa French may pinpoint the 'advantage for documentary directors of being female' (2018, 18).[18] This research insight chimes with the remarkable proximity that the *Después de...* team seem to share with their interviewees, which leads, on many occasions, to astoundingly frank revelations. Selva i Masoliver attributed the intimate nature of the interviews to a particular shooting pace:

> la paciencia de la cámara, el tiempo que se les da y la confianza en la capacidad que los autores dan a los y las entrevistadas, para que sus opiniones, coincidentes o no con la suya, puedan desplegar los significados que tienen y convertirse en reveladoras y sintomáticas de lo que estaba ocurriendo. (the camera's patience, the time they are given and the confidence that the authors have in the men and women interviewed, so that the significance of their opinions, which may or may not match the authors' own, can unfold and become revealing and symptomatic of what was occurring.) (2001, 273)

While we must avoid the dangers of essentialising in relation to gender, French's research might allow us to suggest that it is the presence of Bartolomé as a female director that also made the difference here. In the photographs of the *Después de...* filming team contained in Cerdán and Díaz's 2001 volume (22, 62–3, 66, 73), the physical presence of the bespectacled and slightly framed Bartolomé alongside the three men stands out (during the shoot of the second film Bartolomé was also visibly pregnant). In addition, over the course of the shoot, her pregnancy became more and more visible. I thus suggest that her presence in the interviews, even if she was not always the one asking the questions, may have drawn out deeper levels of intimacy in interviewees. Take, for example, the case of the older lady, a relative, we are told, of Blas Infante, at the Government of Andalucía meeting. She shies away from the camera with a 'yo... no...' (I... I don't...) (even after a friend or relative has adjusted her earring for the visuals of the shot), but is then drawn out to speak. Or consider the case of the previously mentioned Basque woman who begins with 'no quisiera yo hablar delante de éstos' (I didn't want to talk in front of these people (the Bartolomé filming team)), and then does. The confidence inspired in interviewees, and the oftentimes extraordinary frankness yielded by the interview, constitute, I suggest, part of the feminist aesthetic of Bartolomé's documentary practice.

I locate the feminism of Bartolomé's street filming both in her ear for picking up the telling details revealed by interviewees in speech, but also in her eye for the telling details of the context. When filming a tense street riot like the Día de Andalucía (Andalusia day) (Part II), perhaps many directors would, like Bartolomé, have picked out the significance of an anonymous rioter's clenched fist, the fingers wrapped around a stone, about to be hurled in anger, as she does in close-up. But who else would shoot the aftermath of this unsettling sequence of stone-throwing, murderous chants and police brutality with an image of an anonymous woman, sweeping up the debris and broken glass in the street in front of her shop (Figure 5.2)?

Editing

As we have seen, with such a compact production team, Javier Morán was able to edit in sequence. Perhaps the urgency of the

Filming between the jaws of the wolf   131

Figure 5.2 Anonymous lady clears up after street riots in *Después de… segunda parte: Atado y bien atado* (1983)

shoot, and the belief in immediate release and thus participation in debates on the 'street', meant editing was rushed. Some critics, therefore, found the film to be incoherent in places (Fernández Colorado offers an account of these, 2001, 66–7), while others suggest that the films might have benefitted from more material being cut (Selva i Mosoliver 2001, 276; Minguet 2001, 78). It may be pointed out that this incoherence in fact matches well Bartolomé's aesthetic of the 'street' and the quotidian. But the overall impression should not detract from a number of instances where editing effectively creates meaning, and enables critique.

This diptych of films is all about Franco, but, other than the previously mentioned glimpse of his shadowy profile in the early NO-DO at the Azatar Dam of Part I, he physically never appears in them. Yet the 'después de' of both titles refers to the period after him; the colloquial phrase of the first subtitle, 'no se os puede dejar solos', refers to loneliness without him; and that of the second is a quote famously attributed to him, as he deluded himself that his legacy was to leave behind him a country in which everything was 'atado y bien atado'. In such a context, the representation of all political leadership in the films refers back to the Franco model, and an examination of editing in particular demonstrates the Bartolomés' interest in how such figures wield power. I will examine the portrait of the obvious Franco successor figure, Blas Piñar, leader of Fuerza Nueva, in my final section, but focus here on the portrait of young actor and activist Charo Reina.

Actor, singer and leader of Fuerza Nueva, Charo Reina, who turned her back in later life on the politics of her youth, was just nineteen when the Bartolomés interviewed her on the banks of the river Guadalquivir in Seville, the second sequence of Part II of the documentary. What is memorable, unsettlingly so, in her address to camera is her ready facility with rhetoric. Bartolomé opens this section with her, still a teenager, delivering a speech to the party in the Las Ventas bullring in Madrid to wild applause, or, in her words, 'moví las masas' (I moved the masses). In interview to camera she also uses rhetoric to stress her politics. Take the use of repetition in her apparently spontaneous address to camera: 'si defender la unidad de la patria es ser fascista..., yo lo soy; si defender la justicia o amar a la justicia es ser fascista..., yo lo soy; si defender nuestros ideales contra viento y marea es ser fascista..., yo lo soy' (if defending the unity of the patria means being fascist..., then a fascist I am; if defending justice or loving justice means being fascist..., then a fascist I am; if defending our ideas against hell and high water means being fascist..., then a fascist I am). At this point the audience is viewing a singer-actor turned political youth leader; where the film creates meaning in through cross-cutting. Each cut in the montage here creatively matches the rhetorical repetitions ('yo lo soy') we have just heard. Thus editor Morán intersperses Reina as speech-making politician at a rally, with Reina as popular actor on stage. This, the Bartolomés suggest, is how populism functions: popularity in another area of activity, like acting, is blurred and fused with politics with great success by Reina here. History tells us that media-savvy populist politicians across the globe have made the same move with great success both before and since. However, the sequence ends by damning the consequences of such populism through montage. When Reina-political leader admits to fascist violence ('somos violentos, sí' (we are violent, yes)), we cut to the rapturous applause that Reina-singer-actor receives for a theatre performance; but then Bartolomé and the team deliver the killer cut in the editing: 'un joven comunista, muerto a puñaladas en Madrid [por] varios individuos, al parecer de filiación pronazi' (Young Communist, Stabbed to Death in Madrid [by] Various Individuals, Seemingly of Pro-Nazi Affiliation) is the newspaper headline of the next image. In the sequence that follows, Bartolomé also pointedly contrasts Reina's defence of violence, with PCE leader Santiago Carrillo's call for moderation and for no return to the 1930s. (It has to be said that the anonymous interviewees in the crowd Carrillo is attempting to calm with these soothing words reveal that they are not convinced by peaceful means at all.)

The montage of the Reina sequence is the most interesting stand-out use of editing in the films. Elsewhere it is deployed to contrast opposites, or suggest cause and effect. To the fury of Right-wing commentators like Pedro Crespo, it has to be said that the Right usually emerges less favourably from the juxtaposition. But Fuerza Nueva is an easy target. The Bartolomés in fact offer a far wider fresco of mid-Transition life. Thus there is a telling juxtaposition that reveals the various activities of the Catholic Church in the period. In a central sequence of Part I, we witness the sermon of the fire-and-brimstone priest at the Almudena service, attended by new Madrid mayor Enrique Tierno Galván, in which he rails against freedom, modern society and any attack on the sanctity of Spanish family. There is then a cut that links this sermon (the loftiness of the pulpit from which the priest preaches is underscored by Bartolomé's low angle shot) to the positive work on the ground performed by 'los nuevos cristianos' (the new Christians). The Almudena priest may defend the Spanish family in the abstract, but grassroots priests offer support to actual families left homeless by slum clearance in Madrid, among whom an anonymous woman specifically calls for the decriminalisation of abortion and free contraception for women. The justification for this call is suggested in Bartolomé's juxtaposition of this scene with the next: the poverty of one of the twenty-six large families made destitute by the clearance is so deep that their ten-month-old baby has just died.

The condemnation of violence is also not limited to the activities of Fuerza Nueva: *Después de...* is an important witness to the grip in which Basque separatist terrorism held the country in the period. The Bartolomés' street interviewees include terrorists. A particularly chilling example of these is one anonymous interviewee's matter-of-fact declaration that, on the assassination of a Spanish police officer or Guardia Civil, 'nos alegramos y tomamos champán' (we are happy and we drink champagne). The Bartolomés then cut to a newspaper report of the death, admittedly not of a police officer or Guardia Civil, but of the Socialist worker Germán González, and the wave of peaceful protests that followed, including clear-sighted and level-headed appeals to cease violence.[19] Particularly distressing for a delayed, 2020s, viewing here is our subsequent knowledge of how long terrorism would last and how many more lives would be lost to it.

A delayed viewing also means we bring our subsequent knowledge to bear on other warnings conveyed through montage. Key among these is the juxtaposition, at the end of Part II, of the speech of army General Milans del Bosch, in a powerful leadership role, to new recruits completing military service, in which he calls for the army to take up arms to defend the 'patria' if necessary, and the speech of Alcobendas Police Commissioner Jesús Merino, who was disciplined for supporting the democratic Constitution. The juxtaposition between the two men is not through cutting directly between them, as the film cuts first to newspaper clippings to which the added voiceover explains the situation. But cinematography underscores their juxtaposition. Merino is captured in medium shot, in which we see many others in the room, which conveys that his views are as widely shared as they are briefly articulated by him with '¡viva la democracia!' (Long Live Democracy!) and '¡viva la libertad!' (Long Live Freedom!). Milans del Bosch, meanwhile, is shot in low-angle close-up with no others visible in the frame. He offers a lengthy speech, which is peppered with rhetorical flourish, like the bizarre and unsettling suggestion that the military service recruits might perform their duties 'con aire de pasodoble torero' (with the gestures of a bullfighter's pasodoble dance). Noteworthy here too is the editing. While there is no cut after Merino speaks, with Bartolomé holding the image on the applause he receives, when the General delivers the instruction to the recruits to take up arms if need be, the editing cuts dart between the various, and variously nervous, military leaders present at the scene after this instruction is issued. We now know that, only a few years later, Tejero, Milans del Bosch and others would repeat such a call to arms for real, triggering the coup itself. For the intended viewer of 1981 this contrast between a servant of the state who supports democracy being sanctioned, and another who threatens it remaining in post, would have been deeply worrying. But of course even the viewers of the 1983 Madrid Groucho cinema screening could be reassured by just how firmly established democracy had become in Spain over these two short years, for the Tejerazo quickly failed.

Black humour

Thus far, the reader who has yet to see the films might imagine rather earnest pieces: feminist in their insistence on the quotidian; strident in the contrasts they draw; and cause-and-effect in the suggestions they make through editing. But Bartolomé's trademark humour is at work here, even in this genre of documentary, which in other hands may be given to sobriety. The humour of the *Después de…* diptych also allows us to appreciate just how far it departs from the seriousness of *La batalla de Chile* (Blázquez Carretero 2014, 143; Nair 2021). Years later, Chilean editor Menz would compare the approach to humour in the two countries:

> Los problemas siempre tenían en Chile un tono serio, dramático y monocorde; mientras que [en España] siempre había una tendencia hacia el humor en la situación o en el modo de expresarse, un humor a veces muy negro, pero humor… y por supuesto, inesperados excesos. (Problems always had a serious, dramatic and univocal tone in Chile; whereas [in Spain] there was always a tendency to lean towards the humour of a situation, or the humour of a way of speaking, humour that was sometimes very black, but still humour… of course, it also emerged in moments of unexpected excess.) (quoted in Blázquez Carretero 2014, 143)

Let's deal with the most frequently cited example of the deployment of humour in *Después de…* first: the diatribe of the Fuerza Nueva older lady, with which the Bartolomés close Part I. Having already examined just how vitriolic the words spoken by the woman are, which reveal just how deep her fury at the current democracy runs, it is clear that we are dealing with a case of excess. Josexto Cerdán and Marina Díaz explain that, more than excess, or exaggeration, this is *esperpento*:

cuando en el mismo Valle de los Caídos Cecilia Bartolomé cede su cámara a una militante de Fuerza Nueva que hace de su discurso puro esperpento fallero (aunque dicho final todavía hoy estremece al espectador, no hay duda de la fuerte carga tragicómico con que Cecilia Bartolomé lo inserta en el film.) (when in the very Valle de los Caídos itself Cecilia Bartolomé yields her camera to the Fuerza Nueva militant, who makes a speech that is pure exaggerated esperpento farce (even though that ending still makes the spectator shiver today, there is no doubt about the heavily tragi-comic way in which Cecilia Bartolomé inserts it into the film.) (2001, 16)

Let's look closely at the agency implied by the grammar here: that the director 'yields her camera' implies little agency, even though she is the subject of the verb. It is then the Fuerza Nueva speaker who is the active subject of 'hacer' – it is she who makes her speech an *esperpento*. Note, though, that Bartolomé is again the subject of 'insert […] in a heavily tragi-comic way'.

I would suggest that what is going on here is not that the older lady consciously delivers a speech that she makes an *esperpento*; the dark, tragic humour here comes from Bartolomé as artist. Writing more recently, Belén Puebla Martínez pinpoints the way Bartolomé creates *esperpento* in this sequence through her manipulation of film form:

> el discurso de la militante se toma aún más histriónica con el acercamiento excesivo de la cámara y el uso de un montaje que intensifica el ritmo y la emoción del discurso expuesto, lo que provoca una sonrisa irónica en el espectador. (the militant lady's speech becomes even more histrionic through the excessive proximity of the camera, and the use of montage that intensifies the rhythm and emotion of the speech, which triggers an ironic smile in the spectator.) (2012, 3)

If the filmic techniques of cinematography and editing create *esperpento*, we are thus able to identify other instances of it in the film and demonstrate how Bartolomé has created them. Perhaps less memorable, as they are not delivered direct to camera, and thus do not break the fourth wall, are the five speeches made by various male leaders, including Blas Piñar, at the Fuerza Nueva rally of Part 2;[20] but in fact the deployment of *esperpento* here is also wickedly funny and devastating in its critique. Of course, the low-angle shot comically exaggerates the importance of this series of Right-wing extremists whose own inflated rhetoric inflates their own sense of their importance (in practical terms, the filming team would have needed a crane to shoot them from any other angle anyway). What stands out in this sequence is Bartolomé's ability to take advantage of a completely unplanned moment, which recalls the overhead helicopter that interrupts her second, silent Film School short, *Cruzada del Rosario* (1963) (Chapter 1). Here the unexpected concerns the technical problems with the microphone. As the military men bark out the tired old Francoist rhetoric, Bartolomé's camera's attention is clamped on all the fuss created by the faulty microphone: an anonymous technician tries to adjust it, crouching to avoid being hit by the arm-waving gesticulations of the enthusing José Evaristo Casariego. An unrepeatable, spontaneous moment, Bartolomé's eye for detecting and homing in on the ridiculous effectively sends up both the pomposity of the speakers, but also the threatening content of their words.

Bartolomé's humour, in *Después de...*, is not limited to *esperpento*. Her camera roves the scenes she records in search of telling details. Thus when new mayor Tierno leaves the previously discussed Almudena mass, Bartolomé's focus is not on the religion of the devout, nor the statesmanship of the mayor, even as the voiceover attempts to stress this by explaining how impressive is his willingness to attend mass as a gesture of reconciliation. Instead, Bartolomé focusses on the gypsy women selling Virgin Mary calendars to the churchgoers as they leave: the woman's need for money to eat, and the consumerist predilections of the faithful, replace lofty matters of Church and State. Another might be the Fuerza Nueva Valle de los Caídos sequence: for all the fear the team felt when filming among neo-fascists and extremists, this did not stop Bartolomé picking out the telling detail of a dog dressed up in the Spanish flag!

Amusing, too, is the NO-DO spoof with which Bartolomé opens Part II. The addition of the voice-over may have occurred against the director's will, but here she uses it to great comic effect. The setting is Madrid's swanky Hotel Ritz,[21] the music is the French Baroque that recalls the aristocracy before the Revolution, and the politicians and financiers are briefly filmed hard at work in a plenary meeting to approve support for Spain from the Trilateral Commission, which, the voiceover somewhat lamely quips, is also known as the 'Comité Ejecutivo del Internacional *Capitalista*'

(Executive Committee of the *Capitalist* International). Bartolomé then cuts to a tracking shot that pans over the financiers' desks, allowing her to take in the detail that one of them has tucked a copy of the sports news behind the financial papers! She enjoys herself even more when filming the drinks reception after the meeting, complete with cocktails and canapés. To *épater la bourgeoisie* in this way may be an easy target. The sequence takes on more importance by spoofing the Francoist NO-DO. At its end, the voiceover reports that Spain has succeeded in gaining Trilateral support with words that seem to be addressed to a school pupil: 'el examen es satisfactorio' (the exam result is satisfactory). Here we are reminded of the ways dictatorship infantilised its citizens and its propaganda infantilised its audience: but now we are summoned to reject both.[22]

Bartolomé's ear, as well as eye, for telling spontaneous detail is also evident in the darker moments of the films. After the impassioned discussion of the UCD's neglect of agriculture, the tractor drivers set off for a rally in Zamora. She keeps the cameras rolling to include a fairly banal question by one, '¿nos invitan a comer?' (do you think they'll give us lunch?), but then also the amusing 'alguna hostia es lo que vas a comer' (a knuckle sandwich is what you're going to have for lunch) quip by another (Part I). Even in the chilling interviews with ETA terrorists, somehow Bartolomé manages here, in this most unlikely of scenarios, to pick up a comic detail. In a sober reflection on his rejection of the Spanish state, one anonymous interviewee is comparing Spanish Galicia and French Brittany, which he cites as both equally meaningful to him as he holds no allegiance to Spain. Only Bartolomé could end this sequence, with its weighty subject of the justification of terrorism, with the young man musing 'aunque son un poquito más bajitos los gallegos, igual' (even though Galicians are maybe a bit shorter), here shifting gear from a discussion of violence against the state to a totally irrelevant spontaneous comment on comparative stature!

The wolf

Employing an aesthetic of the everyday that interweaves individual interviews with contemporary leaders into a vast fresco of anonymous interviews in order to capture the 'word on the street'; editing the material to evoke eloquent juxtapositions that demonstrated, in many cases, the violent consequences of a rhetoric of violence; and adopting a quirkily humorous tone to send up authority: these were highly risky creative moves in the Spain of 1979 to 1981. Indeed, so risky were they that the films fell victim to neo-Francoist censorship.

Writing twenty years on, Luis Fernández Colorado's interpretation of *Después de...* historicised the films, noting their montage would have been very different had they been made after the coup d'état (2001, 69). Stressing the 'discursive confusion' that was an inevitable consequence of filming the 'confused and slippery' ideological terrain of mid-Transition Spain (2001, 66), he salutes the 'contemplative and respectful' positions the Bartolomés were able to adopt, even when the views expressed to them were far away from their own (2001, 69). Since Cerdán's and Díaz's edited volume in the 'Los olvidados' series of 2001, the little that has been published on these films has continued to stress the frustrations with a 'desmemoriada' (forgetful) Spain (Blázquez Carretero 2014, 149), in which the films remain 'forgotten'. With such close ties to contemporary transnational currents like militant Latin American documentary, *Después de...* may be reframed in the context of world cinema. Beyond the new focus on the 'now' of 1970s Spain, which marked *Después de...* out among contemporary Spanish documentaries that turned to the past, this Chapter has located the originality of these films in Bartolomé's feminist aesthetic of the quotidian; her eloquent editing; and her particular recourse to humour, including the *esperpento*. These make a distinctive contribution to better-known documentaries filmed on the street at times of political tension, like *La batalla de Chile*, which charted the years before Pinochet took power, in an earnest tone. They also influence later documentary approaches, both within Spain (for example Ana Asensio tracks her influence on Basilio Martín Patino's *Madrid* (1987) (2022)) and beyond (for example in more recent films about the Arab spring).[23] But the dangers of that filming moment, principally that of 1979 Spain, must not be dissolved in this wider transnational context. Echoing the richness of the title of her Film School medium-length film *Margarita y el lobo / Margarita and the Wolf* (Chapter 2), Bartolomé describes the shoot and subsequent censorship of *Después de...* as filming between the 'jaws of the wolf', jaws that subsequently closed around them: 'Nos taparon la boca, porque rodamos ante la misma boca del lobo' (they shut our mouths because we were filming between the jaws of the wolf) (quoted in Fernández-Santos, 1983).

Notes

1 For an account of how other contemporary documentaries fared, see Riambau (2001, 126–7). The Bartolomés were certainly not the only directors to experience delays in exhibition.
2 Josexto Cerdán describes these as a 'flood', perhaps not in reference to the number of them, but their significance after so many years of state propaganda (2013, 533). They include: *El desencanto / Disenchantment* (Chávarri 1976); *La vieja memoria / The Old Memory* (Camino 1977); *Raza, el espíritu de Franco / Race, the Spirit of Franco* (Herralde 1977); *Ocaña, retrat intermitent / Ocaña, Intermittent Portrait* (Pons 1978), with the exception of the latter, all of these look back in time in an effort to settle accounts with the dictatorship (Cerdán 2013, 533). Elena Blázquez Carretero adds to this group *Informe general (…) / General Report (…)* (Portabella 1976), *¡Arriba España! / Long Live Spain!* (Francoist slogan) (Berzosa 1976), *Entre la esperanza y el fraude / Between Hope and Fraud* (Cooperativa de Cine Alternatiu de Barcelona 1977) and *El proceso de Burgos / The Burgos Process* (Uribe 1979) (2014, 141). Prior to this period, anti-Franco directors had to work creatively to fold their dissent into fictional film genres that were acceptable for the regime (for the successes, frustrations and contradictions of this situation, see Faulkner 2006).
3 See Appendix Interview (p. 216) on Bartolomé's extraordinary experience of working with this Extreme Right production company. Immediately prior to *Después de…*, they had produced a number of *destape* soft-porn pictures.
4 I therefore use Bartolomé in the singular in this text to refer to Cecilia, unless the creative effort is clearly joint, for which I use the surname in the plural.
5 For the history of these, and alternative, light, portable equipment, see McLane (2023, 236–7).
6 *El País* journalist Juan Bedoya names the members of this Board as J.L. Tafur, José Sámano, Miguel Picazo, Fernando Méndez Leite, Serrano de Osma and López Lemente (Bedoya 1982).
7 A third screening in Seville is mentioned in *Efe*, which may be an error (Anon. 1983).
8 In a review published on the film's delayed release, Galán is able to condemn the UCD's 'censores nostálgicos' (nostalgic censors), for whom

the films 'despertar[on] sus instintos mal reprimidos' (awoke their scarcely repressed instincts) (1983).

9 Elsewhere, José Juan mounted a defence against criticism of other omissions – for example both state and extra-judiciary torture and detentions – explaining that the team shot what was happening in the moment of the shoot, which did not include these (quoted in Blázquez Carretero 2014, 146). (The question of the release of prisoners is included in an interview with the anonymous girlfriend of one such prisoner in the 'Hijos de Agobio' section of Part I.) We might also add the omission of LGBTQ+ experience from the film, about which the response might have been the same. Journalist Mikel Insausti warns that the 'enormes presiones de toda índole' (enormous pressures of all types) that come to bear on documentaries about this period means that all are bound to fail (quoted in Fernández Colorado 2001, 67 n. 6).

10 José Antonio Primo de Rivera was the founder of the Falange Española, later the Falange Española de las Juntas de Ofensiva Nacional Sindicalista (FE de las JONS), one of the parties that merged with others to support Franco.

11 This is also the title of a 1950 film by Luis Buñuel.

12 See for example Annette Kuhn's tracing of a lineage between the interior, domestic focus of *Janie's Janie* (Ahur 1971), *Women of the Rhondda* (Capps et al. 1973) and *Union Maids* (Klein, Reichert and Mogulesco 1976). These immediately preceded *Después de...*, and likewise deployed 'Direct Cinema' / cinéma vérité techniques and interviews (1994, 142–50).

13 In order to aid future study of the films, I list, in order of appearance, the key names and quote their roles at that time in brackets, as they are stated in the films. The length of this list is also useful for getting a sense of the vast ideological terrain covered by the films. Part I: Antoni de Senillosa (Diputado de Coalición Democrático (Representative of the Democratic Coalition Party)); José Pérez Guerra (Editor, *5 Días*); Manuel Vázquez Montalbán (Escritor y Dirigente Comunista (Writer and Communist Party leader)); Ricardo Areste (Alcalde de Paracuellos, Elegido por la lista Comunista; Hijo del Alcalde Republican fusilado en 1939 (Mayor of Paracuellos, Elected for the Communist Party; Son of the Republican Mayor, who was shot in 1939)); Nino, Quintín (both: Sacerdote Dominico (Dominican priest)). Cristina Alberdi is in fact not given an individual name, but appears alongside two colleagues with the title Colectivo de Abogadas Feministas (Feminist Lawyers Collective). Some of these figures reappear, as well as new ones in Part II: Charo Reina (Actriz y Dirigente de Fuerza Nueva (Actor and Fuerza Nueva Leader)); Santiago Carrillo (Secretario General del Partido Comunista

Español (General Secretary of the Spanish Communist Party)) (who is filmed giving a speech, rather than interviewed); Felipe González (Secretario General Partido Socialista (General Secretary of the Socialist Party)); Blas Piñar (Presidente de Fuerza Nueva (President of Fuerza Nueva)) (also not interviewed); Mario Onaindia (Euskadiko Eskerre (Basque Country Leftist Party)); Rosa Olivares (Movimiento Comunista de Euskadi (Basque Communist Movement)); Miguel Castell (Diputado por Herri Batasuna (Basque Coalition Party Representative)); Carlos Garaikoetxea (Partido Nacional Vasco (Basque Nationalist Party)); Txiqui Benegas (Partido Socialista de Euskadi (Basque Socialist Party)); Alejandro Rojas Marcos (Secretario General de Partido Socialista Andaluz (General Secretary of the Andalousian Socialist Party)); Perico Solabarria (Obrero y diputado de Herri Batasuna (Worker and Basque Coalition Party Representative)); Jordi Pujol (Secretario General de Convergencia Democrática de Cataluña (General Secretary of the Catalan Nationalist Party)); Joan Raventos (Secretario General del Partido Socialista de Cataluña (General Secretary of the Catalan Socialist Party)); Santiago Martínez Campos, José Evaristo Casariego, Luis Jaudenes, José Antonio Girón (no affiliation given; part of Francoist rally) Rafael Arias Salgado (Dirigente de Unión Central Democrático (Leader of Union of the Democratic Centre Party)); Comandante Luis Otero (Expulsado del Ejército por pertenecer a U.M.D. (Expelled from the Army for being a member of the UMD (Unión Militar Democrática (Democratic Military Union))); Jesús Merino (Comisario de Policía (Police Commissioner)).

14 In fact, the Bartolomés use a wide variety of settings, with different purposes. We meet Felipe González and the Feminist Lawyers Collective in their offices; a number of the Basque and Andalusian leaders are filmed in interview outside, against a building site and a rural landscape respectively. There are standout exceptions, like Antoni de Senillosa, shot against a dragon sculpture in Barcelona's Park Güell, or Luis Otero, pointedly located in a domestic setting, complete with family photos as well as photos of his younger self in various roles in the Army, from which he has just been expelled.

15 Robert Bahar and Almudena Carracedo's documentary, produced by the Almodóvar brothers, *El silencio de los otros / The Silence of Others* (2018) also begins with the body and voice of an older lady, weakened, but not yet silenced, by age, a descendant of Republicans who had similarly received only unmarked burial. Director Pedro Almodóvar takes up the story in the fictional feature *Madres paralelas / Parallel Mothers* (2021), in which Julieta Serrano plays an elderly Republican

descendant. We met this actor in her then youthful portrayal of the hippy Paula in ¡Vámonos, Bárbara! (Chapter 4).
16 The bill was finally passed as the Ley Orgánica 10/2022, in August 2022.
17 Ana Asensio notes the similarities between the way the Bartolomés shoot the Bilbao rally and the inclusion of a similar rally, similarly shot, in Varda's L'une chante, l'autre pas / One Sings, the Other Doesn't (1977) (2022).
18 Lisa French (2018, 18). French, whose analysis is based on interviews with female directors at the International Documentary Film Festival, Amsterdam 2014, is judiciously cautious in her analysis, which relies on cis identification of women and cannot account for trans experience.
19 These sequences were shot in Zumaya, where Bartolomé recalls no journalists were present, only an older man who was the correspondent for the BBC (Prieto 2018, 4).
20 The names are given as: Santiago Martínez Campos, José Evaristo Casariego, Luis Jauderes, José Antonio Girón and Blas Piñar. The wild gestures and barking rhetoric of these figures is perhaps easy to single out for critique today. More insidious, perhaps, is the level tone adopted by others to deliver unsettling content. At the meeting of the government of Andalusia in Part II, an anonymous speaker appeals to a maniqueism that George W. Bush would make famous in his 2001 speech on the War on Terror: 'quien no está con la Junta de Andalucía está en contra de Andalucía y los andaluces' (if you're not for the Andalusia Junta, you're against the Andalusia Junta and Andalusians). Chilling too is the reasonable tone of a Basque construction worker as he explains that, just as he has to accept running the risk of falling from a building and dying as a hazard of his job, so a Spanish state Civil Guard should likewise accept running the risk of political assassination as a hazard of theirs. As in the sequence with the older lady Fuerza Nueva militant at the end of Part I, Bartolomé draws in to a close-up here to stress the extremism of this view.
21 Fernández Colorado includes a photograph of the shooting team decked out in their finery in order to gain access to the Ritz to film this first meeting of the 'Trilateral' in Spain. The men wear suits, and Bartolomé, a fur coat, but the smirking expressions on their faces give away the fun they intended to have with this sequence (2001, 66)!
22 One of the individual interviews of the films is with José Pérez Guerra, editor of 5 Días, who uses the metaphor of infantilisation to describe the need, in the Transition, for citizens to shift from being 'niños' (children), to 'mayores de edad' (grown-ups) (Part I).

23 In 2008, *Después de…* was subtitled into Arabic for a screening in Cairo; Bartolomé commented that in Egypt 'están luchando contra el fundamentalismo igual que nosotros luchábamos contra una dictadura. Así que han visto un paralelismo' (they are fighting against fundamentalism just as we fought against a dictatorship. Thus, they have seen the parallels) (Contreras de la Llave 2008, 39; see also Zecchi 2014a, 87 n. 15). My thanks to Clara Kleininger-Wanik for suggesting that Jehane Noujaim's *The Square* (2013), about the Egyptian revolution, which also deploys extensive street footage, may reveal the influence of *Después de…*.

6

'Es que no sabéis mirar': colony and memory in *Lejos de África*

When the opportunity finally came to make a feature-length fiction film with the relative freedom and certainty afforded by her own production company (Cecilia Bartolomé P.C.), how typical it was of Cecilia Bartolomé to choose such a tricky topic as Spain's colonial history in Africa. This chapter will explore whether the audacity of the choice paid off. There is a balance to be struck between charting the originality of *Lejos de África / Far from Africa* (1995), the first Spanish film since democracy to address the nation's former imperial territories in what is today Equatorial Guinea,[1] yet also assessing shortcomings. The film's main aim, to explore the final decades of Spain's possession of territories in the Gulf of Guinea before independence as Equatorial Guinea was won in 1968, from the perspective of a young girl, then teenager, then young woman, is brilliant. But the unevenness of *Lejos de África* stems from some at best odd, at worst weak, aesthetic choices, as well as the ways the film was presented to audiences. In a typical interview, Bartolomé complains 'Me irrita que los jóvenes no conozcan el colonialismo español en el continente [africano]' (It annoys me that young people don't know about Spanish colonialism on the [African] continent) (Anon. 1997c). Though using this comment as the article title may have been an editorial choice by *Ya*, the overall marketing approach that stressed unfamiliarity for audiences did not work. We can only conjecture whether one that had stressed familiarity, like the film's connections to popular transnational films about the continent, might have fared better. Sydney Pollack's *Out of Africa* (1985), for example, achieved nearly three million spectators in Spain. Such a presentation of *Lejos de África* to audiences might have stressed narrative and formal similarities with Pollack's film; released in Spain as *Memorias de África*, it even shared a similar title (Santaolalla 2005, 247). Alternatively again, Bartolomé's film might have been presented to audiences in a way that stressed its differences from earlier national traditions of dictatorship-era colonial cinema. Emphasising unfamiliarity and educational need did not work.[2]

The didactic aim of *Lejos de África*, which was in part an autobiographical film for Bartolomé, who, like her protagonist Susana, had spent her own girlhood on the island of Fernando Poo (now Bioko), might not necessarily have been a flaw. Placing this aim to teach audiences about Spain's colonial history in Africa in an accessible period melodrama, *Lejos de África* might be described as a middlebrow film, which is to say, one with a didactic message, high production values and an accessible address to audiences. I have argued elsewhere that the middlebrow should not automatically be dismissed as unadventurous or superficial. Middlebrow films often constitute the most successful work in world cinema, connecting effectively with audiences, who value quality and familiarity – even if, often, film critics who prize originality are less sympathetic.[3] However, where didacticism tips into superficiality, and where a picture fails to connect with audiences, these potential weaknesses of the middlebrow may be pointed out.

For all Bartolomé's plans to engage a wide, especially youth, audience, *Lejos de África*, like the director's other films, did not achieve box office success. Once again we find a Bartolomé out of step with contemporary currents in the national cinema. If an earlier film like *¡Vámonos, Bárbara! / Bárbara, Let's Go!* was also out of step, the younger director, as we have seen (Chapter 4), countered this by conceding multiple interviews in which she explained her original fusion of feminism and humour, encouraged potential audiences to see the film's connections with transnational, if not national, trends, and did offer them familiar anchors by describing her inspiration in figures and tendencies like Berlanga and the *esperpento*. There is less evidence of this marketing savvy with *Lejos de África*. This may be surprising given the use of her own production company, in contrast to the obstructive producer she had to handle with *¡Vámonos, Bárbara!*, as we have seen (Chapter 4). Indeed, one particularly awkward moment, which illustrates the way the director and this film are somewhat out of step, is captured in what should have been the publicity splash of a four-page spread in the national daily *ABC* (Guzmán 1997). A photograph of Bartolomé is juxtaposed with one of new director Fernando León de Aranoa, who was releasing his début, *Familia / Family*, also a melodrama, at the same time as *Lejos de África*. But the sizes of the photographs are oddly uneven as Bartolomé is in a medium close-up, while León de Aranoa is in a full-length shot. León de Aranoa's film, unlike Bartolomé's, though, connects effectively with the 'cine social', the contemporary Spanish genre that updated the Left-wing traditions of Italian Neorealism for Spain's 1990s, which contemporary audiences and critics were beginning to know and admire (Faulkner 2013, 230; in connection with León de Aranoa, 239). *Lejos de África*'s comparative unlocatability, if originality, compares unfavourably. Thus while León de Aranoa would go on to great commercial and critical success in the 1990s and new millennium with ten further films to date, *Lejos de África* would be Bartolomé's last. This chapter will, then, account positively for the ways that Bartolomé is ahead of her time in stressing in her film the intersectionality of gender and race, and in exploring interracial relationships, even if, despite these decolonising efforts, I will argue that the film ultimately adopts a Eurocentric approach.[4] However, a recognition of these strengths must be balanced with an account of the film's flaws.

Before beginning this analysis, it is important to note that the Republic of Equatorial Guinea now, at the time of writing (2023), has had fifty-five years as an independent nation and endured two violent and repressive dictatorships (Francisco Macías Nguema was succeeded by his slightly less authoritarian nephew Teodoro Obian in 1979, after a bloody coup d'état), which have sanctioned some of the worst human rights abuses in the world. This post-1968 history is not the focus of *Lejos de África*, which addresses the Franco-colonial era between 1950 and 1961, which Bartolomé herself spent with her family on the island of Fernando Poo, after her parents were posted there as teachers. However, Francoism's woeful legacy in these territories of subsequent political instability and authoritarian abuse (these began in precisely the years that Spain itself was priding itself on a supposedly peaceful Transition) forms part of the context of this film. Its appeal to nostalgia, and evocation of a childhood idyll – if one that is not always peaceful – is contradicted by what some of the 1996 audience might have known of subsequent, bloody collapse.

If the viewer, then, approaches the film with some wariness, its nostalgic tone, which is created by a fusion of narrative focus and aesthetic choices, works to suspend their knowledge of this subsequent future. Presented in three parts by intertitle, 'Colonias españolas en el Golfo de Guinea, África' (Spanish Colonies in the Gulf of Guinea, Africa), 1950, 1956 and 1961 respectively, each part corresponds to periods of the girlhood, then young womanhood, of protagonist Susana, played in Part I, when she is eight, by Alicia Hernández Díaz, and in Parts II and III, at fifteen and twenty, by Alicia Bogo. Placing the activities of the adult characters in the background – Susana's father Gonzalo (Xabier Eloriaga), a doctor, his medical colleagues, and housewife mother (Isabel Mestres), and her leisured friends – the film promisingly places Susana centre stage, focussing on her interracial friendship with Rita across the three parts (played by Isabel Derrick in Part I, Yanelis Bonicacio in Part II, and Ademilis Hernández in Part III), and romance with Diego (Patricio Wood) in the final part. Thus, as the harmony (Part I), frictions (Part II), then imminent collapse (Part III) of colonial life occupy peripheral adult characters, Bartolomé may focus on wider questions of interracial relationships through her child, teenage and young-adult protagonists. These include the positive portrait of the close friendship between the girls, Susana and Rita; the mutual understanding between Susana and the Nigerian family cook, Silvano (Idelfonso Tamayo), in part owing to a shared knowledge of the English language; and the comradeship between the three friends Susana, Rita and Diego. However, of these three interracial friendships, the fact that the only one to survive to the end of the film is that between Susana and the cook – who is, after all, a paid servant of her family – is a depressing indictment of colonial relationships. With regard to the first friendship, Spanish Susana and Bubi Rita may attend school together, and thus share a peninsular education complete with fascist salutes at the start of the school day (Figure 6.1), and may play together as girls, and thus share Rita's induction of Susana into Bubi beliefs and magic; but their relationship ends with betrayal and fracture. When Rita returns to Fernando Poo after studying in Spain, and steals away Diego's romantic affections from her friend, there is an initial reconciliation between the three

Figure 6.1 Susana (Alicia Hernández Díaz) and Rita (Isabel Derrick) at school in Fernando Poo in *Lejos de África* (2006)

when they share a three-way embrace (see Figure 6.2 of Susana, Rita and hand-me-down boyfriend Diego). However, the film ends with Susana's departure from the island without them: much as she might search the crowds at the port for Rita and Diego, they do not show up to see her off. Silvano's presence at the departure, when he gives her an African talisman as she steps onto the Spanish ship, may indicate the positive impact of Susana's stay in Africa. It is for the viewer to note how this girl Susana's individual legacy – her interracial friendship with Silvano – contrasts so starkly with the wider legacy of Franco's Spain as a colonial power.

From worries to word-play: missed opportunities in the Spanish press

Read retrospectively through the film's subsequent commercial failure (25,464 viewers (Santaolalla 2005, 252)), hindsight allows us to see that the director's approach to the press interviews that might have enticed her audiences failed to connect with them. Her evocation, for example, of a 'mundo desaparecido, del que no queda ya ni el recuerdo' (world that has disappeared, of which not even a memory remains), may be heartfelt, but audiences may have found that her further worries tipped into too much into earnest fretting. 'Si bien los ingleses y los franceses han recuperado la parte colonial de su historia, España no lo ha hecho nunca; [...] el asunto guineano fue materia reservada durante veinte años, hasta 1988, porque la descolonización se hizo tarde y mal' (If the British and the French have recovered the colonial part of their history, Spain hasn't done this ever; [...] the Guinean question was off-limits for twenty years, till 1988, because decolonisation happened late and badly) (Guzmán 1997). Bartolomé may not have been in control of the *Ya* editor's choice of the previously discussed concern 'me irrita que los jóvenes no conozcan el colonialismo español' as the title for their review of the film, but irritation concerning audience ignorance clearly did not encourage those young folks to go to the film theatres. Bartolomé is absolutely right about 'la amnesia histórica que sufrimos' (the historical amnesia that we are suffering from) (Anon. 1997c), an amnesia that includes Spain's history of Civil War and dictatorship on the peninsular territory too, but being right did not prove an effective media strategy.

Nonetheless, the reviews selection available for consultation today[5] reveal a largely sympathetic press. The successful performances of the older Susana (Parts II and III), by Spanish Alicia Bogo, and older Rita (Part III), by Cuban Ademilis Hernández, which speak of the quality production values typical of the middlebrow, are widely admired (Torres 1997; Anon. 1997a; Alonso 1997; Anon. 1997d). The rather less specific qualities of 'authenticity' (Torres 1997) and 'simplicity' (Alonso 1997) are also appreciated. Outliers *El País* (in a review by novelist Adelaida García Morales (1997), whose *El silencio de las sirenas* (1985) Bartolomé intended to adapt) and *La crónica 16 de León* (Anon. 1997d) swing from lavishly praising Bartolomé's 'maestría' (brilliant ability), to scathingly slating the film as a mere 'panfleto' (pamphlet). The reviewer of *ABC* (Anon. 1997b) might be closer to the mark than both these extremes by noting that *Lejos de África* is uneven overall, punning that 'está la colonia, pero no el perfume' (the colony is there, but not the cologne). What emerges is a film that is something of a unicorn in the national context: it connects neither with contemporary Spanish trends like 'cine social', nor, and perhaps surprisingly, with the contemporary rise of Spanish women directors (see Introduction). A further difficulty is that viewers are unable to

'*Es que no sabéis mirar*' 151

place *Lejos de África* in the context of the director's own previous work, which remained, as we have seen, little known – only *El País*'s Augusto Torres (1997) mentions any of Bartolomé's earlier films. While, as we have remarked with regards to *¡Vámonos, Bárbara!* (Chapter 4), such unlocatability might resonate in the similarly 'unlocated' context of the 1970s Transition, by the 1990s, it led to a failure to connect.

Critical approaches, from auteurism to transnationalism

Writing in the decade following the film's release, subsequent scholarly criticism has partly performed this labour of connection. Contributors to Josexto Cerdán and Marina Díaz's 2001 edited volume mount an argument for *Lejos de África* as part of the director's auteurist trajectory. Juan Carlos Ibáñez, for example, suggests that Susana's characterisation inherits the questioning outlook of Ana of *¡Vámonos, Bárbara!* (2001, 25). (Typically, as we have seen (Chapter 4), this focus on Ana obscures the role of Bárbara in the earlier film, whose age and girlhood might connect her more readily with Susana.) Further critics detect Bartolomé's trademark humour in the characterisation of Silvanus (Cerdán y Díaz 2001, 16). While the director has affirmed that the character was based on the cook of her own childhood household, who also set up a brothel in the patio and refused to use the pressure-cooking pot (Ortega 2001, 90 n. 7), this character is also similar to the portrait of the family cook of French director Claire Denis's 1988 *Chocolat*. Denis, like Bartolomé, spent her childhood in colonial French territory (Cameroon), and the portrait she paints of that girlhood from a nostalgic perspective was surely an inspiration to Bartolomé. Denis's Anglophile and English-speaking African cook amusingly bickers with the European girl protagonist's mother over French cuisine, just as Bartolomé's Silvanus does with Susana's mother over Spanish.

In addition to the portrait of Silvanus, which fuses Bartolomé's trademark humour with wider European films about Africa, María Luisa Ortega also points more widely to the comedy of Bartolomé's film. The director mischievously portrays Spain's imposition of various peninsular spectacles on African territory, like the Falangist

'Marcha de juventudes' (Youth March), or Catholic 'Semana Santa' (Holy Week). Her exaggeration of these spectacles evokes the *esperpento*, a particularly effective example of which is the scene that portrays the peninsular Catholic prudery that leads to the mass introduction of white bras for half-naked Black island women at public processions. Ortega summarises such scenes as 'Los esperpénticos esfuerzos de los colonos, que con ironía nos muestra la película, por imprimir el más genuino sello imperial español en los cuerpos y las almas de los colonizados' (the film ironically shows us the *esperpento* (grotesequely exaggerated) efforts of the colonists to imprint a genuine Spanish imperial stamp on the bodies and souls of the colonised) (2001, 84).

Also adopting an auteurist approach, Ana Martín Morán rightly connects *Lejos de África* to earlier work like *¡Vámonos Bárbara!* in the refusal of both films to foreground the 'Grand Narratives' of History. Thus, in the first film, as we have seen, Bartolomé offers no pamphleteering dismissal of patriarchy; nor does she, in the second, simply reject colonialism. In both, her preference is for apparently minor, domestic stories that cast the contradictions of those 'Grand Narratives' of patriarchy and colonialism into a new light. Martín Morán's description of the distinction between approaches works more elegantly in Spanish than English through the polysemous play on 'historia'. Reprising the distinction Cerdán and Díaz make in their Introduction, that Bartolomé's films create 'una mirada que perpetre nuevas identidades en los sujetos de la Historia y de la historia' (a look that brings about new identities in both wider history and particular, personal stories) (2001, 15), she argues that Bartolomé 'logra transmitir la historia con minúsculas que no aparece en ningún sitio y revelar la trastienda de la gran Historia que cuentan los libros' (manages to transmit particular, personal stories, that have never been seen before, and to reveal the backdrop of the wider History written about in books) (2001, 100).

There has been some debate among critics concerning this suggestion that the thematic content of the film 'no aparece en ningún sitio'. Ortega, for example, insists on this argument. For her, *Lejos de África* is an 'orphan' film as it does not connect – and therefore did not connect for potential audiences – with any filmmaking tradition concerning colonial Africa in Spain. Certainly, Spain's brief period of Francoist missionary films set in Equatorial Guinea would scarcely be known by anyone but film historians with access to archives (*Afan Evu* (Fernández Flórez 1945); *Misión blanca / White Mission* (Orduña 1946); *Obsesión / Obsession* (Ruiz-Castillo 1947); *A dos grados del ecuador / Two Degrees from the Equator* (Vilches 1953); *Cristo negro / Black Christ* (Torrado 1963)). Ortega also argues that *Lejos de África* cannot be likened to its two most obvious Hollywood and French predecessors, Sydney Pollack's *Out of Africa* (1985) and Renais Clair's *Indochine* (1992). Even though all three share a reminiscing female perspective, conveyed by an adult voiceover, and, as we have seen, *Lejos de África* has a similar title to the distribution title of Pollack's film in Spain, Ortega rightly argues that Bartolomé's film lacks the transcendental sweep of these earlier evocations of the British and French empires. Somewhat contrarily, the critic perceives *Lejos de África*'s disconnection, or orphanhood, as a positive, as the lack of a frame of reference means that Bartolomé can fashion 'una mirada nueva, insólita, fresca y sugerente' (a new, unusual, fresh and suggestive gaze) (2001, 87). However, as we have also seen, this originality, without a shrewd marketing campaign, failed to encourage audiences and condemned the film to oblivion. More combatively, Ortega also argues that this oblivion is in fact a positive too, as it meant the film could not be subjected to Cultural Studies approaches (2001, 81)!

Isabel Santaolalla is more nuanced in refuting this theory of orphanhood and rightly restores *Lejos de África* to its place in wider, transnational histories of postcolonial cinema – and does so by effectively deploying, precisely, a Cultural Studies approach. For this author, the similarities in title, the intertwining of the female perspective, the use of voiceover, and the evocation of nostalgia all link Bartolomé's film 'estrechamente' (closely) to Pollack's (2005, 247–8). Further connections include the development of each protagonist's knowledge of the continent via a romantic affair – Karen Blinx (Meryl Streep) and Denys (Robert Redford) in Pollack's film; Susana and Diego in Bartolomé's. Bartolomé also adds a deliberate homage to the earlier film when we share a point-of-view shot with the child Susana as she is driven through the streets of Santa Isabel, then capital of Fernando Poo, just as the audience of Pollack's film shares that of Karen as she is driven through Nairobi (Santaolalla 2005, 248). Furthermore, Santaolalla rightly notes the importance of Denis's *Chocolat*, as well as Marie France Pisier's *Le Bal du gouverneur / The Governor's Ball* (1990), as precedents (2005, 251–2). Placing Bartolomé's film in this wider transnational frame also allows Santaolalla to assess the film's treatment of race. Despite its decolonising aims, she argues, as do I, that *Lejos de África* ultimately settles on the Eurocentrism (2005, 256) that also characterises its transnational antecedents.

While this chapter covers some of the same postcolonial conceptual terrain as Santaolalla, it will also reprise elements of the auteurist approach we have analysed from Cerdán and Díaz's volume. However, while auteurist studies generally trace, and celebrate, the consistency of a director's creative trajectory, in this penultimate chapter I will deploy it somewhat perversely also to yield insights into inconsistencies with previous films and point to opportunities not taken, where we might argue that they might have been taken previously. Working through Bartolomé's auteurist hallmarks of feminism (including Girlhood) and Francoism, and the use of humour and music, I will lay out her decolonising, yet ultimately Eurocentric, approach. I thereby seek a balanced response to a brave, if uneven, attempt to tell in the Spanish language the story of Europe's colonial presence in Africa – a story that has so often been told in English and French, and, increasingly, in other languages, such as Portuguese.

Feminism and Francoism

The keystones of Bartolomé's conceptual world, as argued in this book, are (pro-)feminism and (anti-)Francoism: these are both evident in *Lejos de África*. We have seen that its female perspective draws on preceding films that adopt an adult woman's point of view, *Out of Africa* and *Indochine*. Further inspirational precedents – both, as it happens, by Francophone female directors – help pinpoint Bartolomé's move from female perspective to feminism.

While the Spanish Ministry of Culture and Sport Database states that only later films by Martinican director Euzhan Palcy and French director Claire Denis were released in Spain,[6] the parallels between Palcy's *Rues Cases-Nègres / Sugar Cane Alley* (1983)[7] and Denis's *Chocolat* (1988) – the latter explored by Santaolalla – are highly suggestive. Both these antecedents were widely commercially distributed in both France and the United States, and the timing of their releases coincides with the years that Bartolomé struggled to direct feature films following the distribution difficulties of *Después de*, but was planning *Lejos de África*. Palcy's *Rues Cases-Nègres* particularly influences the opening Part I of Bartolomé's film, and perhaps helps explain the director's move away from the teenage child of ¡*Vámonos, Bárbara!*, to the younger child of the later film. Palcy's 1983 film returns to 1930s Martinique and chooses a Black male child protagonist, twelve-year-old José, played by Gary Cadenat, to open the viewers' eyes to the racism that surrounds him. While a child-focussed film is not necessarily feminist, in Palcy's hands it becomes so – and herein the inspiration for Bartolomé – when she uses it to critique the intersection of colonialist and patriarchal ideologies of the white French men of the colony. Focussing on the white female child Susana, daughter of white Spanish colonists, the influence of Denis's *Chocolat*, which focusses on the significantly named female child 'France', daughter of white French colonists, is more obvious. And where Denis's and Bartolomé's film also share a loose tie to each director's biography, what Palcy's film brings to *Lejos de África* lies in the director's development of the character of Susana's childhood friend, Rita. If Susana's immediate cinematic sister is Denis's 'France', Rita offers a Spanish Guinean female version of José. Education within a European colonial system is the key for both José and Rita's social mobility; and for both this is counterbalanced by the importance of a Black male elder. In Palcy's film, while José is cared for by his grandmother – a devastatingly effective performance by Darling Légitimus – the knowledge and guidance provided by the village elder Médouze (Douta Seck) constitute a vital connection to African traditions for the child. In *Lejos de África*, Rita's Grandfather (Jorge Prieto), is similarly the link to her culture: the Bubi language (which is not subtitled in the instances it is spoken in the film) and, what she describes as 'magic', or Bubi rituals.

On certain measures, *Lejos de África* may compare unfavourably with *Out of Africa* and *Indochine*. Susana played by Bogo, an unknown young television actor, hardly compares to the international star power of a Meryl Streep or a Catherine Deneuve. Susana's love triangle, which only occurs in Part III, also scarcely possesses the scale of the Hollywood and French predecessors. However, it is Palcy's and Denis's earlier films that offer more relevant inspiration, especially in the area of Bartolomé's feminism. *Rues Cases Nègres* may have suggested to the Spanish director the intersectional power of the child's perspective to critique both gender and race, while with *Chocolat*, as Santaolalla points out in a comparison that includes *Le Bal du Gouverneur*, 'todas ellas usan la relación interracial y la perspectiva femenina para "deconstruir" el convencional discurso colonial patriarchal, de larga tradición literaria y visual' (they all use an interracial relationship and a female perspective to 'deconstruct' conventional, colonial, and patriarchal discourse, which has a long literary and visual history) (2005, 252). And if there are no previous Spanish films that stage aggressive colonial masculinity in former Equatorial Guinea specifically, audiences can surely make the connection with portraits of such behaviour in other Spanish colonial contexts, not least the American ones that had particularly featured on national screens in the run-up to, and following, the five-hundred-year centenary of 1992, like Carlos Saura's *El Dorado* (1988). Santaolalla singles out a shared, gendered, approach in these Spanish films about empire that cluster around 1992, which differs so much from *Lejos de África* and the Francophone cinema that I have discussed:

> responden a una estructura convencional que da prioridad al punto de vista y la voz de un protagonista masculino, español y blanco, permitiendo solo, en el mejor de los casos, que algún personaje 'racial' secundario cumpla un papel activo dentro de la acción. (they follow a conventional structure that prioritises the point of view and voice of a male, Spanish, and white protagonist, only allowing, at best, the odd 'racial' secondary character to have an active role in the action.) (2005, 229)

As we might expect, Bartolomé's feminist critique of masculinist colonialism also extends to Francoism. Gone, in this film, however, is the acerbic edge that we have previously seen. Not only is this because the dictatorship has become distant in time from the 1996 of the film's release, nor is this because the African setting is distant in space, as the 'lejos' of the title suggests, from the imperial metropolis, or 'península', as it is referred to in the film. Bartolomé chose not to, but she might have focussed on the authoritarian

'*Es que no sabéis mirar*' 157

political practices that equipped the future independent nation of Equatorial Guinea so poorly. Writing of Franco's political legacy, Susan Martin-Márquez bitterly notes the similarities between the newly independent country's dictator and his Spanish predecessor. Instituting a single-party system, refusing democracy, pursuing political enemies with brutality and promoting, especially through education and censorship, a new myth of the nation and of himself as figurehead, 'In many respects', she writes, 'Macías Nguema resembled no one so much as Franco' (2008, 299).

This horrendous future is only glimpsed in Diego's brief comments about the gathering forces of independence, or Susana's father Gonzalo's concerns that lead to the family's departure. Setting these largely aside, Bartolomé focusses instead on the limited influence of the dictatorship she herself saw as a child, teenager, then young adult. The Catholic Church, for example, which, as we have seen, was excoriated for its intervention in women's private lives in the treatment of marital separation in an earlier piece like *Margarita y el lobo / Margarita and the Wolf* (Chapter 2), becomes a different institution once severed from Spain in Africa. Alongside Susana's kindly, compromise-seeking father, Gonzalo, the other white male Spaniards that are positively portrayed in the film are Catholic missionaries. Mild-mannered Father López, for example, is, admittedly, rather insipid. He is dismissed as a 'child' by one of the gossipy colonial housewives, and even his clothing (white tunic and black sash) recalls that of Susana's own dress as a little girl, a monochrome outfit also worn by her doll. On the other hand, he is accepting of the links between Bubi and Catholic practices and respectful of the Bubi 'morimo' site he visits with a group of children in Part I. (As we will see, though, his respectfulness does not extend to his actually intervening to stop Susana's brothers and their male friends from smashing it up.) As Bartolomé reasons,

> he tocado con mucha suavidad el tema de los misioneros. Porque, junto a una parte negativa de algunos [...], siempre hubo muchos francamente interesados. Las personas que más se interesaron por la cultura y las creencias, las verdaderas investigaciones serias, el verdadero acercamiento hacia los africanos, de estudiar sus costumbres y sus creencias con respeto, parte de los misioneros, no parte de los civiles. (I've been very careful with the question of the missionaries. Because, alongside the negative aspects of a few of them [...], there

were always many who were frankly committed. The people who were most committed to the culture and the beliefs, those who did the really serious research, who really got close to the Africans, who respectfully studied their traditions and beliefs, were the missionaries, not members of civil society.) (interview with María Dolores Fernández-Figares, quoted in Martín Morán 2001, 101 n. 7)

Thus, rather than the head-on confrontations with Francoism that we see in the earlier films, and the ensuing battles with state censorship – under both dictatorship and democracy – here the approach is different. We know from interview that, growing up in Africa, Bartolomé experienced what she subsequently realised was a more modern, diverse (in terms of both different nations and different religions) and technologically advanced society than the one she was to discover in Spain on her return in the 1960s. Far from the centre of empire being 'el epítome de la civilización' (the epitome of civilisation), she met instead with an 'asfixiante catolicismo' (asphyxiating Catholicism): 'el viaje a la Península suponía en cierta forma el regreso a un mundo provinciano y menos cosmopolita y "moderno" que la colonia' (travelling to the peninsula meant, in a certain way, going backwards to a provincial world, which was less cosmopolitan and 'modern' than the colony) (Ortega 2001, 87, 91 n. 13). Certainly, the relative freedoms enjoyed by the girls Susana and Rita, especially in the central Part II that corresponds to the 1950s, compare favourably with the restrictions placed on Spanish girls, especially those portrayed on Spanish screens, in the same period: just imagine Marisol engaging, half-naked, in local African anointing ceremonies! The sexual freedoms implied by both Susana and Rita's physical encounters with Diego in the 1961 of Part III are also a far cry from the timid nature of any portrayal of burgeoning heterosexuality in contemporary peninsular films like *La gran familia / The Great Family* (Palacios 1962) or *Tiempo de amor / The Time of Love* (Diamante 1964).

However, it should be noted that such a critique of Francoist prudery is indirect. More direct critique takes the form of the Francoist school teacher, of Part I, captured in low-angle shots as she barks at a group of primary school children to sing 'Cara al sol' (Facing the Sun (Francoist fascist anthem)). She constitutes an exaggerated portrait of castrating authority that fits into the *esperpento* efforts identified elsewhere by Ortega (2001, 84). Another example might be the conversation between Susana and the local press censors, in Part II, which uses an accessible conversation format to name-check censorship on the peninsula (though the point made about the magazines passing Francoist censorship but needing censorship in the colony – perhaps a nod to the contemporary 'apertura' – contradicts Bartolomé's memories of a more liberal society). Such instances are isolated, however, meaning *Lejos de África*'s continuation of the anti-Francoism that characterises the director's earlier oeuvre relies largely on the film's critique of the intertwining of patriarchy, dictatorship and colonialism.

Interracial friendship between girls: Susana and Rita

Considered within the auteurist framework developed in this book, Bartolomé looked set to make an important contribution to on-screen representations of interracial friendship between girls in this 1996 feature. The results here are valuable in the context of an area scarcely explored in Spanish cinema, but, again, uneven in comparison with her earlier work. Her portrait of Cristina Álvarez's teenage Bárbara, as we have seen (Chapter 4), explored multi-faceted examples of adolescent in-betweenness brilliantly to explore the very in-betweenness of the Transition. What was left relatively unexplored in *¡Vámonos, Bárbara!* was friendships between girls – Bárbara's key on-screen relationship was with her mother Ana; her friendship with Paula's daughter Esther was largely developed off-screen. *Lejos de África* brings Susana's relationship with Rita on-screen and to the centre of that screen. Previous scholarship on the film has concurred that the choice of the girl protagonist is the key to exploring what we have seen Martín Morán describe as 'historia con minúsculas' (particular, personal stories) (2001, 100). Where *Lejos de África* does not emerge well from a comparison with *¡Vámonos, Bárbara!*, however, is in the choice of Susana's ages in the three Parts of the film: eight, fifteen and twenty. These choices, perhaps driven by the ages of actors Hernández Díaz and Bogo that casting director Elena Arnao was able to find, miss out the early teen years, and cusp between childhood and adulthood, that Bartolomé explored so effectively in the 1978 film. Notwithstanding this, the strength and originality of *Lejos de África* lie in its rare exploration of interracial cohesion, tension and rupture from the perspective of the Girl. I will examine the key moments that portray these three, one from each of the three Parts, before noting that the fact that the perspective is that of the white European girl is problematic.

Yet the film begins with a promise of a balanced representation of European/African perspectives in Part I. An equilibrium is struck when we consider all of the elements of film form that are deployed in the film's opening. First, we hear an unsubtitled female voice sing 'Ebula lobelo', a popular Bubi song (Santaolalla 2005, 256); next we hear the adult Susana's voice – it is in fact casting director Arnau's – retrospectively describe in voiceover her arrival at the island Fernando Poo 'La primera vez que vi llorar a mi madre [...] fue cuando arivamos a aquella isla, perdida en el corazón del África negra' (The first time I saw my mother cry [...] was when we arrived on that island, lost in the heart of Black Africa).[8] (The balance on the soundtrack is upset somewhat by the fact that one language is not subtitled, thus only accessible to Bubi-speakers; with Spanish, of course, accessible to speakers in Spain, the country where *Lejos de África* was released.) There is a similar balance of European and African perspectives on the image track. After a panoramic, aerial tracking shot of the island port Santa Isabel, which corresponds neither to a subjective perspective from the land itself, nor to one from the Spanish ship on which Susana and her family arrive, there follows an intertitle in Spanish 'Colonias españolas...' (Spanish colonies...). Following this, there is, as Ortega notes (2001, 87), a remarkable use of perspective. The audience might well expect a point-of-view shot of the island from Susana's perspective. First, this would be in keeping with the intertitle 'Colonias españolas...' (Spanish colonies...), written in the colonisers' language of Spanish; and second, it would give narrative explanation for why her mother is crying. Instead, we witness the arrival of the Spanish ship from the anonymous perspective of someone inland, on Fernando Poo. Again, then, this achieves a balance of European and African perspectives. Continuing with this equilibrium of perspectives via point of view, Bartolomé then follows the unidentified inland island perspective of the Spanish boat with subjective shots of the streets of Santa Isabel that are easy to identify as those of the somewhat bewildered young Susana.

The first key moment of interracial alliance in the film, found in Part I, maintains the equilibrium of perspectives established in the formal choices for both audio and visual tracks of the opening sequences. Corresponding to a memory captured in a photograph in Bartolomé's own family album (reproduced in Ortega 2001, 86–7), the moment concerns an early visit by Susana's family to the missionaries' settlement in the heart of the jungle. While Susana's parents are persuaded by the bickering women of their fellow colonial families to take a siesta after lunch, Father López takes the children, including Susana, her brothers and Rita, to explore the nearby waterfalls. Hinting at the racial fracture that is ahead, when the group reaches a viewing point, it is only little Rita who can see her grandfather's Bubi village in the distance: much as her white companions, including sympathetic Susana and the missionary priest, might look, they are incapable of seeing it. 'Es que no sabéis mirar' (It's that you don't know how to look) is Rita's dismissal of their efforts, by which scriptwriters Cecilia and brother José Juan convey, first, the future break-down of Bubi-Spanish colonial co-existence, and transmit, second, a call to the viewer to engage and look. With release planned only in Spain, this call must have been aimed at the Spanish, and thus possibly Eurocentric, viewer.

Indeed, in the very next sequence, that call to question Eurocentrism and engage with Africa is strongly made. The priest and the group of children take refuge in a cave during a storm shower, to discover there the site for Bubi rituals – or 'cosas del Diablo' (Devil's things), as one of the Spanish boys of the group puts it, matching the racism we hear throughout the film from the lips of their colonist parents. Father López respectively, if Eurocentrically, renames the site with the Christian term 'capilla' (chapel). However, all the boys in the group react to the discovery of animal skulls and bowls of fruit by violently smashing them up. While the Spanish priest is sympathetic to indigenous beliefs, even if he can only interpret them in a Catholic framework, he looks on at the vandalism absent-mindedly, and fails to stop it. Poignantly, it is Rita who defends the site, and pieces back together the smashed-up shards of the bowl she recovers. As she does so, Susana looks on intently, learning, I suggest, to 'mirar' in the way her compatriots fail to. The sequence shares some characteristics with a similar trip to a missionary settlement by 'France', her mother and Proto in Denis's *Chocolat*. The French precedent ends with a significant moment of physical touch between 'France' and Proto, who smears her small hand with the blood from an animal sacrifice: this is an excellent example of the saturation of such moments of physical intimacy with interracial meaning that Laura Marks identified in her 2000 *The Skin of Film: Intercultural Cinema, Embodiment and the Senses* (though *Chocolat* is not one of the films Marks analyses). However, at this point in the Spanish film, Bartolomé chooses to focus on sight, 'mirar', rather than touch as the key means to interracial communication.

As well as this appeal to vision, Bartolomé chooses extra-diegetic music and sound to portray the destruction/reconstruction of the site, but here the choices have very uneven results. Extra-diegetic music acts as a commentary on the sequence. Both drums and string instruments, rather one-dimensionally coded as 'African' or 'European' throughout the film, can be heard during Father López's explanation of the site to the children – he relates the Bubi belief in the figure 'morimo' to the Spanish-Catholic fear of the devil. When the Spanish boys destroy the site, only European string music can be heard. And when Rita reconstructs it, the African drums return. Thus far, then, the equilibrium that Bartolomé seeks is in evidence. However, the scene ends in such a way that a Eurocentric perspective dominates with a particularly odd choice on the extra-diegetic soundtrack that literally silences Rita's voice. As the young girl explains Bubi beliefs to Susana, her voice is drowned out by the addition of the adult voice of Susana in voiceover. The adult voice may be articulating post-colonial guilt about 'la sensación de que aquella tierra no era nuestra' (the feeling that that land was not ours), but its presence in the film, silencing the voice of Rita, the voice of that 'tierra', in fact acoustically enacts a colonial barbarism that is not unlike the boys' visually violent destruction, even as it regrets it.

This attempt to convey an interracial equilibrium, which is undermined by Eurocentric choices in film form, continues throughout *Lejos de Africa*. Part II ends with a moment of touch that Marks, as we have seen, finds so significant in films that explore race. The scene begins with the primary school performance of the Nativity and, in particular, the moment that Jesus, who has no terrestrial biological father, is born. The Spanish-coded biblical story is then linked to an individual African story, as Rita's maternal grandfather interrupts the performance to take his granddaughter away, arguing, in Spanish, that she has 'padre ninguno' (no father) – like the infant Christ. The character Dr Oyono (Alden Knight), who has been previously introduced as Rita's father, then argues with her grandfather over custody of the child. String instruments and a Bubi singing voice clash on the extra-diegetic soundtrack, here, as in the cave scene, acoustically to convey the confrontation. A moment of equilibrium is achieved, however, between the young girls Susana and Rita as they touch by holding hands, while the adult male relatives and officials argue about Spanish and Fernando Poo custody laws. However, choices in both extra-diegetic soundtrack and cinematography mean the scene ends with a strikingly Eurocentric perspective. While reviewers and critics insist that Bartolomé avoids exoticising camera shots that adopt a Eurocentric perspective throughout (Ortega, for example, admires its refusal of a 'mirada exótica' (exotic gaze) (2001, 82)); Cerdán and Díaz, meanwhile, salute its avoidance of 'el virtuosismo del cine de pasajes que busca acomodos y contrastes tropicalizantes' (a virtuoso landscape cinema that seeks tropicalising matches and contrasts) (2001, 19)), and I have also argued that this is the case in the opening scene, there are exceptions, and one occurs here. Having temporarily won custody of the child, the grandfather leaves the colonial island capital with his granddaughter for the Bubi village by boat. To begin, the perspective adopted to portray the departure is Eurocentric, if not exoticising. We share Susana's perspective from the island as she watches the boat leave (though this makes narrative sense, it is unlike the more interesting choices we have seen concerning the arrival of the Spanish ship at the start). Then, as in the cave scene, Bartolomé allows music editor José Antonio Quintano to shift from the combination of the African singing voice and the European strings that accompany the argument, to the drowning out of the voice by the strings. Adult Susana's voiceover is then introduced to explain the scene of her friend's departure. Even more remarkably, Bartolomé even allows the director of photography, her son Pancho Alcaine, to finish the scene with a long take of a picturesque sunset, into which the African characters sail. Lasting a full six seconds, this conclusion to Part I tips from problematically Eurocentric to questionably exoticising.

Part II, which corresponds to 1956, when the girls are fifteen, returns to the tricky terrain of Bubi beliefs through Susana and Rita's developing friendship, which is now also overlain with their curiosity about sexuality. Rita has returned to the Santa Isabel capital city from her grandfather's village, but is determined to maintain her Bubi roots by enacting what she calls its 'magic' herself. Susana resists the active and passive acts of racism in the adults who surround her, and remains a key bridge between races in the film. In some scenes, this is successful, especially when Bartolomé is on her trademark terrain of comedy. We witness in Part II, for example, one of a number of arguments between Susana's Spanish mother Marina and her Nigerian cook Silvanus. When Marina asks one of the Bubi house servants to enter the kitchen, Silvanus amusingly defends his domain in his Spanglish: 'Cocina is mine! ¡Cocina mía!'. It would be too simplistic to read this as an African defence of their territory from colonisers. More interestingly, Bartolomé explores instead power dynamics between empires: Silvanus is proud of his membership, as a Nigerian, of the British empire, 'Yo English', he pronounces, extravagantly holding a finger aloft, 'de ¡gran imperio!' It is for Susana to step in and bridge both races, and different colonial communities, speaking both Spanish and English, and winning Silvanus's friendship.

She is also willing, if not always keen, to participate in her friend Rita's magic, and thus Susana forms another bridge between cultures in these scenes. However, the one in which the two girls sacrifice a chicken (borrowed, already dispatched and plucked, from Silvanus's kitchen) is a particularly tricky one to handle and Bartolomé achieves only mixed results. No comedy here: the tone is, rather, earnest. When Susana finds her friend, Rita is already stripped to the waist, and she requests that Susana also strip. The two teenage girls, naked from the waist up, then engage in mutual anointing as part of the Bubi magic. It is problematic to watch, as the viewer is not sure where exactly he or she is situated in relation to the scene. Earlier, the film encourages us to adopt a female perspective, yet seems to suggest, here, that we adopt the heterosexual male gaze of classic Hollywood cinema (Mulvey 1975). The unsubtitled African singing voice 'Ebular lobelo' returns to the soundtrack, coupled with adult Susana's voiceover, which does, here, act as a bridge by explaining in Spanish the Bubi practice we see. The Europe-coded strings then return, expressing Susana's discomfort as she strips, and the girls begin anointing each other as part of the ritual. Interracial bridging may be pinpointed in the interesting overlap the girls themselves identify between the Bubi 'morimo' that protects and watches over Rita, and the Spanish-Catholic 'ángel de la guardia' (guardian angel) that cares for Susana. However, the medium shot long take of two semi-naked teenage girls smearing each other with a semen-like ointment, as the European-coded string music soars, is uncomfortable to watch, including as it does two lengthy close-ups of their matching breasts. There is also a hint at Rita's lesbianism as a further close-up captures the image of her hand as she lowers it down Susana's abdomen, before her friend pushes her away. If the departing boat scene of Part I engaged, consciously or not, in a Eurocentric exoticisation of the African landscape, this naked Bubi ritual scene engages here in a masculinist eroticisation of women's bodies, of all skin colours.

Part III, which corresponds to 1961 and focusses on the girls at twenty, is more successful at avoiding such awkward moments of cinematography, though odd choices in the music score maintain an undermining Eurocentric tone. Nonetheless, Part III contains the most successful scene, in my view, of interracial integration, followed by a somewhat uneven conclusion. Twenty-year-old Susana is still played by Bogo, and the character now has a boyfriend in Diego, played by Wood, and described by Ortega as a rare and fascinating portrait of a Spanish 'colono' (colonist): of Spanish heritage, yet entirely rooted in Africa (2001, 91 n.11). Santaolalla applauds Bartolomé's choice to replace Bonifacio with Hernández to play the twenty-year-old Rita and, indeed, the Cuban actor brings a power and poise to her performance that convey well Rita's transformation, following her studies on the Peninsula, into a confident young woman. Here *Lejos de África* echoes the approach of *Indochine* in exploring interracial relations through a love affair between members of two races, and, like Clair, Bartolomé also frames this as a more interesting love triangle. In fact, both draw on Jean Renoir's *The River* (1951), frequently named by Bartolomé (and indeed her contemporary Josefina Molina) as her favourite film (e.g. Iglesias 2020). In *Lejos de África*, the focus is not on Diego himself, but rather on how his presence disrupts and perhaps destroys, the girls' friendship, just as Jean-Baptiste comes between mother Éliane and daughter Camille in the French film. However, before Diego and Rita's act of betrayal towards Susana in failing to see off her boat as she leaves Africa forever, there is an interesting scene of reconciliation between the three.

The scene occurs at the governor's ball, whose significance is underlined by Marie-France Pisier's choice of that phrase for her 1990 film. Just seven years before independence in 1968, the viewer witnesses the beginning of the dismantling of colonial power in the election of a Black mayor (Dr Oyono). I am interested in the way Bartolomé chooses to yoke this announcement to the declaration of Diego and Rita's interracial engagement: as the governor says, they are 'dos acontecimientos muy importantes' (two important events). Susana has previously learned of Rita's betrayal in stealing Diego when she catches the two canoodling on his boat; we note that the film presents the friendship between the girls as the primary relationship, thus this moment is not presented as Diego's betrayal of Susana in abandoning her for Rita, but Rita's betrayal of Susana. At the announcement at the ball, Susana is to learn of the couple's engagement. Bartolomé begins the scene of reconciliation between the friends with the local Fernando Poo band playing Mexican composer María Grever's 1930s bolero 'Lamento gitano' (Gypsy Lament). Attuned as we are at this point of the film to appreciating the racial significance of musical choices, the audience might note the fusion between the Black African female vocalist (we have heard a female voice sing 'Ebular lobelo' throughout the film) and Black musicians playing Europe-coded string instruments here. However, the choice of a Mexican bolero, especially one that is about Spain's primary mixed-race Roma community, is a successful choice in a film that is generally far too maniquean in the racial connotations of its musical score.

As the lyrics of the bolero concerning lament ring out, Susana approaches the newly engaged couple. Subjective cinematography is deployed with interesting ambiguous effect here, for while we see Susana stare intently at the couple, and we see both Rita and Diego stare intently back, it is only with the final cross-cut that we learn that the shared gaze is one between Susana and Rita, ignoring Diego; likewise, the embrace between the three (Figure 6.2) begins as one between the two women only. Diego then enfolds both women into his arms, but this does not undermine the primacy

'Es que no sabéis mirar' 167

Figure 6.2 Diego (Patricio Wood) (left), Susana (Alicia Bogo) (centre) and Rita (Ademilis Hernández) (right)'s reconciliation in *Lejos de África* (2006)

of their female friendship: given that we now know that the intense gaze was one shared between them, it suggests, rather, that friendship between women may withstand romantic disruption, it is the two women that 'saben mirar' (know how to look).

The contradictions of Bartolomé's 'corte clásico' (classic approach)

As noted in the previous section, it is frequently the case that odd choices in film form lead to an overall unevenness in the film. At times there is a successful fusion between the interracial equilibrium that the script explores, and the formal devices deployed, as in the three-way embrace of the Governer's ball, but too often formal choices undermine this overall intent. Returning to an auteurist approach we may pinpoint these areas. Indeed, Bartolomé does this herself, and perhaps despite herself, with her comment in interview on the film's release. It is a film she describes as 'de corte clásico' (adopting classic approach) – not a genre or tone the director has ever employed before – because, she explains, 'ya he hecho muchas cosas de rompepelotas' (I've already done lots of ball-breaking things). However, it was precisely in the areas of 'rompepelotas' – both *esperpento* comic genre and irreverent tone – where she had had such success before.

Beginning with genre, the glimpses of Bartolomé's wicked humour enhance the film, but are too infrequent. This Chapter has previously examined individual instances that surround the character Silvanus, but even more successful is Bartolomé's ability to draw on the crowd. In frequent interviews, Bartolomé generously attributes this use of the chorus to the inspiration of her 'maestro' Berlanga; I would argue that she fashions the chorus into something new. Few directors portray a group of gossiping women as effectively as Bartolomé – perhaps only the early Almodóvar does, on the street corners, or in the knitting classes and dress-making scenes of films like *Pepi, Luci, Bom y otras chicas del montón / Pepi, Luci, Bom and Other Girls on the Heap* (1980) or *¡¿Qué he hecho yo para merecer esto!? / What Have I Done to Deserve This!?* (1984), scenes which perhaps, in fact, betray the influence of the older director. In Bartolomé's work, she uses scenes of such groups to skewer the excesses of the machismo and racism that surround them. Ana's childhood friends on the Tarragona beach, or the older women on the bus in *¡Vámonos, Bárbara!*, lampoon a patriarchy in which contraception and divorce are not available to women (Chapter 4). In *Lejos de África*, however, the perspective shifts, for we do not sympathise with the colonial housewives of Santa Isabel. The film may begin in melodramatic mode with Susana's mother's tears, but its representation of women's domestic lives then proceeds in a sardonic, comic vein. The bored, bourgeois colonial housewives are the mouthpieces of the racism that was about to self-destruct as the colonies achieved independence.

However, in other areas of film form, as we have seen, odd choices mean that the film falls into a Eurocentrism it seems to set out to query. First, as noted, in cinematography, the results are mixed. There are interesting choices – for example the opening shot of the Spanish ship from the perspective of the island, or the medium shots that convey Susana and Rita's bewildered entrapment in the jungle when they get lost looking for the grandfather's village. However, an exoticising, even eroticising, approach, presumably sanctioned by the director, conflicts with her overall subject matter. Perhaps Bartolomé allowed these in the spirit of making a film 'de corte clásico'. Again, this tone seems to explain why, at two hours, the film is over-long (as Augusto Torres points out (1997)). Perhaps seeking this 'classic' broad sweep is why Bartolomé allowed lengthy exposition, which she would surely have cut down in her earlier films (¡*Vámonos, Bárbara!* is only ninety-four minutes long). It is difficult not to conjecture too that appointing her own son as director of photography had mixed results. There may have been a close working relationship between the two on the shoot, but it is difficult not to wonder if Bartolomé felt less able to cut footage shot by her own son at the editing stage (though she could when that footage was shot by her then husband José Luis Alcaine in her earlier work).

Most surprisingly, and disappointingly, come the choices in sound and music. *Margarita y el lobo*, as we have seen (Chapter 2), is a tour de force in its deployment of a knowing and ironic soundtrack. Yet in *Lejos de África*, Bartolomé, working with music editor Quintano, allows the development of a rather manichean Eurocentrism. Drumbeats and an unsubtitled female singing voice connote colonised Africa; classical string instruments, the colonial power, Europe. As we have seen, the second, European music, frequently drowns out the African music, enacting a kind of auditory colonisation. If there are important exceptions, like the previously discussed 'Lamento gitano' bolero, it has to be noted that the film ends with precisely such a moment of Europe-coded strings silencing African-coded song. As Santaolalla writes, this moment of shift from the African song to the European string score summarises both the problem with, and the future fate of, the film: 'Aquel intento educativo de borrar las diferencias entre las niñas fracasó y cayó en el olvido, igual que la música de África es, finalmente, acallada por las cadencias europeas' (That educational attempt to erase the differences between the girls failed, and fell into obsolescence, just as, ultimately, the African music is silenced by the European cadences) (2005, 256).

Finally, Bartolomé's previous ability to draw out her desired performances from actors seems underpowered here. It is telling that the most successful performances are those of the secondary characters, well-known to Spanish audiences as television stars from familiar programmes, like Mestres and Elorriaga: Susana's mother Marina and father Gonzalo. The praise heaped by the press on Bogo, who plays Susana in Parts II and III, may have been exaggerated. Her performance is good enough, but *Lejos de África* would be her only work in film. Like Mestres and Elorriaga who play her parents, she seems more comfortable on the small screen. Herein, perhaps, lies a contradiction that Bartolomé fails to resolve. Given that the history of Spain's presence in Equatorial Guinea is so little known, it is wise that she allowed casting director Arnau to choose familiar television stars to engage audiences. However, the goal to forego the wider history (Historia) of empire to explore the particular, private story (historia) of the interracial friendship of two girls, was so novel that it needed stronger performances by the female leads. Had they only been the right age, we might imagine a very different film if Arnau had been able to cast a fifteen- or twenty-year-old Julia Peña, Amparo Soler Leal or Cristina Álvarez.

Overall, I suggest that *Lejos de África* is admirable, but flawed. Bartolomé grapples with an extremely tricky subject. In the wider geo-political context of my time of writing, 2023, in which former colonial powers debate reparations for slavery and exploitation, Bartolomé anticipates this move by stressing, nearly thirty years ago, that it is vital for Spain to address its colonial legacy. Her middlebrow approach to this subject matter was not necessarily an erroneous choice.

The flaws of *Lejos de África* spring from some odd choices in film form. Under the cover of reporting what 'malas lenguas' (nasty gossips) say, Carlos Alonso somewhat spitefully accuses the film of being a 'película familiar' (film that keeps things in the family) (1997), with her brother as co-scriptwriter, and a son as director of photography – he fails to spot that a second son seems to be present too in an administrative role. However, many of these odd choices relate to music, soundtrack and casting, where Bartolomé's family members were not present. Instead, I attribute the film's flaws to the wrongly placed attempt at a 'classic approach'. In pursuit of this, Bartolomé seems to have allowed flawed contributions by members of her production team to pass. Unfortunately, in places, some crude choices, especially in the extra-diegetic music, convey a Eurocentrism that undermines the film's overall aim, to explore Spain's scarcely known colonial history in Africa through a sensitive portrait of interracial relationships from the original perspectives of girls and young women.

Notes

1. It was followed by *Palmiras en la nieve / Palm Trees in the Snow* (González Molina 2015). María Miró's *Los baúles del retorno / Luggage for Return* (1995) and the short film *Lalia* (Munt 1999) concern the disputed territory of the Sahrawi Arab Democratic Republic. For films made in Equatorial Guinea see the Asociación Cinematográfica de Guinea Ecuatorial https://acige.wordpress.com/¿que-es-acige/, accessed 30 November 2022.
2. A marketing campaign that focussed on developing connections with films like *Out of Africa* that Spanish audiences did know, rather than one lamenting the amnesia of those audiences concerning Spain's colonial history in Africa, may have been more successful. Such was exactly the strategy of marketing-savvy Portuguese director Miguel Gomes, who, in 2012, released *Tabu*, a film about Portuguese colonialism made legible to transnational audiences through references to specific, widely known, films, like F. W. Murau's *Tabu: A Story of the South Seas* (1931), which it evokes through its title; *Out of Africa*, which it evokes through female characterisation and voiceover; and to general aesthetic moments in film history, like silent film (see Faulkner 2015).
3. See, for example, Faulkner (2016).
4. I am grateful to Will Higbee for his discussion of this aspect of the film with me, in the light of Shohat and Stam (1994).
5. At the Filmoteca Española archive, Madrid.
6. https://sede.mcu.gob.es/CatalogoICAA, accessed 6 December 2022.
7. I am grateful to Will Higbee for pointing out the significance of this film to me.
8. Note that the 'blackness' of the original title of the film, *Black Island*, refers to the colour of the sand and soil of the volcanic island of former Fernando Poo (Asensio 2022; Appendix Interview). It may also refer to skin colour in this line of the film voiceover.

7

The Admiral and the Alcántaras: political biopic meets popular soap in 'Especial Carrero Blanco: El comienzo del fin', *Cuéntame cómo pasó*

After a filmmaking career strewn with obstacles, authoring a key episode of Radio Televisión Española (RTVE, Spanish State Television)'s multi-award-winning *Cuéntame cómo pasó / Tell Me How It Happened* (various authors 2001–) in 2005 at last brought Cecilia Bartolomé the opportunity to reach the mass audience that her accessible filmmaking had always sought. The invitation to make Special Episode 113 of Season 7, which was the series' milestone moment of 'El comienzo del fin' (The Beginning of the End) of Francoism, feels like some sort of retribution. It came a year after the first public screening of *Margarita y el lobo / Margarita and the Wolf* at the San Sebastián festival of 2004, when, as we have seen (see Chapter 2), her treatment under dictatorship began to be more widely known through interview (Yoldi 2004), and when the *Cuéntame* commissioners perhaps also noticed her talent (Asensio 2022). An audience of over four million tuned in to 'El comienzo del fin' (a 25 per cent audience share) at the series' 10 p.m. broadcasting slot on 8 December 2005,[1] multiplying many times over the contemporary audiences Bartolomé managed to reach in the fraught circumstances of each of her preceding films' screenings.

This chapter continues its advised auteurist approach, applying it here to television. This Film Studies methodology is justifiable, first, as the episode is a 'Special', with a veteran filmmaker as both co-scriptwriter and director,[2] and is thus clearly a standout event.[3] In any case, it seems perverse to distinguish between media when Bartolomé's own career criss-crossed between them. Just as she considers her early years in theatre as fruitful for subsequent film work (see Appendix Interview), the experiences she gained during the many years she made a living from television advertising (see, again,

Appendix Interview) likewise enriched her film work. And it is not the case that fruitful creative enrichment must necessarily go in this direction. In Bartolomé's work there is no hierarchy between the two. Indeed, at the start of her career, as we have seen, she engages creatively with television as early as the *Bugs Bunny* sequences in *La noche del Dr Valdés / Doctor Valdés's Night* (1964) (Chapter 1). In an interview on the release of *¡Vámonos, Bárbara! / Bárbara, Let's Go!* the following decade she is asked by Juan Hernández Les and Miguel Gato whether she agrees whether television is jeopardising film as a 'fenómeno mágico, que consiste en que un espectador, al apagarse las luces, se aisla de todo y de todos establieciendo una comunicación íntima y profunda con la pantalla' (magic phenomenon, whereby a spectator, when the lights go down, transcends his or her surroundings and enters into an intimate, deep communication with the screen)? She makes short work of dismissing such misty-eyed cinephilia. 'Creo que no. Ese fenómeno lo perdemos porque no sabemos ver TV' (I don't think so. We lose this phenomenon because we don't know how to watch TV' (Hernández Les and Gato 1978, 40).[4] Showing such early understanding of the medium, it is no wonder that nearly thirty years later she would work within it to such brilliant effect in 'El comienzo del fin', revealing that she knows *how* to watch television, and trusting her audiences do too. Finally, forty or so years on, she reveals that, of all of her projects, this television episode is the piece of work of which she is most proud (Bermejo 2017, 11).

Thus in 'El comienzo del fin', Bartolomé's auteurist 'signature', perfectly legible across film and television media, may clearly be read. Indeed I would argue that its aesthetic attention to documentary, humour and music make it more typical of the director's work than the deeply personal, even autobiographical, film made with her own production company, *Lejos de África / Far from Africa* (Chapter 6). Whether the episode is successful because of, or despite this, is open to debate. It may be the case that Bartolomé in fact smuggled her auteurist film vision into an exceptionally popular television series and thereby pulled off a career high: exploring her creative vision before a mass audience. 'El comienzo del fin' thus denounces Francoism and claims feminism, the twin creative commitments of Bartolomé's career, while adopting a relatively accessible format, deploying documentary techniques and employing humour, the three formal traits of her signature. Accessibility for audiences is ensured partly by interweaving historical events with a selection of seventeen previously broadcast events in the lives of the Alcántara family, just as ¡*Vámonos, Bárbara!* had explored the to-and-fro between the fictional family and the political Transition (see Chapter 4). Second, Bartolomé's belief in documentary, to which she brings her own feminist 'street' aesthetic of combining interviews with well-known interlocutors and interviews with anonymous members of the public on the street, is fundamental to 'El comienzo del fin', and clearly recalls the oral history approach of the *Después de*.... diptych (see Chapter 5). Third, Bartolomé's trademark humour, which we have seen throughout this book, is also evident in her ability to select archive footage and pinpoint the amusing phrase or sequence in longer recordings, and in her ability to make mischievous meaning from choices in *mise en scène*, camera work, editing and extra-diegetic music. This chapter will introduce the television series as a whole before exploring in detail these traits.

Cuéntame cómo pasó and the might of the middlebrow

For the first time in her career, rather than fight for an audience – against sexist Film School teachers, against a Francoist Film School Director, against dictatorship censorship, against obstructive producers, against the neo-censorship of early democracy or against the tide of contemporary Spanish film trends – Bartolomé was here gifted it ready-made. The extraordinarily successful series *Cuéntame cómo pasó*, which, at the time of writing, screens weekly on the Televisión Española first channel's (TVE1) primetime Thursday evening slot, is currently in an unprecedented twenty-second season, making it the longest-running series in Spanish television history; its twenty-third has recently been announced to be its last (Llanos Martínez 2023).[5] Based on an original idea by Miguel Ángel Bernardeau, which is inspired by the US series *The Wonder Years* (Black and Marlens 1988–83), the series portrays late Francoism with a thirty-two-year time delay. It follows the lives of the fictional Alcántara family, whose principal figures, in 2005, were: father, Antonio (played by Imanol Arias); mother, Mercedes/Merche Fernández (Ana Duato); grandmother, Herminia

(Mariana Galiana); and children: Carlos, the on-screen child of the fictional present played by Ricardo Gómez; the future off-screen adult who is the series' narrator in voiceover, by Carlos Hipólito; Inés (Irene Visedo); and Toni (Pablo Rivero). These different generations enjoy distinct narrative threads that intertwine to attract audiences from different age groups, thereby achieving the sweet spot of family entertainment. This family appeal, which intertwines one generation with the next, is underscored by the time delay chosen. According to recent statistics, the average age to become a mother in Spain is thirty-two.[6] The most common temporal dividing line between generations, for Spanish women who are mothers, at least, is thus, also, thirty-two. Fictional storylines concerning the aspirant middle-class Alcántara family, which has migrated to Madrid in the 1960s in search of a better life, like so many families in Spain's city suburbs, are also intertwined throughout the series with actual historical events. These events are not simply referred to in the narrative. RTVE archive footage of them is threaded through the fictional events through editing. In addition, at key moments, the series fictional characters are themselves also added into archive material, a technique made famous by *Forest Gump* (Zemeckis 1994). This technique allows, for example, family patriarch Antonio to go on a hunting trip with none other than General Franco himself in Season 2, Episode 6.

Accusations of political prejudice were perhaps inevitable for a series that recreates Spain's intense, often violent, years of political change, from 1968 onwards. It may be noted too that *Cuéntame* has also been broadcast in the years of similarly intense, though non-violent, debates about memory, from 2001. The new millennium saw the establishment of the Asociación para la recuperación de la memoria histórica (Association for the Recovery of Historical Memory) in 2000, just months before *Cuéntame* first broadcast; then the passing into legislation of the Ley de Memoria Histórica (Law of Historical Memory) by the Partido Socialista Obrero Español (PSOE; Spanish Socialist Party) in 2007,[7] its repeal by the Partido Popular (PP; Spanish Conservative Party) in 2013, and replacement as the Ley de Memoria Democrática (Law of Democratic Memory), again by the PSOE, in 2022. Often accusations of political bias levelled at *Cuéntame* turn around the perceived political role of state television. Manuel Palacio's broad-brush summary of the situation is that, when the PP is in power, as when the series was launched, the Left-wing press accuses the show of conservatism, and vice versa when the PSOE are in power (2012, 356–7). If we examine these accusations in more detail, a more troubling picture emerges. With no named historical advisor (Palacio 2012, 363), and no open archive of RTVE material available to the public,[8] the series' creators are reliant on what anonymous RTVE archivists select for them (Sevillano Canicio 2010, 350).[9] In addition, much of this archive is made up of the Noticiarios y Documentales (NO-DO) newsreels, which were themselves dictatorship propaganda (they were screened, as previously noted, in cinemas before feature films from 1943 to 1981, obligatorily so to 1975). *Cuéntame*'s creators thereby choose from archive material that has in some cases already been doubly filtered: in the case of the NO-DO, by the regime's propaganda; then the selection made by the RTVE archivists. In such a context, Bartolomé's ability to draw new meaning from possibly compromised archive footage through techniques of selection, editing and the addition of extra-diegetic music, is key.

Critics, both television scholars and historians, furthermore, note a particular reluctance to represent Francoist repression in the series, though this reluctance must in part be explained by the show's pitch as primetime family entertainment. The reluctance is pinpointed by Smith, for example, in the sequence where Antonio is present as the Francoist police violently repress student protests (Season 1, Episode 8). He shuts his eyes to 'the horrible spectacle just out of shot', meaning neither he nor we see it (2006, 22). Víctor Sevillano Canicio observes a similar reluctance in Season 7, Episode 7, when Antonio's eyes are again shut tight: this time he is sleeping and has a nightmare about faceless members of the Francoist police beating him up: 'las fantasías de miedo deben ser suficientes para describir el sistema represivo' (fantasies of fear have to be enough to describe the repressive system) (2010, 352). As we will see, Episode 113 may offer a corrective. Bartolomé does not shut her, or her audience's, eyes. While she does not fictionally recreate this repression, remarkably, in this 'Special' of a popular family soap screening at primetime, she does incorporate interviews with former victims of it, including former ETA terrorists who were in prison at the time of the Carrero attack (Teo Uriarte and Javier Elorrieta). If the imprisonment of terrorists is hardly a clear-cut example of state repression, like the police beating up demonstrating students is, Bartolomé also pays attention to the imprisonment of Marcelino Camacho through interviews with his wife Josefina Samper and sister Vicenta Camacho. Camacho was one of the Comisiones Obreras trade unionists of the 1972 '1001 Trial'; the group was imprisoned by the regime simply for meeting together.

Where some creative projects fail owing to bad timing, I suggest that at least one of the reasons why the *Cuéntame* series as a whole prospered was good timing. Its middlebrow approach, which seamlessly fuses didactic content with high quality, accessible form, was not new in Spanish audiovisual history.[10] In particular, a middlebrow approach to screening Spain's fraught twentieth-century history through historical recreation and costume drama was not new. It was tried in the 1980s in the films subsidised by the cultural policies of both the Unión de Centro Democrático (UCD; Union of the Democratic Centre Party) ('el concurso de los 1.300 milliones' (the 1,300 million competition)) and the PSOE (the ley Miró (Miró Law)) governments. For example, Mario Camus's UCD-funded *La colmena / The Beehive* (1982) anticipates *Cuéntame*'s aesthetic approach by combining images from the NO-DO archive with fictional recreations of the period to bring a sense of historical 'authenticity' to the fictional tale of Cela's original polyphonic novel (Faulkner 2004, 24–33), though the novel's portrait of despairing anomy is somewhat undercut by the casting of a host of Spain's star actors of the time (Faulkner 2013, 177). Despite the bid for authenticity and the presence of familiar stars, 1982 Spanish film audiences, in a post-censorship, post-protectionist era of attractive, skilfully dubbed, international fare, were lukewarm. In the 1990s, Bartolomé's own attempt to recreate the dictatorship era in film, *Lejos de África*, also failed to appeal, despite its original and urgent aim to portray Francoism not as it was lived on the peninsular, but in the colonies. Its attractive interweaving of family life with historical events, and shrewd casting of television actors that were familiar to audiences, did not connect with 1996 audiences either (Chapter 6). The reason for both these big screen failures must be that the material found a better home on the small screen, which reached audiences.

RTVE's comparatively flawed *Los años vividos* (1992), for example, achieved an audience of some two and a half million (Sevillano Canicio 2010, 347). A clear precedent for *Cuéntame*, each of its ten episodes moves through time from the 1920s to the present and draws on the RTVE archive. However, its rather flat, talking-head-style interviews with journalists, politicians and artists who recall the period, have none of the emotional pull of the Alcántara family. *Cuéntame*, whose producer Grupo Ganga had tried to secure backing throughout the 1990s, was finally supported by RTVE in 2001. Its winning formula fused the partial successes of earlier attempts: star film actors, familiar television actors, interweaving family and historical lives, and adding in archive materials, now with the addition of special effects that allowed the insertion of fictional characters into archive footage. Particularly important were its high production values. The show lovingly recreates period detail in *mise en scène*, and uses catchy theme music that links one episode to the next. All this prompted a nostalgic response as never seen before on large or small screen. Laura García Pousa, series scriptwriter from 2004 to 2010, and in fact Bartolomé's co-scriptwriter on 'El comienzo del fin', also identifies self-reflexivity as part of the success. Besides faithfully recreating historical settings and props, as, for example, Camus had done in *La colmena*, *Cuéntame* also evoked audiovisual memories of the period in a process she names 'una proyección *vintage* de la memoria del espectador' (a 'vintage' projection of the spectator's memory) (García Pousa 2011, 57). Thus the series evokes Spanish costumbrista films of the 1950s and 1960s (whose familiar stars, like Fernando Fernán Gómez and Tony Leblanc, it also casts), as well as television footage of famous figures of the same period, when broadcasting in Spain began and the Alcántaras themselves bought their first television set. Thus mother Merche's hairstyle imitates then Princess Sofía's blonde wavy look; or father Antonio's hairstyle and suits recall those of UCD President Adolfo Suárez, transforming them, in Laura García Pousa's words, into 'character-objects', who co-exist in the fiction with historical personages and thus gain a 'nuevo estatus ontológico' (new ontological status) (García Pousa 2011, 57).[11] The public service mission to inform audiences about difficult and potentially still divisive political change was being fulfilled too, but the point is that the multiple elements of nostalgic enjoyment engaged audiences. Writing of Eduardo Ladrón de Guevera's efforts to weave his own anti-Franco militancy into the programme, Paul Julian Smith summarises that 'the bitter pill [...] of disenchanted didacticism is sugared by the nostalgic reaction of older viewers' and thus 'intellectual understanding is replaced by emotional empathy' (2006, 17; 20–1). It has been pointed out too that this 'sugared', 'emotional' appeal to look back was particularly welcome at the precise moment *Cuéntame* first screened. On 13 September 2001 audiences were keen fictionally to retreat from the terrifying present that followed the 11 September Al Quaeda terrorist attacks on the New York World Trade Center (Palacio 2012, 335).

Episode 113: 'El comienzo del fin'

However, by the time Bartolomé directed the 113th Special Episode, four years on, far from soothing audiences in the context of the rupture of world order in the present, she in fact took them back to a rupture in national order that was both past and present. Basque terrorist group ETA assassinated Franco's government President, Admiral Luis Carrero Blanco, on 20 December 1973; but, in 2005, its campaign of violence remained active. I suggest that the timing was just right for this challenging portrait of rupture. Over four years, the series had already built up a loyal audience that could be relied on to tune in on a Thursday in their millions. Any risk associated with disturbing the fictional flow with a 'Special' episode was also mitigated by the fact that this had already occurred with 'Háblame de ti' (Tell Me About Yourself) (Series 1, Episode 33, 2002, led by journalist Victoria Prego; see Pousa 2017). In addition, 'El comienzo del fin' was located between two episodes that were also focussed on the attack, Episode 112, 'Dos días de diciembre' (Two Days in December), directed by Agustín Crespi and scripted by Ladrón de Guevara; and 114, 'El día de la bomba, el día después' (The Day of the Bomb, the Day Afterwards), directed by Sergio Cabrera and scripted by Ladrón de Guevara; 112, 113 and 114 together therefore making up a Carrero trilogy.

The timing was right for Bartolomé as director, too, for at this point in her career she was able to deploy her considerable experience to innovate, in both the *Cuéntame* series in particular and Spanish television as a whole. While the combination of archive footage and interviews concerning the Carrero assassination of *Los años vividos*, Episode 7 (broadcast 1 March 1992), may have been an influence, Bartolomé's combination, alongside events in the Alcantarás' lives, is far more original. Located in carefully chosen settings, and captured at various camera distances, 'El comienzo del fin' includes twenty interviews with named interlocutors who had lived through the event. These range from the highly personal, like the Admiral's own son, also called Admiral Luis Carrero Blanco Pichot (his mother's surname Pichot added to his father's name), to the highly political, like contemporary Francoist minister Manuel Fraga (then Spanish Ambassador to the UK, but in the Madrid embassy, according to the interview, at the time of the magnicide), or former ETA terrorist Teo Uriarte (in jail in Burgos at the time, having been arrested in the 1970 trial). On the other hand, and in keeping with her feminist commitment to the everyday that she refined twenty-six years earlier in *Después de…*, Bartolomé includes some twenty-seven interviews with anonymous interviewees in the street: young, middle-aged and older adults, both men and women, some of whom lived through the events, some too young to have done so.

What audiences would have found when they tuned in on that 8 December evening, then, would have differed considerably from earlier episodes (the previous 'Special' had innovated with the introduction of the journalist Prego, but kept the focus on the Alcántaras). Here, instead of archive material illustrating the Alcántaras' lives, this is reversed: events from the fictional family's lives illustrate those described by interviewees (Pousa 2017, 10). 'El comienzo del fin' may begin, and effectively so, with footage repeated from the end of Episode 112 when the fictional family witness the explosion, but what follows is far more political biopic of the Admiral than popular soap about the Alcántaras. With unprecedented access to intimate items like the Carrero family photograph album, which replaces the Alcántara album in the opening credits, the episode surveys the naval officer, then Admiral, then politician, then President's life (1904–73). The sensitive interview with his son yields telling personal details. These are then folded into the archive footage of public events, which, for obvious reasons of Civil War and Transition, focus in particular on the 1930s and the 1960s to the 1970s. If the footage we see of the two sides in the war (1936–39), or the footage we see of the announcement of the restoration of the monarchy (1969), are familiar, the information about the role Carrero played in each is not. Though there are conflicting accounts, from both sides, of Franco's infamous meeting with Hitler at Hendaye, both Carlos's voiceover and historian Ricardo de la Cierva reveal that the report Carrero wrote for the Caudillo was critical in ensuring that Spain did not enter World War II, an assertion backed up by Carrero's son's memory of his father writing it. Carrero's advice to Franco was instrumental too in the naming of then Prince Juan Carlos as successor.[12]

The extreme nature of Carrero's death, at such an extreme moment of Spain's history, has overshadowed public knowledge of the rest of his life. It cannot be denied that the magnicide was spectacular: the force of ETA's 'Operación Ogro' (Operation Ogre) bomb on Madrid's Claudio Coello street was such that it caused Carrero's Dodge Dart car to be propelled into the air, sweep up the side of the six-storey Palacio de los Jesuitas building, and land on a ledge on its interior patio, with all three passengers killed (Carrero; police officer Juan Antonio Bueno Fernández; and driver José Luis Pérez Mogena). Bartolomé's intention, then, is to look beyond this dazzling spectacle to rescue the historical personage from the shadows.

'El comienzo del fin' submits both Carrero's death and, importantly, life, to what Bartolomé intends as balanced scrutiny through archive footage and a panoply of interviews. The description of the series that RTVE released in advance, quoted by television journalists in printed schedules for the broadcast date (e.g. Aniorte 2005 in *ABC*), no doubt mindful of accusations of political bias, stressed this balanced approach. It aims to 'ser honesto con él y con la Historia' (be honest with him and with History), which echoes Bartolomé's goal of impartiality in the *Después de...* documentaries, 'y mostrar a las nuevas generaciones una parte importante de nuestro pasado más reciente' (and show younger generations an important part of our most recent past), which also recalls the director's pedagogic ambition to inform younger audiences of Spain's colonial history in *Lejos de África*.

For all this care over balance, though, a contemporary press clipping and online blog give an indication that audiences may have been somewhat perplexed. *La Vanguardia*'s Salvador Llopart, in a piece titled 'Dictadura en la picota' (Pilloried Dictatorship), and illustrated with a photograph of Franco and

Carrero, does not even mention that number 113 is an episode of *Cuéntame*, describing instead that 'TV1 ofrece… un programa documental' (TV1 offers… a documentary) (2005). Blogger 'El descodificador', whose posts were hosted by *El mundo* at the time of publication, was also confused. Describing the episode as 'extraño' (strange) in which the combination of interviews and Alcántara footage produces an 'ensaladilla' (hotchpotch), he is particularly perturbed by the 'mal gusto' (bad taste) of the music tracks chosen, entitling his review 'El Almirante y la folclórica' (The Admiral and the Folkloric Singer). Picking up the irony of Bartolomé's musical choices seems to have eluded him, even as his blog promises 'los ídolos de la caja tonta pasados por la "turmix" de la ironía' (idols of the telly put through the 'food blender' of irony) (Pérez de Albéniz 2005). Moving from these two particular voices that respond to this individual episode, to general surveys of audience response to the series as a whole, we might conclude that, for 2005 audiences, Episode 113 lay somewhere between the pleasure in nostalgia that surveys about *Cuéntame* revealed in 2008 (Grandío 2008), and the grumbling about an excessive focus on the dictatorship mentioned in those published in 2009 (Corbalán 2009).

Accessible format

Bartolomé does not worry too much about grumbling. At no point in her career has she compromised her commitment to telling her own stories; but this does not preclude her commitment to doing so in a format that is accessible to audiences. Having fought for a mass audience with such difficulty, she was not going to waste it here. Later publications by her co-scriptwriter García Pousa give some insight into how Bartolomé may have struck this balance with 'El comienzo del fin'. On the one hand, García Pousa notes that the '*background*' established by previous episodes allowed creators to be 'más libre – incluso experimental' (more free – even experimental) (García Pousa 2011, 64) in the trilogy of episodes that cover Carrero Blanco's magnicide. On the other hand, in a later work, she cautions against extensive interviews in television, as audiences find them boring (Pousa 2017, 15).

Before examining what García Pousa describes as Bartolomé's 'bet' (García Pouza 2011, 66) on the documentary approach, it is worth stressing that audience interest in the Alcántaras is still respected in 'El comienzo del fin' by intertwining interviews and archive footage with the lives of the fictional family. However, rather than archive footage illustrating the Alcántáras' lives, here the interviews and archive footage take first place, illustrated, secondarily, by fictional family events. Some instances of this are particularly effective. Bartolomé and García Pousa wisely repeat the sequences from the end of Cabrera and Ladrón de Guevara's Episode 112. Our attention is perhaps at best distracted when husband, wife, son and friend Miguel (Juan Echanove) chatter about Antonio's medical appointment in the city centre as the four get in the car on the morning of 20 December 1973, begin their journey, then get stuck in a traffic jam while Carlos complains about being late for school, with authenticity added here by inclusion of contemporary footage of Madrid traffic jams. So dull, in fact, is the domestic detail that our attention might wonder before the jolt of the explosion triggers the propulsion of Carerro's car into the air (the footage of this is in fact taken from the fictional source *Operación Ogro / Operation Ogre* (Pontecorvo 1979), to which we will return) then the ensuing chaos. The fictional family has been jolted out of their mundane morning tasks, we as viewers have been jolted out of our distraction from dull details about domestic duties and a traffic jam, and Spain as a whole is jolted out of the stasis of the continuation of the regime that was supposedly 'atado y bien atado' (all tied down) for the future: this, indeed, is the beginning of the end.

The traffic jam is also a brilliant touch as it introduces the moment when the series changes its temporal pace. Previously its chronology had developed in linear time, in lock-step with the time of broadcast thirty-two years ahead. Harnessing the widely known everyday experience of time slowing down when one is stuck in a traffic jam, at the end of Episode 112, authored by Crespi and Ladrón de Guevara, time likewise stretches and slows down, a process García Pousa compares to Argentine Julio Cortázar's 1966 short story 'La autopista del sur' (The Southern Highway) (García Pousa 2011, 66).

With fictional time opened up in this way, Bartolomé's focus is the interviews, footage, editing and music. There are in fact only fourteen more cuts to the fictional family (as three refer to the traffic jam sequence), and one wonders whether these inserts interested the director less. Wrested from their place within the fictional flow of early episodes, sequences like Antonio's illustration of press censorship at the printing press where he works, or his 'mansplanation' to his wife of the reasons for Franco naming Carrero President, while undressing in the marital bedroom, seem rather heavy-handed in their didacticism. Disappointing too is the inclusion of the climactic sequence where Don Pablo (José Sancho) reveals to Antonio that he killed his father in the Civil War. The intention is to show that the slaughter of war, or, more accurately, the tardy revelation of partial responsibility for slaughter in war, is devastating for actual families. This is hardly surprising information. More effective, I suggest, is Bartolomé's selection of music score to accompany archive images. The lyrics of the anonymous popular copla, 'El barranco del lobo', especially the line 'pobrecitas madres, cuánto llorarán' (the poor little mothers, they will cry so much), not only convey this devastation for families, but also make a point about the repeated futility of armed conflict, given that they refer to an earlier conflict (the 1909 battle of Melilla), but are equally applicable here.

Documentary

If the example of the 'El barranco del lobo' fuses an emotional response (mothers will cry) with an intellectual one (the futility of slaughter in repeated wars), 'El comienzo del fin', as a whole, flips the previous prioritisation of emotion over intellect in the series. This documentary is a 'Special', a one-off: the material is accessible, but Bartolomé's didactic aim to portray a life that has been obliterated from public knowledge owing to the spectacle of a death prioritises the intellectual over the emotional. Mitigated by the fictional focus of Episodes 112 and 114 that precede and succeed it in the trilogy, it seems to be the case that this prioritisation could be sustained for one episode only: Bartolomé was not invited to direct or script any more episodes.

For followers of Bartolomé's career, the interviews of 'El comienzo del fin' recall those of *Después de*.... In both, she mixes named interlocutors, some of whom are located in their offices, and anonymous individuals, all of whom are filmed on the street. The key difference is that while the interviewees of *Después de...* recount social and political change as it occurred, those of 'El comienzo del fin' recall events thirty-two years on. With viewer accessibility in mind, Bartolomé's first interview is with one of her best-known figures. Punningly named, in a translation into English of his first surname, Forges (Antonio Fraguas de Pablo) was cartoonist of *El Diario* in 1973, a role he held at *El País* from 1995 onwards. So well-known are his black-and-white cartoons of a series of amusing, recognisable national types (he explains one depicting the funcionario (Civil Servant) during the episode) that he might be said to have attained the status of national treasure. Thus, after the opening tedium of the 'fictional' traffic jam – in fact, partly presented through 'real' footage of contemporary vehicles – then the jolt of the 'real' bomb – in fact partly presented through the 'fictional recreation' of it in the film *Operación Ogro* – we hear the familiar sound of 'fictional' Carlos's voiceover, advising us that 'hacía un frío que pelaba' (it was absolutely freezing), who here then shifts into a 'real' role of documentary commentator 'esa misma mañana podía decirse que fue el comienzo del fin' (you could say that that very morning was the beginning of the end) (García Pousa 2011, 64). From the chaos surrounding the Alcántaras immediately after the blast, we cut to the intertitle '32 años después' (thirty-two years afterwards), then to the plaque on Claudio Coello street that bears official witness to the event, then to Forges. While the interweaving of fictional and factual may look awkward on the page, it is seamlessly merged on the screen and thus the interviews and archive footage of 'El comienzo del fin' are presented to the viewer in an accessible way. Perhaps only on a second or third viewing might the viewer spot the wink to the unreliability of sources when the second named interviewee, journalist Manuel Marlasca, recalls that the hole made by the bomb obliterated half of the street, then the footage shows us this was an exaggeration.

Yet even this wink at unreliability cannot prepare us for the mistakes and lack of knowledge exhibited in the episode's central section of the anonymous street interviews. This section should be obligatory viewing for anyone interested in teaching the history of Spain, for there is a direct relation between the age of the interviewees and their knowledge. The older individuals who had lived through the Transition could recall who Carrero Blanco was, and, in broad strokes, what his politics and roles were in connection with the dictatorship. Those without lived knowledge of this period either have no idea who the Admiral was, or muddle him up with someone else: he thus becomes, by turns, 'el que impulsó la democracia' (the one who was the impetus for democracy), or even 'el primer presidente de la democracia' (the first President of democracy). Bartolomé's indictment could not be clearer: the young are either not taught or cannot recall being taught their country's recent history at school; and they do not read or watch the cultural products that explore it as young adults afterwards. Knowing this very well from her own experience of the failure of *Lejos de África* to find an audience, the director could not have been keener both to present the problem and simultaneously to address it by making this 'Special' for the mass audience of the television series.

While the interviews with anonymous interlocutors on the street were a driving force of *Después de...*, here, then, they merely confirm a depressingly familiar situation. Where Bartolomé's skills in interview shine in 'El comienzo del fin' is in fact in conversation with the named individuals. In many of these, Bartolomé, first, gains the trust of interlocutors in the moment of the interview itself, so that many offer revealing conversations, rather than being talking heads. Second, in the editing, Bartolomé selects footage to alight on the telling detail, or juxtaposes elements to create meaning. The standout example of the revealing conversation, which speaks to a high level of trust, is the interview with Carrero's son. An elderly man himself by 2005, he is formal and somewhat stiff in conversation, but Bartolomé sympathetically chooses a domestic backdrop, with family photos and a cheerful flowerpot, and yields his surprisingly emotional admission that, even after thirty years, he sees his father's coffin 'como si fuera hace poco y me sigue impresionando muchísimo' (as if it had happened just recently and it still has a big effect on me). Only in later footage does she pull the camera back to medium shot to reveal that the son is sitting before the portrait of the stern visage of Carrero, though the intimate family details remain, as one of his father's own paintings is also included in the frame.

If this all sounds rather sentimental, Bartolomé seizes on the detail of the heavy eyebrows that gave Carrero's face its sternness also to explore the terror that surrounded the President, who was the dictator's right-hand man. Writer Jorge Martínez Reverte introduces this nickname with his colloquial description of the day of the attack (as conveyed to him by his wife) 'ha llegado hecho cachitos el cejas' (eyebrows-man has been blown to pieces). Particularly effective, though, is Bartolomé's footage of the three women sitting at a table on the street before the Communist flag (Figure 7.1): Julia Peña, whose role is given here as a therapist, though she is of course the former actor and star of *Margarita y el lobo* (Chapter 2); Gloria Berrocal, Alianza de Intelectuales Antiimperialistas (Alliance of Anti-Imperialist Intellectuals, a 2002 reformulation of the famous Alianza de Intelectuales Antifascistas (Alliance of Anti-Fascist Intellectuals) formed in 1936); and Elena Arnao, casting director (whose films include *Lejos de África*, as we have seen (Chapter 6)) and Izquierda Unida militant. Here there is a touch of the fun Bartolomé had with the choral function of groups of women seen in her earlier work. In fact, the footage could perhaps have been longer, so that we could have experienced more than just a glimpse of their interaction, as when Peña tries to interrupt or calm Berrocal, who gets upset when she recalls the fear they lived through in the period. What is captured, though, is the way an

Figure 7.1 Gloria Berrocal, Elena Arnao, and Julia Peña, 'El comienzo del fin', *Cuéntame cómo pasó* (2005)

everyday conversation yields the telling detail (as it did so often in *Después de...*): those eyebrows are for these women not a joke, but a synecdoche for the terror of the period. Interestingly too, it is also as part of this everyday conversation that we see the importance of the fairy tale emerge once again, those tales from childhood that are sewn into the very fabric of our imaginations. ETA may have named their operation 'ogro' (ogre), but it is only when Berrocal uses the term to refer to Carrero, as part of the discursive weave of this everyday conversation between women, that it acquires its full emotional force. The effect of her references to wolves, which are also particularly meaningful throughout Bartolomé's earlier work, is similar.

My focus on the telling details yielded by everyday conversations illustrates Bartolomé's feminist aesthetic of the quotidian that I defined in my analysis of *Después de...* in Chapter 5. In the context of the lack of knowledge about the period revealed by the anonymous interviewees, the director could not rely on such telling details alone, however, so the interviews with historians, journalists and politicians of the period are lengthier. Thus, historians Cierva (also a politician under dictatorship), Eduardo González (Centro Superior de Investigaciones Científicas) and Ascención Tejerina (a specialist in Masonery) are included, though Cierva, perhaps as he is a witness from the period, receives far more screentime. The focus of these interviews is the delivery of information, like Cierva's revelations about Hendaye, González's about student and trade union demonstrations and repression during the Transition, and Tejerina's scepticism over the blacklists of illegal Freemasons held by the regime. Information is also delivered by voiceover, as we have seen, and fictional narrator Carlos, here transformed into a documentary narrator delivering information, outlines Carrero's establishment of the secret police, his defence of Spain's African colonies, and his roles in the infamous Burgos and 1001 Trials (of 1970 and 1972 respectively).

Important as the delivery of information is, from the perspective of the creative handling of documentary form, other interviews are more interesting – in particular, those interviews where the interlocutor was politically active at the time of the magnicide, and who, at the time of filming, also holds roles in democracy. Those which stand out are with Manuel Fraga, former Francoist minister and

The Admiral and the Alcántaras

Ambassador to the UK, though in Madrid at the time of the attack, and President of Galicia at the time of the interview; Teo Uriarte, former ETA terrorist jailed as part of the Burgos trial, and thus in prison in Burgos at the time of the attack, and Director of the Fundación para la Libertad (Foundation for Freedom) at the time of the interview; and Joaquín Leguina, living in Chile at the time of the attack, the first President of the Community Madrid from 1983 to 1995, and a PSOE representative at the time of the interview. Professional politicians with public personae all three, it is trickier here for Bartolomé to draw out original telling details as all three are adept at presenting a public façade to camera. Some of their revelations, therefore, seem rehearsed, like Fraga's nonetheless shocking claim that on the day of the attack he assured Ambassadors to Spain that 'incluso, esto, posiblemente facitilará en su momento la Transición' (this, possibly, might even facilitate the Transition when it comes), or that he and Carrero disagreed about Spain's democratic future, 'el tiempo, en poco, me dio la razón' (time, shortly afterwards, would show I was right) (elsewhere Cierva reveals that the two men hated each other). Bartolomé therefore deploys montage to make new meaning. She cuts, for example, from Fraga's assurance about Carrero's death aiding the Transition to Uriarte making the same point: this creates the startling suggestion that Francoist minister and ETA terrorist were in agreement. Next, Bartolomé cuts from Uriarte to Carrero's son, terrorist to victim, lest we forget the human impact of the event. Elsewhere the montage underscores rather than startles. Subsequent knowledge of ETA's campaign weighs heavily on the words spoken by both Uriarte and Leguina. When two anonymous older men in street interviews pronounce the attack beneficial, 'fue una buena noticia para los demócratas' (it was good news for democrats), Bartolomé cuts to Uriarte's warning of the dangers of the 'admiration' for the attack and the facile assumption that 'todo lo que es subversivo es progresista' (everything that is subversive is progressive). She next cuts to images of the hooded men of the group and their arms training sessions, adding the same transient music she had used to score the earlier images of the Civil War, in order to draw a parallel between the two concerning the horror of violence. When the Alcántarás discuss whether the magnicide may have positive consequences, their conversation is juxtaposed with the Leguina interview through editing. Madrid's

President in the years that were blighted by the campaign, he admits that time has taught him to revise the positive reaction everyone on the Left shared on the news of the Admiral's death, for, 'lo difícil' (the hard thing), he now reflects, 'no es coger las armas, es dejarlos' (isn't taking up arms, it's putting them down). After judiciously cutting to two former members of the group, who openly and less openly express their scepticism about the continuation of terrorism into democracy, Bartolomé returns to Lequina. Here the conversation yields expressive insights and everyday phrases that speak to the trust inspired by her interviewing technique. He memorably expresses the dangers of the legitimisation with which the Carrero attack clothed ETA, which then took up its arms against democracy. 'De aquellos lodos vinieron los polvos después' (The chickens have come home to roost), he colourfully concludes, 'las armas, que ya lo decían en mi pueblo, las carga el diablo' (guns, as people used to say in my village, are the devil's work). Bartolomé need then only cut to newspaper reports of multiple deaths to underscore the point.

Humour

With such subject matter, 'El comienzo del fin' seems an unlikely place to find Bartolomé's humour, but, even here, the signature of a director who has spent her career ribbing dictatorship and patriarchy can still be read. Indeed, it is present from the outset: the Alcántaras' fictional witnessing of the explosion may be high on emotional drama, but it is telling that her first interview is with Forges, who cannot resist a joke. Following a serious discussion of why ETA used such a huge bomb to kill just one man (rather chillingly, Uriarte wonders why he was not simply shot with a pistol) the humourist delivers. In the moments before the propulsion of the Dodge Dart into the air was fully understood, Forges recalls how amusing it was to see the city mayor peering into the hole created by the bomb and asking '¿Almirante, está usted allí?' (Are you there, Admiral Sir?). Journalist Marlasca follows up with the joke that did the rounds among Madrid taxi-drivers: following the attack, if they were to ask a customer how far up Claudio Coello street they wanted to be dropped off, the reply would be '¡no se despegue usted del suelo!' (don't leave the ground!). But Bartolomé's humour is not just a matter of including others' jokes. As in her earlier work, it turns around the use of extra-diegetic music for ironic contrast (which so befuddled the *El mundo* blogger, as we have seen) and the deployment of darkly comic exaggerated detail, or the *esperpento*.

On the one hand, where instrumental scores are added to footage, the effect is rather earnest and direct. For example, military drums accompany the yellow-tinted archive footage of Nationalist Civil War victors, which are intercut with the melancholy strings that accompany the blue-tinted footage of Republican defeat and exile. Transient acoustic tones, meanwhile, link Civil War and ETA violence. On the other, Bartolomé takes full advantage of lyrics (see Appendix Interview p. 205). For example, those of Mexican rancheras by José Alfredo Jiménez are exploited for comic effect. When we see the familiar NO-DO archive footage of Franco and his cronies in government, it is animated by the chirpy 'Ojalá que te vaya bonito' (Hopefully everything will go really well for you). The stiffly formal military uniforms of the men, uniforms aimed also at clothing the dictatorship with legitimacy, contrast amusingly with these colloquial titular lyrics. The dictatorship repression that occurs off-screen, meanwhile, is alluded to darkly with the line, 'que acaben tus penas' (may your sorrows come to an end).

Viewers in the 2020s might enjoy in particular the irony of Bartolomé's choice for the footage of the 1969 ceremony when then Prince Juan Carlos signs the succession papers (Juan Carlos's son and heir, the current King Philip IV, is seen in this sequence too as a blond-haired toddler alongside his mother and sisters). Franco and Carrero look on at the Prince. His serious credentials for the role are conveyed through his naval officer uniform, and through the presence of his wife and children, which suggests he is both a family man and a future king with a blood line of succession secured. By the 2000s, though, the king's philandering was a favourite subject of the tabloids; and by the 2020s his abdication and subsequent financial disgrace, which mean he now resides outside Spain in exile in Abu Dhabi, have become infamous. Bartolomé's musical choice in 2005, 'El Rey' (The King), both echoes revelations about Juan Carlos's moral behaviour at the time and seems to predict those concerning his future money laundering and tax fraud: 'Con dinero o sin dinero, yo hago siempre lo que quiero' (With or without money, I always do exactly what I feel like)!

As well as sending up formal ceremonies of the NO-DO archive material through music, Bartolomé also scours the material itself for amusing details. A brief example of this is the contemporary footage of a serious, suited television journalist's interviews with what he believes are eye witnesses of the explosion. 'En la cama' (In bed) might be a reasonable reply to the question '¿dónde se encontraba usted?' (where were you?) at the time, given that the explosion took place in the morning, though the journalist has to revise hurriedly his description of the man from 'witness' to 'audiovisual witness'. The telling detail concerns clothing. In this footage of the immediate aftermath of a terrorist attack that saw the President's car propelled high in the air, Bartolomé brings audiences down to earth by focusing on the interviewer's examination of the fact that his witness is… still in his pyjamas!

Propulsion into the air lies behind the comic content that Bartolomé finds in what seems to be a fact-finding interview with Emilio Ruiz, concerning the apparently gentle subject matter of the construction of film set models. Ruiz is, in fact, the model maker of the previously mentioned 1979 fictional film about the attack, *Operación ogro*. Inclusion of this interview is fundamental to Bartolomé's concerns in 'El comienzo del fin', exhibiting not only her documentary practice in interview technique, and choice of setting, but also demonstrating her wider aim in the episode to look beyond the surface spectacle of Carrero's death to explore the life, and the period he lived through, in depth. This is also achieved partly by examining the spectacle itself. It has been frequently remarked that, where individuals have not lived through an event, their external knowledge of them, and even internal memory of them, are mediated by audiovisual material that may be fictional (an early reflection on this is Rosenstone's, 1995). The bombing of Carrero's Dodge Dart is a particularly representative example of this in Spain, as Gillo Pontecorvo's *Operación ogro* sequence has been so frequently reproduced that it dominates memories of the event (Fernández Soldevilla and García Varela 2022, 63). Its incorporation into the end of Episode 112, repeated at the start of 113, is a good example of how it is the go-to material for film and television creators to reconstruct the event. Stills from this fictional film about the explosion from Ruiz's model in Pontecorvo's film are even used in school history textbooks about the attack (Fernández Soldevilla and García Varela 2022, 77).

It seems, at first, that watching the interview with the elderly Ruiz, who comes across as a kindly aficionado of his model-making craft, will be a gentle experience for viewers. But we gradually realise that Bartolomé is exposing us to unsettling contrasts, which are at times troublingly comic, sitting as they do on the cusp between the intentional and unintentional. Ruiz proudly shows us the special set he constructed for the reconstruction of the attack in the film, in which the buildings look like large dolls houses. He describes how he spent three days measuring buildings, road and pavement on Claudio Coello street so that the recreation would be as accurate as possible. Such was his lengthy attention to detail that a neighbourhood porter reported that residents were getting concerned. Ruiz even steps into one of the doll's house sets to point out details, appearing by turns a Gulliver on his travels, or an Alice in her wonderland (Figure 7.2). As we marvel at the detail, we remember that this dedicated work only came about owing to a terrorist attack.

Figure 7.2 Emilio Ruiz in the model he constructed for *Operación Ogro* (Pontecorvo 1979) in 'El comienzo del fin', *Cuéntame cómo pasó* (2005)

We may shudder as we realise too that Ruiz and his team's careful measuring of the street for the reconstruction matched the ways the terrorists themselves also carefully measured the street to make their tunnel, plant their bomb and calculate at what moment to trigger it as the Dodge Dart passed – no wonder the porter and the residents were alarmed. Worse still is the darkly humorous moment when Ruiz proudly presents us with the black toy car, recalling his joy at finding it in a toy shop as it so perfectly matched Carrero's. When he talks about the moment that the three men lost their lives, Ruiz is so engrossed in explaining the process that he perhaps forgets that Bartolomé is filming him. One of the most momentous moments of recent Spanish history, it is portrayed here, I suggest, as *esperpento*. Bartolomé's close-up stresses the comic exaggeration of the model-maker waving the toy car about from side to side in the air, as he recalls how difficult it was to propel it in the right direction: 'el coche se nos iba pa' acá, otras veces se nos iba pa' allá…' (the car went over here, then other times it went over there…). The subject matter is deadly serious, so the *esperpento* humour of Bartolomé's focus on the doll's houses and the toy car could not be darker.

'Lecho histórico' (historical bedrock)

Perhaps unknown to her at the time, the episode title 'El comienzo del fin' referred both intra-textually to the exploration of the beginning of the end of Francoism; but also extra-textually to the beginning of the end of Bartolomé's own film and television career. In this context, alongside its risky dark comedy, the interview with model-maker Emilio Ruiz also provides a summary of her contribution, both in this episode and as a reminder of the wider goals of her career.

As we have seen, the *Cuéntame* series responds to the fact that, in the audiovisual age of film, television and streaming, an audience's knowledge of a historical period, whether they lived through it or not, is already audiovisual. Thus the show's fictional period settings rely as much on imitating what was seen on-screen on film and television of the time, as on recreating off-screen materiality. Some cultural commentators have been highly critical of the privileged role *Cuéntame* plays in this creation of national memory, rightly pointing to matters such as the use of compromised material and its omissions, as we have seen. On the other hand, others have argued that we should attend to the fact that *Cuéntame* itself is part of the process of memory construction in Spain, broadcast as it is during the debates that surrounded the Law of Historical Memory and Law of Democratic Memory, discussed above. Abi Loxham argues that the series therefore 'approaches memory as it is being created, offering a mnemonic device that is revealed as inconsistent, in the process of creation, the subject of contestation'. The television medium is key as it 'has the ability to provoke debate and extend the argument on memory, media and remediation' (2015, 721). This is surely a more productive approach than criticising *Cuéntame* for bias, as if it were a finished product that has recreated only one, single memory of the period, to the exclusion of others.

A creative practitioner rather than cultural critic, I compare Bartolomé's approach to Loxham's. Just as Francoism is known to audiences who did not live through dictatorship through audiovisual reconstructions like the *Cuéntame* series, Bartolomé addresses the fact that Carrero's magnicide, as we have seen, is known to most audiences through the frequently seen fictional footage of it in Pontecorvo's film. With stills of the moment reproduced in school history textbooks, it is also likely the first encounter of most with the event. 'El comienzo del fin' as a whole shows us how to look beyond the superficial spectacle of the death to the wider depths of the life and the period. But it also examines the creation of that spectacle itself. And how could the fictionality of Pontecorvo's film be more effectively demonstrated than by taking viewers through the minute details of its fictional recreation through Ruiz's construction of the set? While Joan Ramón Resina may comment with some despair that 'our relation to the past has become spectatorial' (2010, 225), Bartolomé recognises this as a creative challenge and instead explores it.

Finally, Bartolomé's choice to explore the creation of spectacle through the role of the model maker is also layered with significance. Firstly, we might read her focus on the labour of the modelmaker as a homage to creativity in classic cinema, before the advent of Computer Generated Imagery. Ruiz is sweetly modest as he speaks with pride about his work, showing no resentment about the fact that his fundamental contribution to *Operación Ogro* is largely unknown (his work provided the publicity poster for the film at the time of release; and is now in the age of online streaming its most frequently viewed sequence). He simply states that he is proud to be there

> a pesar de que muchísimas veces no dan mi nombre, quien es el autor de esto, para mí ha sido una satisfacción tremenda saber que, por lo menos, escondido un poco, yo estoy también en el lecho histórico metido. (even though they usually don't give my name as the author, for me it has been hugely rewarding to know that, at least, hidden a bit, I'm there too, part of the historical bedrock.)

The role of model-maker is a typical below-the-line role in cinema, often uncredited and undervalued. It is, then, the opposite of the above-the-line role par excellence of the director (or, in fiction film, the actors), usually credited first and valued as the leading creative voice. For a director like Cecilia Bartolomé, though, there is something very relevant to her own experience to be found in Ruiz's words. Frustrated throughout her career by difficulties in production, distribution and exhibition – and it is important to note that these held her back under both dictatorship and democracy – Bartolomé carried on. With her contribution only attracting modest attention, thus far, and only later in her life (see Introduction), she, too, is 'escondida un poco' (hidden a bit), but is there 'en el lecho histórico' (in the historical bedrock).

If we look carefully at the closing credits of 'El comienzo del fin', the physical person of Bartolomé is there too, just as she was present physically at the end of what was to be her first feature, but remained the Film School medium-length assessment piece, *Margarita y el lobo*. In 1969, she is present shouting '¡corten!' (cut!) as the camera pulls back self-referentially to capture the fictional actors in the wider context of the whole film crew (Figure 2.2). In 2005, she is there in a series of outtakes shown during the final credits. We cannot hear her words as she chats to various interviewees about their participation – we are busy, instead, appreciating the military connotations of the Pasodoble on the soundtrack – but we see her shake hands in thanks with Fraga (his public façade also sneakily stressed as he is the only figure we see being prepared for the interview by the make-up and wardrobe assistant), with González, Leguina, Samper and Ruiz. It is fitting that the last image we will likely ever see of Bartolomé within one of her own works is this one, with the model-maker. Both have always been there, 'escondidos un poco', in the history of Spain and the history of cinema, in the 'lecho histórico', if we only know where, and how, to look.

Notes

1 I take these figures from https://www.formulatv.com/series/cuentame-como-paso/capitulos/1805/ (accessed 22 February 2023); this is average or above average for the series. According to Héctor Llanos Martínez, the highest figure ever was seven million with a 51 per cent audience share (2023), though Ana Corbalán, using a webpage that is no longer available, cites a record audience of nearly ten million (2009, 341). Bartolomé is proud that the figure beat 2000s transnational television sensation *Gran Hermano / Big Brother* (2000–) (e.g. in an interview with Andrea Bermejo 2017, 11). The episode is currently free to stream (without subtitles), including to territories outside Spain, on the RTVE website: https://www.rtve.es/play/videos/cuentame-como-paso/cuentame-como-paso-t7-capitulo-113/880677/, accessed 17 April 2023.
2 Over its exceptionally long running time, *Cuéntame* has had various scriptwriters and directors (for figures that were accurate in 2012, see Palacio 2012, 359). Bartolomé co-wrote the script for the Special with Laura García Pousa (also known as Laura Pousa), who wrote twenty episodes from 2004 to 2010 and has gone on to publish a number of works on the series (García Pousa 2011; Pousa 2017).
3 Throughout the series, the 'authorial voice' of founding scriptwriter Eduardo Ladrón de Guevara, whose anti-Franco militant politics are explored in print (Ladrón de Guevera 2003), can also be heard (Smith 2006, 20).
4 She continues, 'En cambio, los niños veréis que se abstraen por completo ante la TV, cuando hay algo que les interesa' (By contrast, you'll see that children are completely absorbed when they watch television, if it's something they're interested in), a tendency we first see when the children watch the Western in *Carmen de Carabanchel / Carmen of Carabanchel* (1965). While Bartolomé did not work in children's film and television herself, her comments in 1978 chime with contemporary feminist work in this area in Drac Màgic (see Introduction).
5 The final episode, Episode 8 of Season 23, 'Carlos: El heredero', was screened on 29 November 2023.

6 https://www.elindependiente.com/sociedad/2022/06/15/la-edad-media-de-las-madres-se-dispara-a-326-anos-en-otro-ano-con-minimo-historico-de-nacimientos/, accessed 23 February 2023.
7 Elena Cueto Asín notes that this moment coincided with the fictional 1975 of the series, and was thus able to explore memory, retribution and reconciliation within the fictional text – Antonio and his brother visit their assassinated father's grave – precisely as these were being enshrined in law (2009, 155).
8 More material has been added to the RTVE archive, see www.rtve.es, since scholars lamented this situation (e.g. Smith 2006, 17).
9 To counter these limitations, Víctor Sevillano Canicio (2010, 350) notes that *Cuéntame*, like earlier series *Los años vividos / The Years We Have Lived Through* (Odina, Sánchez Pereira and Ventura 1992) and *La Transición / The Transition* (Andrés and Prego 1995), had to use foreign news archives.
10 For a history of this approach in Spanish film of the 1970s onwards, see my volume, Faulkner (2013).
11 García Pousa shows that a similar approach is adopted in *Mad Men* (Weiner 2007–15) (2011).
12 For further information on Carrero's Hendaye report, see Payne (2008, 95); on his support for the restoration of the monarchy, Preston (1993, 741).

Conclusion: Cecilia Bartolomé and the incomplete history of Spanish cinema

I. Feminist auteur, from 'rose' period to 'blue'

As I have written this book, it has become clearer and clearer to me that there would be two ways of finishing it. The first I subtitle 'Feminist Auteur', as my research into this director has been driven by the determination to include her name among those far better-known figures, in both national and international contexts, to whom this label has been attached. In Spain, these would include the generation that came into prominence in the 1990s, like Icíar Bollaín, Isabel Coixet and Chus Gutiérrez; internationally, her contemporaries, Claire Denis, Euzhan Palcy and Agnès Varda.

Having previously published on her work in Spanish (Faulkner 2022b, 285–309), I have hoped to join conversations concerning her recovery among scholars writing in this language, like Andrea Bermejo and Sonia García López. With the publication of this book, along with my collaborations with students, colleagues and institutions in the United Kingdom to subtitle her work into English,[1] I hope to reach Anglophone readers and audiences who have hitherto been unable to know it. This is important, first, because of her work's originality. As we have seen in these pages, its innovations lie in the topics it explores that others ignored, or simply did not know existed; as well as in the genres and approaches it develops, especially comedy, music and documentary. Yet 'originality' and 'innovation' feel like terms that have been worn out from previous use. A better term might be provocation: her singular vision demands our attention.

Yet, as we know, Bartolomé was thwarted in her provocations, and tracing the processes of that thwarting is a second reason why her case deserves attention. In this book I have explored in meticulous detail the processes of prevention: I have named the opponents she encountered at Film School by drawing on scarcely examined documentation held at the Filmoteca Española; I have demonstrated dictatorship censorship and its use of the 'blacklist'; I have explored her experience of apparently supportive, then bizarrely obstructive producers; extensive press reports and interviews, finally, have allowed me to track the neo-censorship she faced in early democracy. In such circumstances, the fact that she managed to produce as much work as she did is remarkable: the seemingly modest corpus is in fact extensive.

A body of work that is 'provocative', from a director who faced 'processes of prevention' might make it sound as if watching her films would be rewardingly worthy, but rather taxing. In fact, the encounter with Bartolomé's world is a joy for audiences. She is a cineaste of both the cerebral and the comic; her world is one in which both the momentous and the mirthful mingle. From the halls of the Dehesa de la Villa Film School in the 1960s, to the corridors of the Pozuelo de Alarcón Prado del Rey television studios in the 2000s, her twin creative commitments to denouncing Francoism and claiming feminism are constant. Within them, I trace what I identify as two periods in this body of work. The shorts, *Margarita y el lobo* / *Margarita and the Wolf*, the unfilmed scripts *Qué tal Margarita… pero bien* / *What's Up, Margarita…? Not Bad* and *La linda Casilda* / *The Beautiful Casilda*, and *¡Vámonos, Bárbara!* / *Bárbara, Let's Go!* all exhibit an attention to the urgency of the present that dominates her early work. Formally, in this period, the predominant tone is humour, which is exhibited in particular through choices in music (both diegetic and extra-diegetic) and the grotesque exaggeration of the *esperpento*. After the bridging documentary diptych, there follows a later period, made up of *Lejos de África* / *Far from Africa* and 'El comienzo del fin' / 'The Beginning of the End', which mount a fight against forgetfulness, or a focus on the past. In this later period the comic tone remains, and is seen in choices of music, but also of cinematography and editing, though the documentary approach in 'El comienzo del fin' is newly dominant. Threaded through both periods, then, is her filmmaking signature of an accessible approach, an attention to the everyday and an eye and an ear for the comic, whether in the genre of melodrama (*La* *siesta* / *The Siesta*; *La brujita* / *The Little Witch*; *La noche del Dr Valdés* / *Doctor Valdés's Night*; *Carmen de Carabanchel* / *Carmen of Carabanchel*; *Lejos de África*), musical (*Margarita*), road movie (*¡Vámonos, Bárbara!*) or documentary (*Cruzada del Rosario*; *Después de… / Afterwards*, 'El comienzo del fin'). (Had *La linda Casilda* been made, we might have been able to add the Western here too.)

We might thus, rather grandly, but knowingly so, refer to this evolution as a shift from an earlier 'rose' period – ironically enough, a period that chronologically coincides with the repressive years of the Franco dictatorship – that shifts to a later 'blue' period; again, ironically enough, as this period coincides with the supposed freedoms of democracy. With this language of creative demarcation, I thus pointedly claim Bartolomé's place in a lineage of Spanish male artists, from Pablo Picasso to Pedro Almodóvar, to whom the 'rose' and 'blue' periodisation has previously been applied.[2]

In her 'rose' period, the focus is the present of Franco's Spain and the tone lampooning. Bartolomé's 'present' is the 1960s and 1970s work in which she homes in on women's issues: lack of legal birth control for women (both contraception and abortion) (*Carmen*); lack of divorce and the infantilisation of women through the *permiso marital* (*Margarita* and *¡Vámonos, Bárbara!*). The unfilmed scripts also focus on entirely new material in Spanish cinema such as post-natal depression (*Qué tal Margarita*), and female mental health and suicide (*Qué tal Margarita* and *La linda Casilda*). But, of course, issues in the present are inextricable from repression in the past: Bartolomé's feminist claiming of women's rights in the 1960s and 1970s is all about denouncing the Franco regime that removed them in the past, especially its revocation of divorce, which was legal in the Second Republic (the democratic government from which it illegally captured power by means of Civil War). In a similar way, if the present is imbued with the past in Bartolomé's 'rose' period, then the potentially tragic also underscores the divertingly comic in these pieces. We should not, then, be fooled by the witty tone and grotesque exaggeration of the work. The do-it-yourself birth control of *Carmen*, the physical toll of multiple births in both that short and in *¡Vámonos, Bárbara!*, and the lack of attention to maternal mental health in *Qué tal Margarita* are deadly serious. Had Bartolomé been able to film the scripts she wrote in the 1970s, audiences would have born witness to this in the female suicides of Natalia and Casilda.

The shift to a focus on the past and increased use of documentary techniques in the 'blue' period are similarly multi-layered. *Lejos de África* and 'El comienzo del fin' may portray Francoist Africa of the 1950s and 1960s, and Francoist Spain of the 1970s, but these portraits are all about the contemporary audiences of 1996 and 2005. Rather than just bemoaning the 'desmemoria' (forgetfulness) of younger generations, Bartolomé picks up her camera and does something about it. Despite its flaws, had better choices been made in marketing, *Lejos de África*'s accessible family melodrama about the colonial Africa of Bartolomé's youth might have reached a wider audience. The intertwining of different generations of a fictional family and the portentous historical change from colonialism to independence in this 1996 film look forward to the winning formula of one of the most important Spanish television series of all time, *Cuéntame cómo pasó / Tell Me How It Happened*, launched in 2001. Only a one-off episode, Bartolomé's contribution to that series in 'El comienzo del fin' explicitly intertwines past and present through interviews with members of the 'desmemoriada' youth, who do not know about the Transition, and interviews with political protagonists of the period. Unlikely as this melodrama about colonial Africa, and this documentary biopic of Francoist government President Admiral Carrero Blanco, may sound as terrain for amusing mischief, the cerebral and the comic are layered here once again. In the 'blue' period, Bartolomé's eye for the disarming detail, or ear for the telling phrase, accompanied by choices in editing and music, though somewhat hampered in *Lejos de África*, remain as sharp as ever in 'El comienzo del fin'.

In this analysis of a shift from 'rose' to 'blue', finally, *Después de...* may be understood as more than a bridging work: it is rather the creative keystone of Bartolomé's filmography. Focussed on the urgent present of violence and tension of the Transition – elements that are convenient for revisionist commentators to overlook – the past of Francoist repression imbues every image. These include the sense of entitlement mingled with threat among those who supported the dictator, to the sense of possibility mingled with fear among those who opposed him. This diptych of documentaries faces the future (unlike the contemporary documentary films being made in Spain at the time that look back to the past), and even uncannily predicts the major collision of past and present of the Spanish

Transition that occurred days after the films were complete. The dangerous mix of past entitlement, present threat and fear for the future experienced by the Spanish Army that had supported General Franco's military regime exploded in the coup d'état of 23 February 1981 that has come to be known as the Tejerazo. Had circumstances been more propitious, Bartolomé and her brother intended to make a third part to *Después de...*, to be called *¡Todos al suelo! / Everyone Down on the Floor!*, one of Colonel Tejero's cries as he burst into Spain's democratic chamber, his pistol aloft. But this third part was unmade, unfilmed, unfinished or unproduced. Film history might, however, rename the completed *Después de...* diptych as an incomplete triptych, of which two parts are extant, but of which there is a third part, a shadow that throws shade onto the first two, or a ghost that haunts the earlier two from an impossible future.

II. Incomplete

This volume has aimed to justify Bartolomé's place in Spanish film history in the auteurist terms in which that history, or indeed the history of art more generally, has always been written. But Bartolomé's 'fit' within such an approach, as I have been careful to acknowledge, is awkward. Not only is this because her corpus, at six shorts, a medium-length piece, two fiction films, a documentary diptych (triptych) and a television episode, is modest. It is also manifestly a corpus that is unfinished, unmade or incomplete. In *The Cinema of Cecilia Bartolomé: Feminism and Francoism*, I have acknowledged this by including two scripts written in the early to mid 1970s, when the director was on the dictatorship blacklist. The updating of *Margarita y el lobo* into the fiction film *Qué tal Margarita... pero bien* (1974), another melodrama and comedy, and *La linda Casilda* (1976), a Western, yield new and tantalising insights into Bartolomé's creativity, like a focus on mental health and suicide. Chapter 3 is thus shorter than the others, which focus on work that was at least finished, if not always fully exhibited or distributed, but its inclusion is vital to form a more complete picture of the director's creative intentions and trajectory.

Yet perhaps the idea of 'completeness' misses the point. If we consider Chapter 3 in the singular, it does contribute to 'completing' a picture of Bartolomé's creative trajectory. Yet if we step back and consider Bartolomé's career as a whole, the 'incomplete' edges once again into view. The cause to which this volume is committed is the inclusion of Bartolomé's vital work in histories of Spanish cinema in a national context, and in histories of feminist cinema in a transnational context. But this inclusion will never 'complete' any picture. Chapter 3 of this volume strives to ensure that the voice of women directors that political censorship attempted to silence may be heard, even when, by being present in a script, rather than a finished film, the volume of that voice is faint. However, I could only write this chapter because of the existence of an archive that took custody of the scripts. What of all those other projects that do not leave a trace in the archive, like the planned third part of *Después de…*, which are shadows or ghosts? The historian must endeavour to recover as much material for scholarly scrutiny as possible, even if that means including outlier, shorter chapters, like my own Chapter 3. But the 'incomplete', as the feminist scholars of Unproduction Studies I cite in Chapter 3 argue, is in fact the point. Bartolomé's career may be incomplete, darkened by the shadows, or haunted by the ghosts, of her unmade work; but so is the history of Spanish cinema.

Notes

1 See 'Subtitling World Cinema' project (Introduction, note 9).
2 Deployed in art history to describe the two distinct periods of Pablo Picasso's work (e.g. Daix, Boudaille and Rosselet 1967), Paul Julian Smith spotted the reuse of this 'rose' and 'blue' periodisation in connection with Almodóvar in French magazine *Les Inrockuptibles* in 1999. He goes on to connect Almodóvar's 'blue' period with the 'art movie' (2003, 144–67); I have suggested elsewhere that it may also be interpreted as middlebrow (Faulkner 2013, 211).

Appendix: Cecilia Bartolomé interview

Cecilia Bartolomé interview, Sally Faulkner and Núria Triana Toribio, Madrid, 9 June 2022. Translated by Mar Diestro-Dópido.

Songs are very important in your films, for example, in Carmen de Carabanchel / Carmen of Carabanchel (1965). What drove you to use those songs? What were you after?
I've always considered that music with lyrics works really well, things flow better with music. You can say things with songs and the message is conveyed in a much smoother way. For me, the music, the lyrics and the singing style enrich the narrative; in other words, the same thing, conveyed with a song, instead of dialogue, feels better. When I filmed, I would separate out the things that I needed to get across in a more forceful way from the more realistic elements. Then, I would add music to the former. And then both would intertwine.

I started performing in theatre at the school I attended when I was a child. My mother was a teacher there, and the school organised many recitals and small plays. And when we moved to Guinea, I carried on being involved in small shows. For instance, when we were on the boat, I was around nine years old, I managed to get hold of a copy of a Sección Femenina [women's branch of the Falange political movement in Spain][1] magazine. They used to publish children's stories and plays and I staged one called 'La pastorcilla ambiciosa' [The Ambitious Little Shepherdess]; that is where I discovered my vocation as both a director and an actor, because I also performed. I also became aware of my facet as a producer, something I always put first, because I figured out that you have to generate money from the things that you do. I charged an entry fee in order to donate the proceeds to a congregation that had an orphanage in Guinea. At first, we were charging one *peseta* [Spanish currency between 1868 and 2002], but we soon realised that it wasn't profitable. So, we convinced the boat's captain to let us have the music hall, and we invited the captain and his crew and all the rich people on the boat to the performance, then we passed around a hat after the show, which was far more profitable than charging an entry fee, because nobody gave less than a *duro* [five pesetas]. We managed to collect around three or four hundred pesetas, which, at the time, was a fortune, and we sent it to the orphanage. So, as you can see, it was my vocation since I was very little.

And this is the key point, making films costs money and you need finances in order to be able to make them.
Exactly. You need to make money out of a show because it allows you to make more shows.

When we finally settled in Guinea, I carried on setting up shows and my little plays, and when I was fourteen, I discovered cinema, because in Spain we hardly watched any films, and in Guinea, with no other form of distraction, there was a Summer Cinema that we often used to go to.

And what do you remember having watched back then that you liked?
If I'm honest, the first film I watched was when I was ten or eleven and it was *Cobra Woman* (Siodmak 1944), with María Montes in Technicolor. I was fascinated. Later on, I watched one by Bardem, and I didn't like it at all because it was in black and white, and was about social issues.

Did you watch the version of *Sissi – The Young Empress* that was made back then?[2]
Yes, but I think I actually watched it in Spain. I'm talking about the 1950s. And during one of the summers we spent in Spain on holidays, I became enthralled by the big US weepies, like *Gone With the Wind* (Fleming, Cukor, Wood 1939), and not only the spectacular ones, but also the more intimate films, about great passions. That's when I said to myself: 'what I really like is cinema as a narrative medium'. And when I was fourteen, I watched a NO-DO [newsreel] where they played an advert for the recently founded Film School,

which at the time was called the Instituto de Cinematografía/ Institute of Cinematography, and afterwards became the Escuela Oficial de Cinematografía/Official Film School. The advert included images of the students as they were filming, and that's when I said to myself: 'this is what I want to do, and this is where they teach it'. It was a dream come true. So, from the age of fourteen I knew exactly what I wanted to do, and I spent the following three years planning how to convince my parents to let me live in Spain and go to the Film School, because they were never going to let me do so until I had finished secondary school. So, I finished my studies in Guinea and managed to enrol in the Film School.

How did you get the funds to be able to go to the Film School? How did you manage? Did your family pay, or were there any grants?
It cost very little money, because the Film School was really cheap. That was down to Fraga Iribarne, because he wanted to set up a Hollywood-style school. The School hardly made any profits. And it was very disorganised. So, when my parents came to visit, they saw it in a state of collapse and took me back to Guinea. That year and a half that I spent in Guinea was very beneficial to me because an amateur theatre company was being set up and we started performing, and one of the shows was a very Christian play that everybody was putting on at the time – Alejandro Casona's *La dama del Alba / The Lady of the Dawn* (1944). I also gained a degree in Business Consulting after finishing secondary school, and I needed money, so I started working as an accountant in a bank, since I had specialised in accounting. That money allowed me to do my own things: we put on radio shows, and we also had a theatre group called 'Agrupación Teatral de Guinea' (Guinea Theatre Group) and our first show was *La barca sin pescador / The Boat Without a Fisherman* (Casona 1945), followed by other comedies and plays. We also invested the money by converting a place where they dried cocoa beans into a theatre.

Did you have an audience?
We did, there were five thousand people living there, so we'd put on the play and run it for four or five days only – though it was only ever the European population that came – but, even so, we'd sell out because it was a novelty and pretty much everyone had a friend

or a family member in the company. Still, the African population wouldn't come.

What was everyday life like at the Film School? Which subjects did you like best? Which teachers did you get on with best?
There was a period when the School was chaotic, but when José Luis Sáenz de Heredia took charge, the teaching became much more rigorous, and he even created the programme of final-year project screenings.[3] This is where Saura, Borau, Patino, the first generation of the New Wave, came from. During that period, the School achieved a much higher status and became much more selective, because the entry test would be taken by, perhaps, a little over a hundred people, and only ten passed it. Bear in mind that the final year project was a medium-length film, so it was very expensive; the Film School had the same budget as the Faculty of Medicine. They built up a professional studio, editing rooms, sound mixing rooms, etc. They invested a lot in equipment and it became one of the most professional schools in Europe, bearing comparison with the Italian and French schools. So, since we had to have practice-based training and it was so expensive, access was very competitive.

What kind of entry test did you have to take?
You had to write a short script, take a theory exam and write a short film review. Almost everyone would fail the script test, because writing a script in two or three hours is very hard.

Who started with you that year?
Manolo Gutiérrez Aragón, Patricio Guzmán… (My brother [José Juan Bartolomé] started in another year.)

And did you collaborate with each other when you were making shorts?
We did, because when we were in our third year, the students from the first and second years were our assistants. It was a total of three years, and the end-of-year project had to be done as part of the third year. You had to write the script and you were given the means to film it afterwards, and the equipment was of a very high quality.

Tell us a little bit about the shorts you made at the School, for instance, with a short like *Carmen de Carabanchel*, were you told

by the School to film in a particular location, or did you have total freedom?
We did have total freedom on everything except for the budget, which was set, and the practice-based project had to be done with limited film stock and in a given number of days. The practice-based project for the first year was silent and had to be done in one day; the one for the second year did have sound and you had about two-to-three days, but it was a short of approximately fifteen minutes. But in the third year you had to film at a professional level, films of about thirty minutes, like *Margarita y el lobo / Margarita and the Wolf* (1969). Yet in my third year there were only eight of us students left, because the School would be very selective regarding who was allowed to continue. About ten students were admitted in my first year, but comparatively few of them were left by the third year – even in my year group, which had one of the largest numbers of students graduating. When Patino was studying, for instance, only four or five students graduated in the end. The practical exercise in the third year was almost as expensive as making a professional film; and, once finished, it was screened at a cinema. You left the School having learnt how to make cinema, as you were given the opportunity to make a professional film. Those who tried to make shorts by their own means didn't have access to the same kind of equipment, hence the result of these was not as professional.

So, your final year project was a step towards entering the industry, is that right? Except, in your case, they played a dirty trick on you.
Yes, all of us in my year pushed our projects too far, but my film really did rub them up the wrong way, together with José Luis García Sánchez's, who was in the second year. Both our films were censored because Baena had just begun [as Director], and he was evil.

He started off by being very progressive, didn't he?
Yes, yes, he did, he had even joined the Communist Party at some point, but he did have some serious problems of some kind. He got really upset and crossed over to the opposing side.

How did you earn your living when you were told you couldn't make it in cinema? Because, when *Margarita y el lobo* was censored, you

became a person with a degree in film direction, who could not work in the world of cinema...
Yes, I could work. There are many different fields that spin off from cinema, like documentary and advertising, which is what I started doing, basically: filming documentaries and making adverts.

Tell us about the adverts you made.
My work was quite innovative, because the first advert I made was for La Casera [a traditional Spanish brand of soda], and the owners wanted to do something really refined, and I told them that I was going to make something like a Hollywood musical. They had a big budget, they gave me the slogan and what I was aiming for was a fun advert where the protagonist, a boy, was travelling around in a world of dwarves, so we made *The Seven Dwarves*. It attracted a lot of attention, and it allowed me to make a career in television advertising. Those five years before Franco's death were really beneficial to me: I was making adverts, doing some documentaries and I got involved in a project that I really liked, the 'making-of' documentary of *El perro / A Dog Called... Vengeance* (Isasi-Isasmendi 1977). This was a film with a budget of one hundred million pesetas, when the average back then was twenty million, so it could be said that it was planned as if it were a US film. This was all great for me, because I could make the documentary about the difficulties they encountered during the shoot, even though the documentary did not materialise in the end, because the shooting of *El perro* ended really badly. Isasi and the producer fell out, and the latter ended up financially ruined. I always wanted to recover all that material...

How was the shooting of *Carmen de Carabanchel*? What was it like filming in Carabanchel?
We did not film in Carabanchel, but at the place I lived in at the time and in my neighbourhood, which was right where Carabanchel starts. I wanted to make a film that was easy to shoot as I was pregnant. A number of office buildings had been built next to the Manzanares river for the civil servants working at the different ministries. These are located under the Pradera de San Isidro, and right there is where the Carabanchel neighbourhood starts. It was a neighbourhood with families from varied social backgrounds. The more luxurious places that looked over the river were for the civil servants who worked at the ministries. My father, when he was

destined to Guinea, bought two small cheap flats there, so that my siblings and I would have somewhere to live when we were studying; we didn't live in the more luxurious flats. I filmed *Carmen de Carabanchel* there.

And the actors? Were they in the same class as you at School?
No, they were students from the Film School, where you could specialise in camera work, acting, sound, decoration, etc. So, even though the actors were not from my class, they were students at the Film School. And the films embedded within the film[4] are the ones we used to watch at the time. What's funny about such an iron-clad dictatorship is that films sneaked through. For instance, *Diferente / Different* (Delgado 1962) is about a gay relationship, but the censors did not realise that they were gay and let it through: we all watched it stupefied.

We have the feeling that, with your being a woman, the censors would be primed to look for excuses to cut your work.
When I made *Margarita y el lobo*, scenes with naked men were very uncommon in cinema – until Jane Campion arrived and filmed Harvey Keitel's bum in *The Piano* (1993) – so the censors went crazy with my naked bum scene. But, in sex scenes, people need to be naked.

And what about *La brujita / The Little Witch* (1966) and *Plan Jack Cero Tres / Plan Jack Zero Three* (1967)? How did you come up with those shorts? Were you told to work with different genres at the School?
No, no, not at all. We had no creative impositions from the School, aside from censorship, of course, which we were constantly trying to dodge. As I mentioned before, each year had a different budget for different length projects.

And did you edit the films?
When I started at the School, there wasn't yet a specialisation path in editing. There was an editing teacher, Ana María Romero Marchent, who supervised the editing of our films, but we edited them ourselves.

And censorship?
In fact, censorship started with García Sánchez and me, because there was no censorship before that; but neither had previous

students dared to do anything that put them at risk of being censored – they self-censored. And when they wanted to propose issues that would be censored, it was all done very cryptically, as in *La caza / The Hunt* (Saura 1966), for example, where everything was very symbolic. And those of us who started talking about things in a more straightforward way were García Sánchez and me. García Sánchez, in his second-year project, had one of his actors stand right outside the Film School with a huge banner that said 'whorehouse' next to a group of blokes queuing up; obviously, that was inadmissible for the censors at the time…

Tell us about Julia Peña.
She was the actor I chose for *Margarita y el lobo*. Julia was a total myth, an exceptional woman. A militant member of the Communist Party, she was arrested twice. Politically, she was very active in protests against the Francoist regime, and she was very well-respected as an actor. I have a very striking image of her in my mind. In a play with Aurora Bautista,[5] Bautista had given Peña the second lead when the latter had been reported for her political activism. During the performance of the play, the police came into the theatre and blocked all the exits and the backstage so she couldn't escape. When the play finished, Peña came out onto the stage together with the rest of the cast, took a bow and was then taken prisoner. But she had managed to carry on with the play fully aware that she was going to be arrested as soon as it ended.

So, she was the perfect actor to play Margarita…
Yes, of course she was. She wrote much of the script with me, many of the lyrics for the musical numbers, and a lot of the dialogue is hers too.

Did you work together again?
No, we never worked together again… I mean, we were working on *Margarita y el lobo* for a year, of course, tweaking the script so it was smoother and making it feature-length,[6] but it never materialised because of censorship. José Luis Borau, who was my tutor at Film School, helped Julia and I with that script. Borau was very endearing, because he was both very clumsy, but also really intelligent, with his little obsessions and things, but absolutely endearing.

Did you like directing actors?
Yes, I loved it, for me this is the most essential part of cinema. Unlike those who prioritise the aesthetics within the frame, what I most cared about was the actors, because I consider that they are, together with the script, the foundations of a film. You go nowhere with a bad script and bad actors, but, even without an actual film set, you can still make a good film – in fact, there are films and plays that are being made without a set and they work really well.

Who did you like to work with? Did you find it easy working with Amparo Soler Leal when you made ¡Vámonos Bárbara! / Bárbara, Let's Go! (1978)?
It was fantastic, both Amparo and the girl [Cristina Álvarez], who was clever as a fox as well, and such a diva. Amparo was a magnificent woman with a huge sense of humour. I had an argument with Alfredo Matas, the producer, and after the row, he told me that I had to finish filming on a Saturday at 3 o'clock. At 3 o'clock on Saturday afternoon we were about to film the last scene, I had Amparo and the girl sitting in the car to deliver the last line of dialogue, and the production director, Sol Carnicero – we got on really well – told me it was 3 p.m. and she was very sorry, but I had to finish filming. Hence, we decided to ask the lead actor, Amparo, if she wanted to stop filming there, or whether she wanted to continue and finish the final shot. Amparo, who was married to Matas, decided that the final shot had to be filmed regardless of what her husband had said, and that she would deal with him later. And that's how we filmed the last take in ¡Vámonos, Bárbara!. The filming of the final shot was ordered by the lead actor against what had been imposed on us by the producer. Amparo was the one in charge.

One of the things we are fascinated by is the chorus of English women in the film. Where did you find them?
They came from the Paralelo. The Paralelo in Barcelona is an avenue where all the nightclubs were located and the casting director we had in that city was just incredible. I told her we needed older, foreign women and she said, 'Ah, leave it to me, I'll get them. They don't even need to be actual foreigners, I'll find them.' It turns out that they were women who, back in the day, had all worked as dancers in the Paralelo clubs and they were older, but they'd all

been blonde, tall, slim and still had that bearing. In addition, many of them were English and French – they had been the good-looking girls of Paralelo, and were now retired. So, my casting director sent over a group of older, foreign-looking women that looked wonderful.

And Bárbara? How did you find that actor? Were you after a redhead in particular, a girl that looked slightly different?
We found her at a casting session we did looking for girls. And we weren't looking for a red-head in particular, we liked her because she was the best one; though she does resemble Amparo Soler Leal, so she could actually pass for her daughter.

She never did anything else, did she?
Not as far as I know, no. I don't know why.

Bárbara has been interpreted[7] as a guide for her mother who recalls Lazarillo de Tormes [the young, street-wise character who guides the blind man in the Spanish sixteenth-century picaresque novel of the same title], who acts as a guide for a blind man. Did you ever think of her from that angle?
It is true that she's the one in charge and makes the decisions, but I never thought of her as a 'lazarilla' for her mother when we were writing the script.

The film starts, seemingly, as a *destape* film [contemporary Spanish soft-porn film], yet it is very anti-*destape*; it is as if it is mocking the *destape* films that were being made at the time.
Yes, absolutely. The shot was originally wider, with the man standing up so you could see his penis perfectly well, but Matas told me that was inadmissible, whilst his wife, Amparo, was lying stark naked on the bed! And I told him, 'come on Alfredo, why are you giving me trouble over showing the actor's penis, but not the female actor's vagina?' And he carried on saying no, that it was impossible to show the actor's penis. He told me very seriously that: 'it is not the same'. At the time, when we shot the film, we were right in the midst of the *destape*, so women were taking their clothes off all the time in films – for instance, Amparo had already had to take her clothes off in several films. When censorship was abolished in 1977,[8] everyone went crazy about nudity, but it was the women and not the men who took their clothes off. Amparo asked me how

many times she had to take her clothes off in the film, and I told her it was just at the start, and as a joke, as it was going to be the most anti-erotic nude scene ever made in Spanish cinema. We also did the strip scene with the *mantón de manila* [Manila shawl] in a burlesque mode.

I also have a very funny anecdote from the shoot. So, the character of Ana is a bohemian, she is an interior designer and comes from a well-to-do family and we needed an appropriate car. I'd asked for a Citroën 2CV, a functional car, and Matas turned up with a horrible, green, lettuce-coloured S.E.A.T., which was all the rage at the time, but was the shabbiest and tackiest car ever. I saw the car on a Saturday and we were filming on Monday and I told him I was not making the film with that car, that it was impossible that a person like Ana would drive such a tacky car. And he said 'nobody's ever stopped the shoot of one of my films' and I answered, 'Funny that. Well, it's going to be me, the novice, I'm going to be the first to do it, because you are going against your own interests and if you want to commit suicide with this film, go ahead, but I won't'. And he ended up agreeing with me, because he'd not actually seen the car either, a friend of his who had a managerial position at S.E.A.T. had sent it over, and when Matas finally saw the car, he did admit it was 'so green, so awful; let's see how you fix it'. So, we spent the shoot covering it up with soil, mud, dust, anything we could get our hands on. We also spent the Sunday before the shoot sewing new covers for the seats, because they were an awful green colour too!

And did the film do well? Why didn't it have more of an impact?
Because its première was badly organised. For some reason, Matas didn't give it the première it deserved and I got really upset with him, because he thought the film wouldn't work.

Another problem was that I wanted to film it in the two languages spoken in Catalonia at the time: the upper classes spoke in Catalan, and the servants in Castilian Spanish, or with a Southern accent, because they were from the South. I wanted the film to reflect that mix of languages and accents. But Matas wouldn't let me, because he said that it couldn't be done in a commercial film, that mishmash of accents and languages didn't work. And then, when he saw they were dubbing films into Catalan at the time, he told me the film had to be dubbed into Catalan. I refused, because not all characters spoke proper Catalan. So, at his own risk, he dubbed it into Catalan with Amparo and they premièred it in Barcelona in this Catalan version.

What a character, Aunt Remedios. Did you also find her through a casting process?
No, somebody recommended her to me, I was introduced to her, I loved her and gave her the role.

Another aspect of the film that stands out is that, while there were no gay characters in the films made in Spain at the time, you introduce them in ¡Vámonos, Bárbara!, Andrés and Curro, the Andalusian character who cannot reveal his sexuality.
Yes, that was based on true events, on stories I knew; there were many gay men from Andalusia in the clubs in Barcelona at the time, so I thought Curro was a very feasible character. It was also an aspect I wanted to show, the fact that in 1977, when I shot the film, Spanish society was starting to open up and modernise. It really was a transitional period.

When your brother came back from Chile with Patricio Guzmán after doing the sound for La batalla de Chile / The Battle of Chile (Parts I–III, 1975–79) you filmed the documentary Después de… / Afterwards… (1983)
We were able to make that film because initially an extreme Right production company that does not exist anymore, Producciones Cinematográficas Ales S.A., put in the money. And that's what's really funny about the story of that film, because we were looking for funding and went to that production company who became interested in the project because Manuel Summers had just released a documentary that did really well at the box office.[9] And when we finished the films and screened them at the production company, the producer invited two policemen to watch them, because apparently they really liked cinema, and I was in shock. But, as it turned out, they really liked them, and said they were very respectful. You never know with cinema. Another film that was fun to make was Lejos de África / Far from Africa (1996), which we filmed in Cuba, although it was really hard to film, because it was extremely hot, there were tornadoes.

Why did you film it in Cuba?
The story takes place in Guinea, and Cuba was the only place where we could film, because it was inconceivable to shoot in Guinea due to its impossible political situation back then. There was no infrastructure whatsoever to be able to film there, and also the old colonial houses have disappeared, so it was not possible to find the right settings. By contrast, we did find the right locations in Cuba, for example, the waterfalls, and the surrounding undergrowth. The only problem was the colour of the sand on the beaches – it is very white in Cuba, but was black in Fernando Poo, as it is a volcanic island.

A striking scene in *Lejos de África* is the one where the two girls are in a Guinean school with a map of Spain behind them, and, in the heat, the teacher is explaining to them what snow is… We guess that was based on your own experience.
Yes, absolutely. I experienced that there. The books we used were Spanish and weren't adapted, so the teachers found themselves having to explain what snow was, because they didn't know what it was in Guinea.

Do you remember the Portuguese Carnation Revolution? What impact did it have in Spain?
It had an impact, as far as that was possible at the time. We had an event in a stadium, and we all attended carrying carnations. But Franco died in his bed…

With regards to what we were talking about earlier, how Franco's death and the Transition were a period in which everything remained to be done, the feeling was that the new Spain was yet to be settled, the idea of everything being in flux, of change…
Yes, of course you could feel Spain was changing, and the fact that Adolfo Suárez was the first President of the Democracy, a man from the democratic centre, who was accepted by all – except by those in the most radical circles – this helped the Transition to go more smoothly. If the socialists had been in government straightaway, it would have probably been more difficult, because there would have been a sector of society who would not have accepted it. Of course, there were violent episodes, which I filmed in 16 mm in *Después de…*

We always play the scene of the woman at the Valle de los Caídos to our students in class…
Yes, filming that woman is one of the most surprising experiences I've had as a film director. She followed us all around the Valle de los Caídos because she wanted to talk on camera, but we could see how unstable she was. And the Valle was full of fascists at that moment, and we thought, if we film her, surrounded by Francoists wearing Falange uniforms, we will get killed. And, almost at sunset, when there was little light left for shooting, a group of young men in Falange uniform approached us to ask why we didn't want to film the woman, that she wanted to be filmed, and that she had been following us around the whole afternoon. When you are in these situations you have to play it very straight and I told them in no uncertain terms that we didn't want to film her because it would make them look very bad, because she was very agitated and she could taint the image of the beautiful act that had just taken place. That's how clear I was with them. But they kept on insisting that the woman from the village also had the right to express herself. So, in the end, we filmed her surrounded by the fascists, on the insistence of those Falangists.

Another moment in the film that is also very tense is when the workers surround the priest and start insulting him.
Yes, it is a particularly dramatic scene and also quite surreal, because the police had just charged against the protesters quite harshly, you can see the square with the police cars and even that the protesters had set part of the buildings on fire. The police had thrown three smoke bombs to disperse them, and, at that moment of maximum tension, there appears a priest out of the blue – and he was half-drunk too, by the way. The police were already leaving and we were putting the camera away, because we assumed the whole thing had finished, when the priest started crying '¡Viva Cristo Rey! ¡Bendito el que viene en el nombre del Señor! ¡Viva España!' [Long live Christ the King! Blessed is he who comes in the name of the Lord! Long live Spain!], shouting out that kind of fiery speech. A group of demonstrators who had just been charged by the police then lunged at the priest. So, we had to intervene in order to stop it from getting worse.

There's a feeling of constant threat in those documentaries.
Yes, there is a saying in the world of cinema that goes 'blend in with the milieu where you are shooting', do not stand out, the camera has to be as invisible as possible because you never know what's going to happen. For instance, we were filming a demonstration on the 1 May from a bridge, and when there was hardly a soul left and we were looking for the camera cover, a group of men – from the political Left – that were around thought we wanted to carry on shooting, and shouted out 'What's up? So you haven't seen anything bad enough in the demonstration? So now you are filming only the very few that are left so it looks like it was a very small protest, aren't you?' And we had to explain to them that, on the contrary, we'd filmed the whole demonstration and that we were just packing away the camera. Then one of them almost hit us because he thought we were there to discredit them. The risks we were taking when we were filming those documentaries were huge; you always needed to be careful, you always needed to ask for consent.

Did you and your brother follow a script, or were you filming as the events were taking place? We ask this because both films are very balanced.
It was all written in advance, we knew exactly which subjects we were dealing with, in order to get a *fresco* of the Transition and its effects on different social sectors. We wanted to talk about women, workers, the birth of political parties, the military etc. That's why the film was made in two parts, because we wanted to deal with several issues, so the social aspect was dealt with in the first film, and the political one in the second. I remember when the coup d'état took place in 1981, we had just deposited the film footage cans at the Ministry of Culture to be classified for release, and I thought, if the coup goes ahead, we'd be better to get those cans back from the Ministry, hence my brother and I were awake all night so we would be ready to go and pick them up.

How do you link the portrait of Spain in *Después de...* to that of the *Cuéntame cómo pasó* / *Tell Me How It Happened* (various authors, 2001–) episode on Carrero Blanco (2005)? It seems to us that the portraits are similar.
That is one of the most important things my brother and I had in mind when we shot *Después de...*: not to manipulate anything. If

we can look at something properly, we film it properly, even if we don't like it. I may not like Charito Reina, but I had to see her as a talented, entertaining young woman, who, at only nineteen years of age, and with no education, was able to get a standing ovation in a Madrid bull ring when she gave a speech to Fuerza Nueva, and that's how it's shown in the documentary.

The same happens with Carrero Blanco, he's known for the terrorist attack, but you show the background: that he was a cultured and talented person.
Of course, Carrero Blanco was a very educated person who had great talent, yet he has always been described as a dark individual, an ogre, a slave to Franco; but he never was, he was never Franco's friend, he never went to his parties, nor on his hunting trips. He was a political technocrat and a military strategist who specialised in maritime strategy. He wrote a book where he identified the weakest points along the northern Spanish coast that would be vulnerable should there be a British invasion during WWII. His son used to say he was a very kind man, serious, devoutly Catholic, humble, intelligent and very professional at his job. In fact, Carrero Blanco was the person who prevented Franco from forming an alliance with Hitler that would have meant Spain entered WWII – his son told me all this in such a beautiful way – because Franco was going to support Hitler, but he backed out due to a strategic report written for him by Carrero Blanco. His son told me how one night his father phoned his mother and told her he wasn't coming home for dinner, and that he would probably be out all night, because he had to write a very important report for the Caudillo. He spent the whole night writing the report about the Spanish coast in which he demonstrated that if Franco joined forces with Hitler, there was an enormous risk that the UK would invade the northern Spanish coast as a result. And that was the report that convinced Franco not to form an alliance with Hitler. In other words, deep down we need to thank this Francoist Admiral, who was very knowledgeable and very sensible, for Spain not taking any part in WWII.

Did you make the episode on Carrero Blanco on your own accord or were you commissioned to do so?
No, it was a commission from Televisión Española [Spanish State Television]. Each week they shot an episode for *Cuéntame*, and

every so often, after a certain number of fictional episodes, they'd make a documentary, because it was cheaper. So I had a female friend working there who told them I had experience in making documentaries, that I could make an interesting documentary for them on the anniversary of the death of Carrero Blanco; and that's how I got commissioned to make it. It was one of the most fascinating pieces of work I've ever made, one of those where you realise that one cannot be unilateral, reality is always more complex than that, and it has to be looked at from all angles. Carrero Blanco was called the 'ogre' and I tried to find out who that ogre was. His assassination was a bit of a stupid murder, since he was not a warmonger, and it was also quite botched.

Notes

1 Square brackets indicate a translator's note. Dates and directors of films are added in round brackets for ease of cross-reference. Endnotes are the author's notes.
2 This was the title of the second (1956) of a trilogy of films about Sissi by Ernst Marischka.
3 Director from 14 March 1959 to 21 October 1962 (Blanco Mallada 2016, 7).
4 *Reina Santa / The Holy Queen* (Gil 1947) and a Western.
5 In another interview she has named this play as Aristophanes's *Lysistrata* (Bermejo 2017, 9), whose subject matter aptly matches Peña's bravery.
6 This year was 1970, after Bartolomé had graduated from Film School. The title of the feature-length version of *Margarita y el lobo* was to be *Qué tal Margarita… pero bien / What's Up Margarita…? Not Bad*, see Chapter 3.
7 See Parrondo Coppel (2001, 35).
8 Note that *¡Vámonos, Bárbara!* was filmed before this abolition.
9 Bartolomé may be referring to *Juguetes rotos / Broken Toys* (1966). There was also a contemporary boom in documentary film at the time; see Chapter 5.

Filmography

Film School (Escuela Oficial de Cinematografía) (director and scriptwriter)

La siesta / The Siesta (1962).
Cruzada del Rosario (1963).
La noche del Dr Valdés / Dr Valdés's Night (1964).
Carmen de Carabanchel / Carmen of Carabanchel (1965).
La brujita / The Little Witch (1966).
Plan Jack Zero Tres / Plan Jack Zero Three (1967).
Margarita y el lobo / Margarita and the Wolf (1969).

Feature films (director/co-director and co-scriptwriter)

¡Vámonos, Bárbara! / Bárbara, Let's Go! (1978).
Production company: Alfredo Matas P. C.
Producer: Alfredo Matas
Screenplay: Sara Azcárate; Cecilia Bartolomé; Concha Romero
Photography: José Luis Alcaine
Music: Carlos Laporta
Art direction: Josep Rosell
Editing: José Luis Matesanz
Sound direction: Francisco Peramos
Production managers: Carlos Bové; Marisol Carnicero
Script and continuity: Eva del Castillo
Costume: Margarita Sastre
Make-up: Ángeles Otal; Carmen Teran
Principal actors: Amparo Soler Leal (Ana); Cristina Álvarez (Bárbara); Julieta Serrano (Paula)

Después de… primera parte: No se os puede dejar solos / Afterwards… Part One: You Can't Be Left Alone and *Después de… segunda parte: Atado y bien atado / Afterwards…: Part Two: All Tied Down* (Documentaries) (co-directed with José Juan Bartolomé) (1983).
Production company: Producciones Cinematográficas Ales S.A.
Producer: Cecilia Bartolomé
Screenplay: Cecilia Bartolomé; José Juan Bartolomé
Photography: José Luis Alcaine
Editing: Javier Morán

Lejos de África / Far from Africa (1996).
Production companies: Cecilia Bartolomé P. C.; Marea Films; Instituto Cubano del Arte e Industrias Cinematográficas; Era Films; Animatógrafo
Producers: Cecilia Bartolomé; António da Cunha Telles; José Luis Arrojo; Adrian Lipp; Santiago Llapur; Camilo Vives
Screenplay: Cecilia Bartolomé; José Juan Bartolomé
Photography: Pancho Alcaine
Music: José Antonio Quintano
Art direction: Satur Idarreta; Rodolfo Montero
Editing: Luis Villar
Sound direction: Luis Castro; Eduardo Fernández, Pelayo Gutiérrez; Ricardo Istueta; Ricardo Pérez; Nacho Royo-Villanova; José Vinader; Jaume Puig
Production manager: Olga María Fernández
Script and continuity: Ileana Pérez; Bea Revilla
Costume: María José Iglesias; Miriam Dueñas; Maribel Pérez; Elbia Rondón, Caridad Sánchez
Make-up: Grisell Cordero; Rubén Izquierdo; Jorge López; Mar Paradela; Magaly Pompa
Principal actors: Alicia Bogo (Susana); Yanelis Bonifacio and Ademilis Hernández (Rita); Isabel Mestres (Marina); Xabier Elorriaga (Gonzalo)

Television (director and co-scriptwriter)

'El comienzo del fin' / 'The Beginning of the End' (broadcast 8 December 2005).
Season 7, Episode 113, *Cuéntame cómo pasó / Tell Me How It Happened*
Scriptwriters: Cecilia Bartolomé; Laura García Pousa

Bibliography

If no first name is given, this is because it does not appear in the article; if initials only are given, this is because full names are not included. Please note Film School Documentation is listed as a separate entry.

A.-J., M. 1978. *¡Vámonos Bárbara!*: una odisea doméstica. *Arriba*, 5 November 1978, n.p.

Aguilar, Flor. 1978. 'Cecilia Bartolomé y *¡Vámonos, Bárbara!*: feminismo no es agredir al hombre'. *Ya*, 22 October 1978, n.p.

Alonso, Carlos. 1997. 'Dos amigas diferentes'. *Diario de Burgos*, 19 February 1997, 58.

Aniorte, Carmen. 2005. '*Cuéntame...* y el día que mataron a Carrero Blanco, esta noche en TVE'. *ABC*, 8 December 2005. https://www.abc.es/espana/abci-cuentame-y-mataron-carrero-blanco-esta-noche-200512080300-1012844360452_noticia.html, accessed 15 February 2023.

Anon. 1977. '"Punto y coma", nueva revista quincenal del arte y la cultura'. *El País*, 12 December 1977. https://elpais.com/diario/1977/12/13/cultura/250815607_850215.html, accessed 14 April 2023.

Anon. 1978a. '*Vámonos Bárbara*: feminismo colectivo'. *Al día*, 7 May 1978, 8.

Anon. 1978b. '*Vámonos Bárbara*: un caso de cine feminista'. *Fotogramas*, 4 November 1978, 46–7.

Anon. 1979. 'Se rueda *Después de Franco*'. *Mundo Diario*, 3 October 1979, n.p.

Anon. 1981. '*Después de...*, Crónica contemporánea'. *La Vanguardia*, 16 October 1981.

Anon. 1983. 'Próximo estreno de *Después de...*, película española "maldita"'. *Efe*, 4 November 1983, n.p.

Anon. 1997a. '*Lejos de África*'. *El correo español*, 6 February 1997, 47.

Anon. 1997b. '*Lejos de África*: está la colonia, pero no el perfume'. *ABC*, 25 January 1997, 75.

Anon. 1997c. 'Me irrita que los jóvenes no conozcan el colonialismo español'. *Ya*, 24 January 1997, 43.

Anon. 1997d. 'Y sin embargo amigas, Lejos de África'. *La crónica 16 de León*, 4 April 1997, 75.

Arranz, Fátima. 2013. 'No, chicas, no son nuestros amigos: La crisis económico-social y el lugar de las mujeres en el cine español'. *Con la A*, 21. https://conlaa.com/wp-content/uploads/2014/09/21_Otra_mirada.pdf, accessed 1 May 2019.

Asensio, Ana. 2022. 'Cecilia Bartolomé. Nunca es tarde para conocer a una audaz pionera del cine español'. *Atmósfera*, 15 February 2022. https://atmosferacine.com/2022/02/15/cecilia-bartolome-nunca-es-tarde-para-conocer-a-una-audaz-pionera-del-cine-espanol/, accessed 17 April 2023.

Aznarez, Malen. 1978. '¡*Vamos* [sic], *Bárbara!*: primera película feminista del cine español'. *Arriba*, 9 July 1978, n.p.

Bartolomé, Cecilia. 1981. '*Después de...*, un espejo que quisieron romper'. *Madrid Abierto*, 1 June 1989, 4.

Bartolomé, Cecilia, José Juan Bartolomé, José Luis Borau and Julia Peña. 1974. *Qué tal Margarita... Pero bien*. Unpublished script, Spanish National Library, Madrid.

Bartolomé, Cecilia and Manuel Gutiérrez Aragón. 1971. *Historia de Sabigoto, su marido Aurelio, sus primos Félix y Liliosa y Jorge, Monje de Belén, Mártires en la Córdoba de Abderraman II según el memorial de San Eulogio por los cronistas franceses Usuardo y Odilardo*. Unpublished script, Library of the Catalan Film Archives, Barcelona.

Bartolomé, Cecilia and Concha Romero. 1976. *La linda Casilda*. Unpublished script, Spanish National Library, Madrid.

Beaney, Rachel. 2021. 'Orphans at Play in *Cría cuervos* (1976) and *Estiu 1993* (2017): Reconsidering the Playspace'. *Forum for Modern Language Studies*, 56(4): 367–88.

Bedoya, Juan. 1982. '*Después de...*, documental sobre la transición Española, ha sido desposeído de las subvenciones estatales'. *El País*, 7 May 1982, n.p.

Beeston, Alix and Stefan Solomon, eds. 2023. *Incomplete: The Feminist Possibilities of Unfinished Film*. Oakland, CA: University of California Press.

Bermejo, Andrea. 2017. 'Cecilia Bartolomé: la directora más feminista (y censurada) de España'. *20 minutos*, 12 June 2017. https://www.20minutos.es/cinemania/noticias/la-directora-mas-feminista-censurada-espana-85102/, accessed 12 April 2023.

Blanco Mallada, Lucio. 2016. 'La enseñanza oficial de cine en España'. *Área Abierta*, 1(2): 3–12.

Blázquez Carretero, Elena. 2014. '*Después de*... Una historia de la Transición'. *El Futuro del Pasado*, 5: 137–50.

Bond Stockton, Kathryn. 2009. *The Queer Child, or Growing Sideways in the Twentieth Century*. Durham, NC: Duke University Press.

Boyero, Carlos. 1983. '*Después de*... mostraba la crisis del gobierno de UCD'. *Madrid Abierto*, 21 November 1983, 9.

Bradbury-Rance, Clara. 2016. 'Desire, Outcast: Locating Queer Adolescence'. In *International Cinema and the Girl*, eds Fiona Handyside and Kate Taylor-Jones. Basingstoke: Palgrave Macmillan, 85–96.

Bruno, Giuliana. 1993. *Streetwalking on a Ruined Map: Cultural Theory and the City Films of Elvira Notari*. Princeton, NJ: Princeton University Press.

Calpena, Ana. 2022. 'Entrevista a Cecilia Bartolomé'. 'Cecilia Bartolomé en la EOC'. *Filmoteca Española*. https://www.culturaydeporte.gob.es/dam/jcr:2853cdcb-22a8-452f-a165-c2d2d711670c/cecilia-bartolom--en-la-eoc---flores-en-la-sombra.pdf, accessed 12 April 2023.

Camí-Vela, María. 2001. *Mujeres detrás de la cámara. Entrevistas con cineastas españolas de la década de los 90*. Madrid: Ocho y medio.

Camporesi, Valeria. 2001. '"El país patas arriba; hasta tú te estás contagiando": *Vámonos, Bárbara* y la Transición democrática'. In *Cecilia Bartolomé. El encanto de la lógica*, eds Josexto Cerdán and Marina Díaz. Madrid: Ocho y medio, 53–62.

Camporesi, Valeria. 2022. 'Ha llegado la hora de Cecilia Bartolomé, Premio Feroz de Honor 2022'. *The Conversation*. https://theconversation.com/ha-llegado-la-hora-de-cecilia-bartolome-premio-feroz-de-honor-2022-174750, accessed 18 April 2023.

Carter, Angela. 1996 [1979]. *Burning Your Boats: Collected Short Stories*. London: Vintage.

Català, Josep María, Josexto Cerdán and Casimiro Torreiro, eds. 2001. *Imagen, memoria y fascinación. Notas sobre el documental en España*. Málaga-Madrid: Festival de cine de Málaga-Ocho y medio.

Cerdán, Josexto. 2013. 'Shorts, Documentary, Experimental Film, and Animation in Transhistorical Perspective'. In *A Companion to Spanish Cinema*, eds Jo Labanyi and Tatjana Pavlović. Malden, MA: Wiley-Blackwell, 531–42.

Cerdán, Josexto and Marina Díaz. 2001. 'Las rozaduras del agua se hacen de manera invisible: pequeña cartografía para transitar por el cine de Cecilia Bartolomé'. In *Cecilia Bartolomé. El encanto de la lógica*, eds Josetxo Cerdán and Marina Díaz. Madrid: Ocho y medio, 13–22.

Cerdán, Josexto and Marina Díaz, eds. 2001. *Cecilia Bartolomé. El encanto de la lógica*. Madrid: Ocho y medio.
Cixous, Hélène. 1975. 'Le rire de la Méduse'. *L'Arc*, 39–54.
Cleries, Jaume. 1978. 'Es un film sobre tías, sin caer en el panfleto'. *Mundo Diario*, 9 April 1978, n.p.
Contreras de la Llave, Natalia. 2008. 'Entrevista. Cecilia Bartolomé. La linterna de la memoria'. *Quaderns de Cine*, 3(4): 37–43.
Corbalán, Ana. 2009. 'Reconstrucción del pasado histórico: nostalgia reflexiva en *Cuéntame cómo pasó*'. *Journal of Spanish Cultural Studies*, 10(3): 341–57.
Crespo, Pedro. 1978. '¡*Vámonos Bárbara!* de Cecilia Bartolomé'. *ABC*, 27 October 1978, n.p.
Crespo, Pedro. 1983. '*Después de...*, de Cecilia y José Bartolomé'. *ABC*, 10 November 1978, 72.
Cueto Asín, Elena. 2009. 'Memorias de progreso y violencia: la Guerra Civil en *Cuéntame cóm pasó*'. In *Historias de la pequeña pantalla. Representaciones históricas en al televisión de la España democrática*, eds Francisca López, Elena Cueto Asín and David R. George. Madrid-Frankfurt: Iberoamericana-Vervuert, 137–56.
Daix, Pierre, Georges Boudaille, with Joan Rosselet. 1967. *Picasso, The Blue and Rose Periods: A Catalogue Raisonné of the Paintings, 1900–1906*, trans. Phoebe Pool. Greenwich, CT: New York Graphic Society.
Devesa, Dolores and Alicia Potes. 1999. *Seis mujeres guionistas: contar historias, crear imágenes*. Málaga: Ayuntamiento de Málaga.
Díez Puertas, Emeterio. 2012. *Golpe a la Transición. El secuestro de* El crimen de Cuenca. Barcelona: Editorial Laertes.
Faulkner, Sally. 2004. *Literary Adaptations in Spanish Cinema*. Woodbridge: Támesis-Boydell & Brewer.
Faulkner, Sally. 2006. *A Cinema of Contradiction: Spanish Film in the 1960s*. Edinburgh: Edinburgh University Press.
Faulkner, Sally. 2013. *A History of Spanish Film: Cinema and Society, 1910–2010*. New York: Bloomsbury Academic.
Faulkner, Sally. 2015. 'Cinephilia and the Unrepresentable in Miguel Gomes's *Tabu* (2012)'. *Bulletin of Spanish Studies*, 92(3): 341–60.
Faulkner, Sally. 2016. 'Introduction. Approaching the Middlebrow: Audience; Text; Institution'. In *Middlebrow Cinema*, ed. Sally Faulkner. London: Routledge, 1–12.
Faulkner, Sally. 2017. 'Delayed Cinema and Feminist Discourse in *El mundo sigue* (1963/1965/2015)'. *Bulletin of Hispanic Studies*, 94(8): 831–45.
Faulkner, Sally. 2022a. 'Spain's "First Feminist Film": Feminism and Francoism, *Margarita and the Wolf* (Cecilia Bartolomé, 1969)'. *Feminist Media Studies*, 1–16.

Faulkner, Sally. 2022b. *Un cine contradictorio. Ocho filmes españoles de la década de los 1960*. Revised, extended and translated version of *A Cinema of Contradiction*, trad. Manuel Cuesta. Iberoamericana-Vervuert: Madrid-Frankfurt.

Faulkner, Sally and Núria Triana Toribio. Forthcoming. *Entrevistas con las mujeres del cine y de la televisión españoles, 1970–1980*.

Faulkner, Sally, Hilary Owen and Núria Triana Toribio. 2021. 'The Project: Invisibles e insumisas/invisíveis e insubmissas: Leading Women in Portuguese and Spanish Cinema and Televisión,1970–1980'. https://leadingwomenproject.com/the-project/, accessed 14 July 2022.

Fenwick, James. 2021. *Unproduction Studies and the American Film Industry*. London: Routledge.

Fenwick, James, Kieran Foster and David Eldridge, eds. 2021. *Shadow Cinema. The Historical and Production Contexts of Unmade Films*. New York: Bloomsbury Academic.

Fernández Colorado, Luis. 2001. 'Los expositores del imperio'. In *Imagen, memoria y fascinación. Notas sobre el documental en España*, eds Josep Maria Català, Josexto Cerdán and Casimiro Torreiro. Málaga: Festival de cine de Málaga, 65–74.

Fernández Soldevilla, Gaizka and Pablo García Varela. 2022. 'El asesinato de Carrero Blanco. Historia, teorías conspirativas y ficción'. *Araucaria. Revista Iberoamericana de Filosofía, Política, Humanidades y Relaciones Internacionales*, 24(50): 61–83.

Fernández-Santos, Ángel. 1983. '*Después de...*, obra "maldita" del cine de la transición, se estrena con tres años de retraso'. *El País*, 3 November 1983, n.p.

Field, Allyson Nadia. 2022a. 'Editor's Introduction: Sites of Speculative Encounter'. *Feminist Media Histories*, 8(2): 1–13.

Field, Allyson Nadia. 2022b. 'Editor's Introduction: Acts of Speculation'. *Feminist Media Histories*, 8(3): 1–7.

Fiestas, Jorge. 1978. 'Lo prometido es deuda'. *Fotogramas*, November 1978, n.p.

Flecha, Consuelo. 1991. 'Etapas y tendencias de la presencia de la muyer en la Universidad española'. In *L'Université en Espagne et en Amérique Latine du Moyen Age à nos Jours I: Structures et acteurs*, eds Jean-René Aymes, Ève-Marie Fell and Jean-Louis Guerena. Tours: Presses universitaires François-Rabelais, 319–37. https://books.openedition.org/pufr/5876#text, accessed 12 April 2023.

French, Lisa. 2018. 'Women in the Director's Chair: The "Female Gaze" in Documentary Film'. In *Female Authorship and the Documentary Image: Theory, Practice and Aesthetics*, eds Boel Ulfsdotter and Anna Backman Rogers. Edinburgh: Edinburgh University Press, 9–21.

Fuentes, Gumer. 1976. 'La mujer en el cine español: de la represión al destape. La española cuando besa'. *Vindicación Feminista*, 6: 60.
Fuentes, Gumer. 1977a. 'La mujer en el cine español: la caída del sostén y el alzamiento del tampax'. *Vindicación Feminista*, 11: 62.
Fuentes, Gumer. 1977b. 'Mujeres detrás de la cámara'. *Vindicación Feminista*, 15: 14–15.
Fuentes, Gumer. 1978. 'Review of ¡*Vámonos, Bárbara!*'. *Vindicación Feminista*, 23: 14.
Fuertes, Sol. 1978. 'Cecilia Bartolomé: Tengo obsesión por la lógica'. *Diario 16*, 31 October 1978, n.p.
Galán, Diego. 1978. 'Review of ¡*Vámonos, Bárbara!*'. *Triunfo*, 4 November 1978, n.p.
Galán, Diego. 1981. 'Tres años ha durado el rodaje de *Después de...*, una película sobre la España postfranquista'. *El País*, 23 May 1981, n.p.
Galán, Diego. 1983. 'Nuestra reciente historia'. *El País*, 7 November 1983, n.p.
Galán, Diego. 2016. 'Cecilia Bartolomé: cineasta con coraje'. *El País*. https://elpais.com/cultura/2016/01/17/actualidad/1453048289_887821.html, accessed 27 August 2021.
Galindo, Carlos. 1979. 'Cecilia Bartolomé: película-testimonio sobre el cambio sociológico español'. *ABC*, 30 September 1979, n.p.
García, Víctor. 2016. 'Entrevista a Laura Pousa'. *Espectáculos*, 20 August 2016. https://www.meer.com/es/18814-entrevista-a-laura-pousa, accessed 15 February 2023.
García Delgado, José Luis. 1995. 'La economía española durante el franquismo'. *Revista Temas*, 12: 27–32.
García López, Sonia. 2020. '¿Por qué duele el amor? Mujeres en la Escuela Oficial de Cinematografía'. #Doréencasa, Filmoteca Española. https://www.culturaydeporte.gob.es/dam/jcr:146a1a5b-a275-4708-a11a-911dc95ced60/el-dor--en-casa---por-qu--duele-el-amor.pdf, accessed 12 April 2023.
García López, Sonia. 2021. 'Miradas invisibles: mujeres en la Escuela Oficial de Cinematografía (1947–1976)'. *Journal of Spanish Cultural Studies*, 22(3): 1–19.
García López, Sonia. 2022. 'Caza de brujas en las aulas: La censura española en la Escuela Oficial de Cinematografía'. *Studies in Spanish and Latin American Cinemas*, 19(1): 91–108.
García López, Sonia. 2023. 'Margarita, the Big Bad Wolf, and the Film Censor: Film, Feminism, and Dictatorial Repression in Spain'. *Feminist Media Studies*, 1–16.
García Morales, Adelaida. 1997. 'La mirada ingenua de dos niñas'. *El País*, 8 March 1997, 2.

García Pousa, Laura. 2011. 'Proyecciones *vintage*: *Mad Men* y *Cuéntame cómo pasó*'. *Secuencias*, 33: 52–69.

García Sahagún, Marta. 2016. 'La música como reivindicación de género en "Margarita y el lobo" de Cecilia Bartolomé'. *Área Abierta*, 16(2): 71–87.

Gómez Alonso, Rafael. 2001. 'Filmografía de Cecilia Bartolomé'. In *Cecilia Bartolomé. El encanto de la lógica*, eds Josexto Cerdán and Marina Díaz. Madrid: Ocho y medio, 43–8.

Gorina, Alejandro. 1978. '*Anem-nos-en, Bárbara!*'. *Guía de ocio*, 17 April 1978, n.p.

Grandío, Mar. 2008. 'La recepción de series familiares contemporáneas: *Los Serrano* y *Cuéntame cómo pasó*'. In *Series de televisión. El caso de Médico de familia, Cuéntame cómo pasó y Los Serrano*, ed. Mercedes Medina. Madrid: Ediciones Internacionales Universitarias, 133–57.

Granell Toledo, Mónica. 2020. 'París 68-Barcelona 77. Del mayo francés a la contracultura española: la evolución de la revista *Ajoblanco* en la Transición'. *Pasado y Memoria. Revista de Historia Contemporánea*, 21: 225–48.

Guarner, José Luis. 1978. 'Review of *¡Vámonos, Bárbara! / Anem-nos-en, Bárbara!*'. *Catalunya Express*, 8 April 1978, n.p.

Guillamón Carrasco, Silvia. 2015. 'Los discursos fílmicos de las cineastas en España'. *Dossiers Feministes*, 20: 285–301.

Gutiérrez, Irene. 2021. 'Irene Gutiérrez presenta "Después de…" de Cecilia y José Juan Bartolomé'. 'Espacio femenino. Pioneras' Instituto Cervantes programme. https://vimeo.com/521016203, accessed 9 February 2023.

Guzmán. 1997. 'Versión original. Dos islas en el cine español. Cecilia Bartolomé estrena *Lejos de África* y Fernando León *Familia*'. *ABC*, 23 January 1997, n.p.

Hains, Rebecca C. 2008. 'The Origins of the Girl Hero: Shirley Temple, Child Star and Commodity'. *Girlhood Studies: An Interdisciplinary Journal*, 1(1): 60–80.

Handyside, Fiona and Kate Taylor-Jones. 2016a. 'Introduction'. In *International Cinema and the Girl: Local Issues, Transnational Contexts*, eds Fiona Handyside and Kate Taylor-Jones. Basingstoke: Palgrave Macmillan, 1–18.

Handyside, Fiona and Kate Taylor-Jones, eds. 2016b. *International Cinema and the Girl: Local Issues, Transnational Contexts*. Basingstoke: Palgrave Macmillan.

Hernández Les, Juan. 1978. 'Review of *¡Vámonos, Bárbara!*'. *El imparcial*, 5 November 1978, 27.

Hernández Les, Juan and Miguel Gato. 1978. *El cine de autor en España*. Madrid: Miguel Castellote.

Hogan, Erin. 2018. *The Two cines con niño: Genre and The Child Protagonist in over Fifty Years of Spanish Film (1955–2010)*. Edinburgh: Edinburgh University Press.

Holmes, Diane. 1996. *French Women's Writing 1948–1994*. London: Athlone.

Hutton, Margaret-Anne. 1998. *Countering the Culture: The Novels of Christiane Rochefort*. Exeter: Exeter University Press.

Ibáñez, Juan Carlos. 2001. 'Sobre adioses, rupturas y pactos cotidianos: sociedad e identidad en el otro cine de Cecilia Bartolomé'. In *Cecilia Bartolomé. El encanto de la lógica*, eds Josexto Cerdán and Marina Díaz. Madrid: Ocho y medio, 23–32.

Iglesias, Pablo. 2020. 'Pablo Iglesias entrevista a la directora de cine Cecilia Bartolomé'. https://www.youtube.com/watch?v=2900s770-ig, accessed 24 August 2021.

Jenkins, Henry. 2006. *Convergence Culture: Where Old and New Media Collide*. New York: New York University Press.

Kinder, Marsha. 1983. 'The Children of Franco in the New Spanish Cinema'. *Quarterly Review of Film Studies*, 8(2): 57–76.

Kuhn, Annette. 1994. *Women's Pictures: Feminism and Cinema*. London: Verso.

Kunze, Peter. 2017. 'Herding Cats, or, The Possibilities of Unproduction Studies'. *The Velvet Light Trap*, 80: 18–30.

Labanyi, Jo. 2000. 'Feminizing the Nation: Women, Subordination, and Subversion in Post-Civil War Spanish Cinema'. In *Heroines with Heroes: Reconstructing Female and National Identities in European Cinema 1945–51*, ed. Ulrike Sieglohr. London: Cassell, 163–82.

Labanyi, Jo. 2013. '"Chicas raras": The Television Scripts of Carmen Martín Gaite'. In *A New Gaze: Women Creators of Film and Television in Democratic Spain*, ed. Concepción Cascajosa Virino. Cambridge: Cambridge Scholars Publishing, 3–14.

Ladrón de Guevera, Eduardo. 2003. *Cuéntame cómo pasó. Querido maestro*, ed. Emeterio Diez, Madrid: Fundamentos-Universidad Camilo José Cela.

Ledesma, Eduardo. 2014. 'Helena Lumbreras's *Field for Men* (1973): Midway between Latin American Third Cinema and the Barcelona School'. *Studies in Spanish and Latin American Cinemas*, 11(2): 271–88.

Llanos Martínez, Héctor. 2023. 'RTVE confirma el final definitivo de *Cuéntame cómo pasó*: así será su última temporada'. *El País*, 16 February 2023, n.p.

Llopart, Salvador. 2005. 'Dictadura en la picota'. *La Vanguardia*, 8 December 2005, n.p.

Longhurst, Alex. 1999. 'Class'. In *Encyclopaedia of Contemporary Spanish Culture*, ed. Eamonn Rodgers. London: Routledge, 113–14.
López, Silvia. 2022. 'Quién es Cecilia Bartolomé, la directora histórica homenajeada en los Premios Feroz 2022'. *Vogue Spain*, 30 January 2022. https://www.vogue.es/celebrities/articulos/cecilia-bartolome-directora-cine-homenajeada-premios-feroz-2022, accessed 18 April 2023.
Loxham, Abi. 2015. '*Cuéntame cómo pasó/Tell Me How It Was*: Narratives of Memory and Television Drama in Contemporary Spain'. *European Journal of Cultural Studies*, 18(6): 709–23.
Marinero, F. 1978. '¡*Vámonos, Bárbara!* de Cecilia Bartolomé: trampas cotidianas'. *Diario 16*, 25 October 1978.
Martín, Annabel. 2005. *La gramática de la felicidad: Relecturas franquistas y posmodernas del melodrama*. Madrid: Libertarias/Prodhufi.
Martínez, Luis. 2020. 'Cecilia Bartolomé: "Siempre vi normal lo que para los demás era anatema"'. *El mundo*. https://www.elmundo.es/papel/lideres/2020/03/09/5e629628fdddffeeab8b4614.html, accessed 27 August 2021.
Martínez Pérez, Natalia, and Concha Gómez. 2022. 'Ellas escriben: mujeres guionistas en el cine y la televisión'. In *Brecha de género en el audiovisual español*, ed. Concha Gómez. Valencia: Tirant Humanidades, 154–68.
Martín Gaite, Carmen. 1993 [1987]. *Desde la ventana: Enfoque femenino de la literatura española*. Madrid: Espasa Calpe.
Martin-Márquez, Susan. 1999. *Feminist Discourse and Spanish Cinema: Sight Unseen*. Oxford: Oxford University Press.
Martin-Márquez, Susan. 2008. *Disorientations: Spanish Colonialism in Africa and the Performance of Identity*. New Haven, CT: Yale University Press.
Martín Morán, Ana. 2001. '*Lejos de África*: Recuerdos de una vida ajena'. In *Cecilia Bartolomé. El encanto de la lógica*, eds Josetxo Cerdán and Marina Díaz. Madrid: Ocho y medio, 93–101.
Masó, Ángeles. 1978a. 'Anem-nos-en, Bárbara'. *La Vanguardia Española*, 8 April 1978, n.p.
Masó, Ángeles. 1978b. 'Con Cecilia Bartolomé, un cine feminista para mayorías'. *La Vanguardia Española*, 12 April 1978, n.p.
May, Delphi. Forthcoming. *Hybrid Acts: Representations of (Spanish-) Chineseness in Spanish Film*. Oxford: Legenda.
McLane, Betsy A. 2023. *A New History of Documentary Film*. New York: Bloomsbury Academic.
Minguet, Joan M. 2001. 'Tras el Después (El cine, la memoria, el compromiso)'. In *Cecilia Bartolomé. El encanto de la lógica*, eds Josetxo Cerdán and Marina Díaz. Madrid: Ocho y medio, 73–80.

Missero, Dalila. 2022. *Women, Feminism and Italian Cinema: Archives from a Film Culture*. Edinburgh: Edinburgh University Press.
Mitchell, Claudia, Jacqueline Reid-Walsh and Jackie Kirt. 2008. 'Editorial'. *Girlhood Studies: An Interdisciplinary Journal*, 1(1): vii–xv.
Molina, Josefina. 2000. *Sentada en un rincón*. Valladolid: Semana Internacional de Cine de Valladolid.
Montejano, Fernando. 1979. '*Después de...*, un film difícil de Cecilia Bartolomé'. *El Alcázar*, 29 August 1979, n.p.
Mulvey, Laura. 1975. 'Visual Pleasure and Narrative Cinema'. *Screen* 16(3): 6–18. 9
Nair, Parvati. 2021a. 'Parvati Nair presenta "Después de...: Atado y bien atado" de Cecilia y José Juan Bartolomé'. ' Espacio femenino. Pioneras' Instituto Cervantes programme. https://vimeo.com/528735975, accessed 9 February 2023.
Nair, Parvati, 2021b. 'Parvati Nair presenta "Después de...: No se os puede dejar solos" de Cecilia y José Juan Bartolomé'. 'Espacio femenino. Pioneras' Instituto Cervantes programme. https://vimeo.com/525441973, accessed 9 February 2023.
North, Dan. 2008. 'Finishing the Unfinished'. In *Sights Unseen: Unfinished British Films*, ed. Dan North. Cambridge: Cambridge Scholars Publishing, 1–18.
O'Leary, Catherine and Alison Ribeiro de Menezes. 2002. *A Companion to Carmen Martín Gaite*. Woodbridge: Támesis.
Odriozola, Lourdes. 2020. 'Mi relación con la E.O.C.'. *Filmoteca Española*. https://www.culturaydeporte.gob.es/dam/jcr:146a1a5b-a275-4708-a11a-911dc95ced60/el-dor-en-casa-por-qu-duele-el-amor.pdf, accessed 4 January 2022.
Ordóñez, Marcos. 1978. 'Cecilia Bartolomé: ser tía en el cine español'. *Fotogramas*, 12 May 1978, 12.
Ortega, María Luisa. 2001. 'Memorias para una África olvidada, o el discurso colonial imposible'. In *Cecilia Bartolomé. El encanto de la lógica*, eds Josetxo Cerdán and Marina Díaz. Madrid: Ocho y medio, 81–92.
Padura, Monty. 1978. 'Primera película catalana y feminista'. *Catalunya Express*. 6 April 1978, 18.
Palacio, Manuel. 2012. *La televisión durante la Transición española*. Madrid: Cátedra.
Parra, Pilar. 1983. 'Cecilia Bartolomé: "El ministerio de Cultura prohibió terminantemente que se estrenase"'. *Diario 16*, 7 November 1983, n.p.
Parrondo Coppel, Eva. 2001. '*¡Vámonos, Bárbara!*, hacia la libertad'. In *Cecilia Bartolomé. El encanto de la lógica*, eds Josetxo Cerdán and Marina Díaz. Madrid: Ocho y medio, 33–41.

Payne, Stanley. 2008. *Franco and Hitler: Spain, Germany and WWII*. New Haven, CT: Yale University Press.

Pérez, Jorge. 2008. 'Women Behind the Wheel: Gendering the Transition to Democracy in *Vámonos, Bárbara*'. *Revista de Estudios Hispánicos*, 42: 215–36.

Pérez, Jorge. 2013. 'Directoras españolas al volante: la "road movie" como viaje de concienciación ética'. In *Gynocine. Teoría de género, filmología y praxis cinematográfica*, ed. Barbara Zecchi. Amherst, MA: University of Massachusetts, 129–60.

Pérez de Albéniz. 2005. 'El Almirante y la folclórica'. https://www.elmundo.es/elmundo/2005/12/09/descodificador/1134085150.html, accessed 23 February 2023. [See also independent blog: http://www.eldescodificador.com.]

Pérez Guevara, José Antonio. 2018. 'Entrevista a Cecilia Bartolomé'. https://242peliculasdespues.com/2018/08/14/entrevista-a-cecilia-bartolome/, accessed 11 April 2023.

Pousa, Laura. 2017. 'Outra abordagem à série espanhola *Cuéntame cómo pasó*: os episódios especias'. *Matrizes*, 11(2): 1–19. https://www.revistas.usp.br/matrizes/article/view/122895/133232, accessed 17 February 2023.

Prieto, Carlos. 2018. 'Entrevista a Cecilia Bartolomé. La inesperada lección sobre Vox de la señora más franquista de España'. *El Confidencial*, 20 December 2018. https://elconfidencial.com/cultura/2018-12-20/franquismo-documental-transicion-vox-video_1711730/, accessed 6 February 2023.

Puebla Martínez, Belén. 2012. 'El documental en la Transición Española, testimonio de su tiempo. Estudio de caso de *Después de… (No se os puede dejar solos* y *Atado y bien atado)*'. *Revista de Cibercomunicación*, 067: 1–3.

Resina, Joan Ramón. 2010. 'The Weight of Memory and the Lightness of Oblivion: The Dead of the Spanish Civil War'. In *Unearthing Franco's Legacy: Mass Graves and the Recovery of Historical Memory in Spain*, eds Carlos Jérez Ferrán and Samuel Amago. Notre Dame, IN: University of Notre Dame Press, 221–42.

Riambau, Esteve. 2001. 'Vivir el presente, recuperar el pasado: el cine documental durante la transición (1973–1978)'. In *Imagen, memoria y fascinación. Notas sobre el documental en España*, eds Josep Maria Català, Josexto Cerdán and Casimiro Torreiro. Málaga : Festival de cine de Málaga, 125–38.

Ripoll-Freixes, Enric. 1978. 'Dones… feliçment'. *Avui*, 8 April 1978, 22.

Roca-Sastre, E. 1978. 'Review of *Anem-nos-en, Bárbara!*'. *Mundo Diario*, 13 April 1978.

Rochefort, Christiane. 1963. *Les Stances à Sophie*. Paris: Éditions Bernard Grasset.
Rodríguez Merchán, Eduardo. 2007. 'La enseñanza del cine en España: perspectiva histórica y panorama actual'. *Comunicar*, 29: 13–20.
Rosentone, Robert A. 1995. *Visions of the Past: The Challenge of Film to Our Idea of History*. Cambridge, MA: Harvard University Press.
Ruiz de Villalobos, Miguel Fernando. 1978. 'Un acceptable debut de Cecilia Bartolomé'. *Diario de Barcelona*, 9 April 1978, n.p.
Sánchez Biosca, Vicente. 2013. 'NO-DO: The Francoist Newsreel'. In *A Companion to Spanish Cinema*, eds Jo Labanyi and Tatjana Pavlović. Malden, MA: Wiley-Blackwell, 526–31.
Sánchez González, Darío. 2013. 'El documental. Cecilia Bartolomé y los lobos de la Transición'. In *Gynocine: teoría de género, filmografía y praxis cinematográfica*, ed. Barbara Zecchi. Amherst, MA: University of Massachusetts, 187–200.
Santa Eulalia, Mary G. 1978a. 'Cecilia Bartolomé, sexta realizadora española'. *La hoja del lunes*, 1 May 1978, n.p.
Santa Eulalia, Mary G. 1978b. 'Review of ¡*Vámonos, Bárbara!*'. *Ya*, 9 June 1978, 11.
Santaolalla, Isabel. 2005. *Los 'Otros'. Etnicidad y 'raza' en el cine español contemporáneo*. Zaragoza: Prensas Universitarias de Zaragoza.
Santiago, R. 'Review of ¡*Vámonos, Bárbara!*'. *Punto y Coma*, 9 May 1978, n.p.
Scholz, Annette. 2018. 'Mujeres invisibles del cine español'. In *Cineastas emergentes: mujeres en el cine del siglo XXI*, eds Annette Scholz and Marta Álvarez. Madrid-Frankfurt: Iberoamericana-Vervuert, 45–68.
Selva Masoliver, Marta and Anna Solà Arguimbau. 1985–86. 'Los personajes heroicos femeninos en le cine histórico español (1941–1961)'. Unpublished manuscript, Drac Màgic.
Selva i Masoliver, Marta. 2001. 'La palabra necesaria: a propósito de *Después de* (I y II parte)'. In *Imagen, memoria y fascinación. Notas sobre el documental en España*, eds Josep Maria Català, Josexto Cerdán and Casimiro Torreiro. Málaga: Festival de cine de Málaga, 271–6.
Sevillano Canicio, Víctor. 2010. 'Del documental del recuerdo a la recreación ficcional de la intrahistoria de los años sesenta: las series *Los años vividos* y *Cuéntame cómo pasó* de TVE en contraste'. In *Docuficción. Enlaces entre ficción y no-ficción en la cultura española actual*, eds Christian Con Tschilshke and Dagmar Schmelzer. Madrid-Frankfurt: Iberoamericana-Vervuert, 339–54.
Shohat, Ella and Robert Stam. 1994. *Unthinking Eurocentrism: Multiculturalism and the Media*. London: Routledge.
Smith, Paul Julian. 2003. *Contemporary Spanish Culture: TV, Fashion, Art and Film*. Cambridge: Polity.

Smith, Paul Julian. 2006. *Television in Spain: From Franco to Almodóvar*. Woodbridge: Támesis-Boydell & Brewer.
Tejada, Isabel. 2020. 'Fuera del canon: Las artistas pop en la Colección'. Entrevista a Cecilia Bartolomé, Museo Nacional Centro de Arte Reina Sofía, 4 February 2020. https://www.youtube.com/watch?v=PExRGwT9djE, accessed 27 August 2021.
Thomas, Sarah. 2019. *Inhabiting the In-Between: Childhood and Cinema in Spain's Long Transition*. Toronto, ON: Toronto University Press.
Torres, Augusto. 1992. *Conversaciones con Manuel Gutiérrez Aragón*. Madrid: Editorial Fundamentos.
Torres, Augusto. 1997. 'Entrañable evocación'. *El País*, 31 January 1997, 40.
Torres, Augusto. 2004. *Directores españoles malditos*. Madrid: Huelga Fierro Editores.
Triana Toribio, Núria. 2003. *Spanish National Cinema*. London: Routledge.
Triana Toribio, Núria. 2013. 'La igualdad/ En torno a la paridad y la visibilidad'. In *Gynocine. Teoría de género, filmología y praxis cinematográfica*, ed. Barbara Zecchi. Amherst, MA: University of Massachusetts, 129–60.
Tubau, Iván. 1989. 'Informe: Cine catalán y cine de Barcelona'. *El Ciervo*, 38(459): 28–31.
Tuchman, Barbara. 1978. *The Distant Mirror: The Calamitous Fourteenth Century*. New York: Alfred A. Knopf.
Vaquero, Isabel. 1983. '*Después de...*, en las carteleras'. Pueblo, 10 November 1983, n.p.
Vargas, Isabel. 2019. 'A día de hoy, todavía resulta exótico ver a una tía al mando de un equipo de cine'. *Granada Hoy*, 3 April 2019. https://www.granadahoy.com/ocio/Entrevista-Cecilia-Bartolome-Festival-Jovenes-Realizadores-Granada-cine-feminista_0_1342366333.html, accessed 12 April 2023.
Vernon, Kathleen. 2002. 'Screening Room: Spanish Women Filmmakers View the Transition'. In *Women's Narrative and Film in Twentieth Century Spain*, eds Orfelia Ferrán and Kathleen Glenn. New York: Routledge, 95–113.
Vernon, Kathleen. 2011. 'Cine de mujeres en la Transición: la trilogía "feminista" de Cecilia Bartolomé, Pilar Miró y Josefina Molina'. In *El cine y la transición política en España (1975–1982)*, ed. Manuel Palacio. Madrid: Biblioteca Nueva, 145–58.
Viader, Jordi. 1978. '*Anem-nos-en, Bárbara*'. *La Prensa*, 11 April 1978, n.p.
Whittaker, Tom and Sarah Wright. 2017. 'Locating the Voice in Film: An Introduction'. In *Locating the Voice in Film: Critical Approaches and*

Global Practices, eds Tom Whittaker and Sarah Wright. Oxford: Oxford University Press.

Wright, Sarah. 2013. *The Child in Spanish Cinema*. Manchester: Manchester University Press.

Yoldi, Pili. 2004. 'C. Bartolomé: "Me levanta la moral seguir estando en la lista de los incorrectos"'. Interview with Cecilia Bartolomé, *Diario del festival*, 25 September 2004, 17. https://www.sansebastianfestival.com/admin_img/diarios/archivos/diario_53.pdf, accessed 5 January 2022.

Zecchi, Barbara. 2004. 'Mujer y cine: Estudio panorámico de éxitos y paradojas'. In *La mujer en la España actual. ¿Evolución o involución?*, eds Jacqueline Cruz and Barbara Zecchi. Barcelona: Icaria, 315–50.

Zecchi, Barbara. 2013. 'La comedia como estrategio feminista: la recuperación de la risa'. In *Gynocine: teoría de género, filmografía y praxis cinematográfica*, ed. Barbara Zecchi. Amherst, MA: University of Massachusetts, 161–86.

Zecchi, Barbara. 2014a. *Desenfocadas: cineastas españolas y discursos de género*. Barcelona: Icaria.

Zecchi, Barbara. 2014b. *La pantalla sexuada*. Madrid: Cátedra.

Zecchi, Barbara, ed. 2013. *Gynocine: teoría de género, filmografía y praxis cinematográfica*. Amherst, MA: University of Massachusetts.

Zurián, Francisco, ed. 2015. *Construyendo una mirada propia: mujeres directoras en el cine español. De los orígenes al año 2000*. Madrid: Síntesis.

Zurián, Francisco, ed. 2017. *Miradas de mujer: cineastas españolas para el siglo XXI*. Madrid: Fundamentos.

Film School documentation, Cecilia Bartolomé Pina

Anon. n.d. '"Juegos de tarde" de Cecilia M. Bartolomé Pina'.
Anon. 1968a. 'Margarita y el lobo feroz', PRA/9/4.
Anon. 1968b. 'Escuela Oficial de Cinematografía Curso: 1968–69', PRA/9/4.
Anon. 1968c. Informe, December 1968, PRA/9/4.
Anon. 1969a. Reunión preparatoria, 13 January 1969, PRA/9/4.
Anon. 1969b. Nota para el Jefe de Estudios, 30 January 1969, PRA/9/4.
Baena, Juan Julio. 1968a. Letter to Cecilia Bartolomé, 7 December 1968, PRA/9/4.
Anon. 1968b. Letter to Cecilia Bartolomé, 13 December 1968, PRA/9/4.
Anon. 1968c. Letter to Cecilia Bartolomé, 26 December 1968, PRA/9/4.
Bartolomé, Cecilia. 1964. 'Parte de Incidencias', 10 March 1964, PRA/2/1(6/9).

Bartolomé, Cecilia. 1965a. 'Parte de Incidencias del rodaje', n.d., PRA/16/2.
Bartolomé, Cecilia. 1965b. Letter to EOC Jefe de Estudios I, 30 October 1965, PRA/16/2(5/6).
Bartolomé, Cecilia. 1965c. Letter to EOC Jefe de Estudios II, 30 October 1965, PRA/16/2(5/6).
Bartolomé, Cecilia. 1968, Letter to EOC Director, 18 November 1968, 103/30/47.
Bartolomé, Cecilia. 1969a. Letter to EOC Director, 17 February 1969, 103/30/47.
Bartolomé, Cecilia. 1969b. Letter to EOC Director, 5 March 1969, 103/30/47.
Cotoz, Almudena, et al. 2005. 'Parte de incidencias', 22 March 1965, PRA/16/2.
Cunillés, José María. 1969. Letter to EOC Director, 28 January 1969, PRA/9/4.
Daza de Castillo, Juan José. 1964a. 'Parte de Incidencias', 2 March 1964, PRA/2/1(6/9).
Daza de Castillo, Juan José. 1964b. 'Parte de Incidencias', 4 March 1964, PRA/2/1(6/9).
Daza de Castillo, Juan José. 1964c. 'Parte de Incidencias', 6 March 1964, PRA/2/1(6/9).
Diamante, Julio. 1968. 'Ana y el lobo feroz', PRA/9/4.
Flaquer, Alfonso. 1964. Letter to Jefe de Estudios, 11 May 1964, PRA/2/1(6/9).
García Berlanga, Luis, Juan Miguel Lamet and Carlos Saura. 1964. EOC Informe, PRA/2/1.
García Sánchez, José Luis. 1968. 'Ana y el lobo feroz', PRA/9/4.
Jacoste, José Gabriel and José María Cunillés. 1969. Letter to EOC Director, 28 January 1969, PRA/9/4.
Labybam [approximate transcription; name partly illegible]. n.d. Letter, PRA/16/2.
Ochoa, Alberto. 1969. Letter to Inspector de Prácticas, 20 January 1969, PRA/9/4.
Proharam, Miguel Ángel Martín. 1968. 'Ana y el lobo feroz', PRA/9/4.

Index

Note: 'n' indicates chapter endnotes.

abortion 16–17, 30–1, 33–4, 106n13, 128, 133
adolescence 93–4, 101–2
adultery themes 49–50, 70, 86–7
aesthetic of the everyday 138–9
Alberdi, Cristina 128
Alcaine, José Luis 43
Alcántara family (characters) 174–5, 178, 180, 183, 189–90
Aleixandre, Margarita 38, 54, 57–8n13
Alejandro (character) 51, 67–8
Alice Doesn't Live Here Anymore (Scorsese 1974) 6, 76–7, 102, 103–4n1, 107n25
Almodóvar, Pedro 71, 168, 204n2
Alonso, Carlos 170
Álvarez, Cristina 80, 90–1, 93, 96, 98, 159, 213–14
Ana (character) 77–80, 85–6, 85–9, 91, 94, 95, 96–7, 101–2, 151, 168
Ana y el lobo feroz 54
Andrés 50, 65, 67, 216
Antonio (character) 174, 176, 184, 198n7
Antonio Amor, Juan 37
Arnao, Elena *187*
Asensio, Ana 36n6, 139, 143n17
Asensio y de Merlo, Ángela 34
Asociación para la recuperación del la memoria histórica (Association for the Recovery of Historical Memory) 175

Ateneo Feminista de Madrid 5
audience accessibility 182–4
auteurs 60, 76

Baena, Juan Julio, and the Film School 19, 25n2, 37–8, 40–1, 209–10
Baeza, Elsa 22
Bahar, Robert 142–3n15
Bárbara (character) 78, 80, 82, 88–95, 96, 97–8, 100–3, 151, 159, 214
Bardem, Juan Antonio 54
Bartolomé, Cecilia 1, 6, 17, 21, 52, 129, 150–1, 179–80, 196–7, 199, 207–8
awards 12n8
background 43, 92, 122, 157–8, 205–7
blacklisted 9, 15, 23, 37, 59, 61, 64, 72, 76, 200
on *Carmen de Carabanchel* 29
on censorship 19, 28
and feminist counter-cinema 66, 69
hypothetical reception of 39–40, 42–3
interviews 13n12, 37–8, 50, 56n1, 56n4, 72–3, 88, 121–2, 172–3, 197n4, 205–21
on *La noche del doctor Valdés* 24
and Molina 20

pregnancy 23, 29, 33, 130
website 4, 11n7, 118
Bartolomé, José Juan 10, 62, 108, 110–12, 120, 129, 141n9, 219
Bautista, Aurora 212
Beeston, Alix 61, 72–3
Berghahn journal 89–90
Berlanga, Luis García 13–14n20, 15–16, 19, 23, 146, 168
Bermejo, Andrea 13n19, 199
Bernardeau, Miguel Ángel 174–5
Berrocal, Gloria *187*, 188
Blázquez Carretero, Elena 119
blindness 97
Borau, José Luis 19–20, 24, 62, 212
Bradbury-Rance, Clara 80, 93
British film industry 60–1
Bruno, Giuliana 1–2, 61
Bueno Fernández, Juan Antonio 181
Bugs Bunny 32, 173
Buñuel, Luis 16–18, 26, 38

Cabrera, Sergio 179
Calpena, Ana 24–5, 38
Camacho, Marcelino 177
Camacho, Vicenta 177
Camporesi, Valeria 86–9
Camus, Mario 177–8
'Caperucita' ('Little Red Riding Hood') song 55
Caperucita y roja (1977) 39, 53–4
Carabanchel 210–11
Carlos (character) 175, 185, 188
Carmen de Carabanchel (1965) 9, 21, 27–30, *31*, 32–5, 88, 122, 128, 197n4, 201, 208–11
 distribution 4, 56n3, 57n7
 failure of 23, 29, 35
 filming of 24
 and *La brujita* 22
 music of 27, 30–3, 45, 205
 School reactions 16
Carnicero, Marisol 104n2
Carracedo, Almudena 142–3n15
Carrero Blanco, Luis 179, 181–2, 186, 188, 191–2, 195, 220–1

Carrero Blanco Pichot, Luis 180–1, 186–7, 189
Carrillo, Santiago 133
Carter, Angela 9, 39, 43, 53, 55–6
Català, Josep María 120
Catalan Film Archives 73–4n2
Catholic Church 157–8
Cecilia 11n7
Céline and Marriage novel 39, 43, 45, 47–8, 56n4
censorship 2, 15, 25n2, 60–1, 105n12, 109, 118, 200, 211–12
 and Borau 19–20
 in *Cuéntame* 184
 of *Después de…* 112–14, 139
 of *El mundo sigue* (Fernán Gómez, 1963) 16–17
 in *Lejos de África* 159
 of *Margarita y el lobo* 2–3, 9, 15, 19, 21–2, 30, 37–8, 40–1, 51, 72, 209–10
 and soft porn 71, 87, 214–15
 of *Qué tal Margarita… pero bien* 62, 73n1
 and Saura 54
 script fragments 59
 and script-writing 3
 self-censorship 28, 212
Cerdán, Josetxo 119–20, 130, 139, 140n2, 151–2, 163
Chaplin, Geraldine 53
'chicas raras' 92–3, 103, 106n16
Chile 110, 135, 139
chorus 168, 213–14
Churchill, Frank 47
Cierva 188
CIMA 7–8, 41
Cinco horas con Mario (Delibes 1966) 7
cineastes of the quotidian 120–1, 129, 132, 139
'cine con niño' film genre 90–1
'cine social' genre 147, 150
Cixous, Hélène 43
Clair, Renais 153–4, 165
Cobra Woman (Siodmak 1944) 206

Index

Colectivo Cine de Clase 121
Colectivo Cine de Madrid 123–4
colonialism 149–50, 154, 170
Comas i Mariné, Anna 84
comedy 10, 42–3, 59, 66–7, 81, 97, 100–1, 108, 164, 200–1, 215
completeness 3, 60–1
Convergència Democràtica de Catalunya (Catalan Nationalist Party) 113
Corbalán, Ana 197n1
Corona, María Elisa 34
Cortázar, Julio 183
Costalreda, Antonio Pascual 28
costumbrista films 178
Crespi, Agustín 179, 183
Crespo, Pedro 117–18, 133
Cruzada del Rosario (1963) 21, 30, 137
Cuéntame cómo pasó 172, 174–5, 183, 194–5, 197n2, 202, 220–1
  'El comienzo del fin' 2, 10, 172, 176, 179–82, 184–90, 194, 196, 197n1, 200, 219–20
  humour in 174, 190–4
  interviews in 180, 183–7, 193
  music in 174, 176, 178, 182, 184, 190–1
  special episodes 179–80, 186
  use of archival footage in 175–6, 178–81, 191
  see also specific characters
cultural commentaries 118
Cultural Studies approaches to film 153
Curro (character) 107n24, 216

Daza de Castillo, Juan José 24
de Azcarate, Sara 77
de Beauvoir, Simone 65
Decameron (Boccaccio) 54
de la Cierva, Ricardo 181, 188, 189
de la Iglesia, Eloy 71
del Valle-Inclán, Ramón 13–14n20
Denis, Claire 151, 153–5, 161–2

Después de... / Afterwards... 2, 10, 73, 108–10, 124, 127, 130, *131*, 132, 141–2n13, 143n20, 180–1, 202–4, 216, 219–20
  Bartolomé on 139–40, 144n23
  censorship of 112–14
  criticisms of 119, 123
  editing 130–5
  Fernández Colorado on 139
  graveyards 125–6
  humour in 135–8
  interviewees 112, 122–4, *125*, 126–30, 132, 184–6, 217–18
  reporters on 115–19
  screenings 116, 118, 133–5, 144n23
  tractor drivers 138
  see also documentaries
destape 71–2, 87, 93, 105n12, 214
Devesa, Dolores 73–4n2
Diamante, Julio 40
Díaz, Marina 119, 130, 139, 151–2, 163
Diego (character) 148, 165–6, 167
Diferente (Delgado 1962) 211
divorce 9, 37, 46, 47, 69, 77
documentaries 5, 10, 11n5, 21–2, 30, 34, 108–12, 119–20, 140n2, 173–4, 184–90, 202, 210
Drac Màgic 5
Dressel, Teresa 34
  see also Durán Dressel, María Teresa
Dr. Oyono (character) 163, 166
dubbing 29, 41, 48, 78–9, 83–4, 98–9, 104n5, 105n11, 106n20, 106n21, 215–16
Durán Dressel, María Teresa 25–6
  see also Dressel, Teresa
'Ebula lobelo' 160, 164, 166
'El barranco del lobo' 184

El silencio de las sirenas (1985) 3
El silencio de los otros (Bahar and Carracedo 2018) 142–3n15

Equatorial Guinea 145, 147, 152–3, 155, 170, 171n1, 205–7
  see also Lejos de África (1995)
Erice, Víctor 15–16, 21, 77
esperpento 10, 13–14n20, 88, 106n18, 135–7, 146, 152, 158–9, 168, 191, 200
Estiu 1993 (Simón 2017) 101
Eurocentrism 161, 163, 168, 170

failures, criteria for 23
fairy tales 39, 53–6
Falcón, Lidia 5
Father López (character) 157, 161
feminism 9, 65
  and child-focused films 155
  and Francoism 8–9, 39, 49, 52–3, 64–5, 154–9, 173
  feminist counter-cinema 66, 69
  feminist discourses 7, 35, 42, 65, 129, 154
  'feminist trilogy' 71
Fernández, Bernardo 20
Fernández Colorado, Luis 114–17, 139, 143n21
Fernández-Santos, Ángel 116
Fernán Gómez, Fernando 16–17, 178
Field, Allyson Nadia 61, 71
film historiography 8, 59–60
Filmoteca Española 16, 81, 114, 200
Film School 10–11n2, 16, 56–7n5, 200, 206–8, 211
  and anti-Francoism 18, 35
  archives 2, 9, 41
  and Baena, Juan Julio 19, 25n2, 37–8
  as Escuela Oficial de Cinematografía 17, 74n6, 207
  history of 17–18
  hypothetical statements about 39–40
  and undistributed works 16–18
  and women 18–19, 34
Florentina, Fiorella 63
Forest Gump (Zemeckis 1994) 175

Forteza, María 5
Fraga, Manuel 180, 188–9, 196
Fraguas de Pablo, Antonio 185, 190
France, Institut des Hautes Études Cinématographiques 17
Franco, Francisco 6, 96, 123–4, 126, 131–2, 157, 184, 191, 217, 220
Francoism 4, 16, 56–7n5, 90, 110, 155–6, 158, 194–5
  and Cuéntame 176
  and feminism 8–9, 39, 49, 52–3, 64–5, 154–9, 173
  see also censorship
Freeman, Elizabeth 94
French, Lisa 129–30, 143n18
Fuentes, Gumer 5, 57n7
Fuerza Nueva 110–11, 116–18, 120, 124, 126, 132–3, 135–7
Función de noche (Molina 1981) 71, 86

Galán, Diego 82, 115–17
Galván, Enrique Tierno 134
Ganga, Grupo 178
García Escudero, José María 27, 56–7n5
García López, Sonia 15, 18–19, 34, 42, 56n1, 199
García Morales adaptation 11n5
García Morales, Adelaida 3
García Pousa, Laura 178, 182–3, 197n2
García Sahagún, Sonia 42
García Sánchez, José Luis 40, 209, 211–12
Garci, José Luis 63
Gary Cooper, qué estás en los cielos (Miró 1980) 7, 71, 86
Gato, Miguel 173
Girlhood 77, 89, 103, 159–60
Girlhood Studies 9–10, 77, 89–94, 106n14
Girlhood Studies 90
Gómez, Fernando Fernán 49
Gómez, Sara 66, 74n6
González, Eduardo 188

Index

González, Felipe 112, 142n14
González-Haba, Manuela 34
González Sinde, José María 38
Gonzalo (character) 148, 157
Gorocelaya, Aitor 53
Gorospe, José Manuel 25
Grand Narratives 152
Guarner, José Luis 73–4n2, 81–2
Guillamón Carrasco, Silvia 41–2, 49, 55
Gutiérrez Aragón, Manuel 20, 28, 73–4n2, 76, 79
Gutiérrez Caba, Emilio 22
Gutiérrez, José María 73–4n2
Guzmán, Patricio 120, 129

Hains, Rebecca 90
Handyside, Fiona 90, 106n14
Herminia (character) 174–5
Hernández Les, Juan 173
Hipkins, Danielle 12n9, 106n14
Hipólito, Carlos 175
Historia de Sabigoto, su marido Aurelio... 73–4n2
Holmes, Diana 43–4, 57n9
Huarte, Juan 38
Hutton, Margaret-Anne 44

Ibarra, Gabriel 29
incompleteness 3, 61–2, 72–3, 203–4
Inés Alcántara (character) 175
Insausti, Mikel 116, 141n9
interracial friendships 159–66, 167
Iribarne, Manuel Fraga 27, 206–7
Italy 17
Izquierda Unida 187

Jiménez, José Alfredo 191
Juan (character) 30–2, 34
Juan Carlos (Prince) 191
Juegos de tarde script 22–3

Kinder, Marsha 91
Kuhn, Annette 129
Kunze, Peter 60

La batalla de Chile (Parts I–III, 1975–79) 110, 135, 139

La brujita (1966) 21–2, 211
Lacaci, Fernando 28
La caza de brujas (Drove 1967) 25n2
La ciudad no es para mí (Lazaga 1965) 100
Ladrón de Guevara, Eduardo 179, 183, 197n3
La gran familia (Palacios 1962) 36n6
La linda Casilda (1976) 59, 69–73, 71–2, 200, 203
Lamet, Juan Miguel 23
languages 83–4, 98, 104n5
La niña bonita 11n5
La noche del Dr Valdés (1964) 4, 9, 15–16, 21, 23–6, 25–6, 27, 30, 34, 45, 57n7, 173
L'Arrivée d'un train en gare de La Ciotat (Lumière 1896) 25
La siesta (1962) 21–2
Leblanc, Tony 178
Légitimus, Darling 155
Leguina, Joaquín 189–90, 196
Lejos de África (1995) 76, 109, 145, 170, 173, 177, 181, 186, 200, 202
  as autobiography 146, 151, 157–8, 161, 217
  Bartolomé on 145, 157–8, 167–8
  compared with other movies 155–6, 161–2, 165
  'corte clásico' (classic approach) 168–9
  and exaggeration 151–2
  filming 216–17
  and Girlhood 159–60
  humour in 151–2, 168
  imagery of 160, 163, 166, 169
  interracial friendships in 159–66, 167, 170
  magic in 148, 155, 164–5
  music of 160, 162–6, 169
  as 'orphan' film 152–3
  and *Out of Africa* (Pollack 2005) 145–6, 153, 156
  photography director 169

publicity for 145–6, 149–50, 153, 202
screenings 161
secondary characters in 169–70
structure 148
subtitles in 155, 160, 164, 169
unevenness of 10, 145, 150, 154, 159, 162, 165, 167
and ¡Vámonos, Barbara! (1978) 152, 159
and West Africa 10
see also Equatorial Guinea
León de Aranoa, Fernando 147
Ley de Memoria Democrática (Law of Democratic Memory) 175, 195
Ley de Memoria Histórica (Law of Historical Memory) 175, 195
LGBTQ+ themes 71, 74n4, 94, 101–2, 106–7n22, 107n24, 141n9, 216
see also Bárbara (character)
'Libertad condicional' (Conditional Freedom) script 111–14
Lisa, Mariano 121
literary adaptations 43, 52–3
Llopart, Salvador 181–2
Lorenzo (character) 47–8, 64–5, 68, 70
Losey, Joseph 86–7
Loxham, Abi 195
Luces de Bohemia (del Valle-Inclán 1920) 13–14n20
Lucía (character) 25–6, 27
Lumbreras, Elena/Helena 34–5, 120–2

Madre Concepción (character) 25–6
Mallada, Lucio Blanco 18
Marcelino, pan y vino (Vajda 1955) 99
Margarita y el lobo (1969) 15, 21–2, 30, 37–43, 46, 47, 52, 53–4, 57n8, 139, 157, 169, 196, 200–1, 203
censorship of 3, 19, 37–8, 40–1, 51, 72, 209–10
critical reception 41–2
filming of 24, 40–1, 50, 209, 211
music of 42, 45–52, 55, 69
and Rochefort 9, 39, 41–6, 48–50, 52, 62
screenings 4, 12n8, 38, 41, 56n1, 56n3, 172
structure 45
and ¡Vámonos, Barbara! (1978) 59
Mariscal, Ana 5–6, 17
marital separations 46, 47
Marks, Laura 162
Marlasca, Manuel 185
marriage 65–7, 69–70
Martínez, Belén Puebla 136
Martínez Reverte, Jorge 187
Martínez Soria, Paco 100
Martín Gaite, Carmen 92–3
Martin-Márquez, Susan 4–7, 42, 157
Martín Morán, Ana 152, 159
Martín Patino, Basilio 139
Masó, Ángeles 82
Matas, Alfredo 6, 76, 78–9, 81, 83, 213
Matute, Ana María 92
Medio, Dolores 92
Menz, Bernardo 110, 120, 135
Mercedes/Merche Fernández (character) 174, 178
Merino, Jesús 134
middlebrow films/television 146, 150, 177
Miguel (character) 183
Milans del Bosch, Jaime 11n4, 110, 133–4
'mirar' 161–2
Miró, Pilar 6–7, 71, 76, 113–14
mise en scène 97, 174, 178
Mission: Impossible (television show) 46–7
model-makers 196
modernity 25–6, 49, 71
Molina, Josefina 6–7, 13n14, 17, 20, 35, 71
Montejano, Fernando 115
Morán, Javier 111–12, 130–2

Mostra Internacional de Films de Dones 4–5, 11n5
motherhood 175
mother-in-law characters 49
Mulvey, Laura, 'Visual Pleasure and Narrative Cinema' 42
Muñoz, Luisa 28
Murau, F. W. 171n2
music 10, 53, 162, 176, 190, 200
   see also specific productions
Nair, Parvati 34, 128
Natalia (character) 51, 67–8, 71, 201
Negro / Black 11n5
New Latin American Cinema 66
North, Dan 60–1
Notari, Elvira 1–2
Noticiarios y Documentales footage 48, 109, 120–3, 132, 137–8, 176–7, 191–2, 206–7
nudity 105n12, 211, 214–15
'Nuevo Cine Español' (New Spanish Cinema) movement 50–1, 53

'Operación Ogro' (Operation Ogre) 181
Operación ogro (Pontecorvo 1979) 58n13, 183, 185, 192, 193, 195
oral history 129, 174
Ortega, María Luisa 151–3, 158–9, 165

Palacio, Manuel 175–6
Palcy, Euzhan 154–6
Parrondo Coppel, Eva 86–7, 97
Partido Feminista de España (Spanish Feminist Party) 5
Partido Popular (PP; Spanish Conservative Party) 175
Partido Socialista Obrero Español (Spanish Labour Party) 6, 113, 175–6
Patino, Basilio Martín 15–16, 22, 50, 57n11, 209
Paula (character) 87–8
Pellicer, Coral 16, 24–5, 27

Peña, Julia 37, 45, 54–5, 62, *187*, 212
Pérez Guerra José, 143n22
Pérez, Jorge 107n24
Pérez Mogena, José Luis 181
Perrault, Charles 55
Philip IV (King) 191
Picazo, Miguel 19
Pinal, Silvia 16
Piñar, Blas 132
Pi, Rosario 5
Pisier, Marie France 153–4, 166
plays 205–8
Poe, Edgar Allan 24
Pollack, Sydney 145–6, 153–4, 171n2
Ponce, Elvira 28
Pons, Ventura 71
populism 132
Portuguese Carnation Revolution 217
postcolonial cinema 153–4
Potes, Alicia 73–4n2
Pradera, María Dolores 49
Prego, Victoria 179
Prieto, Jorge 155
Primo de Rivera, José Antonio 141n10
Producciones Cinematográficas Ales S.A 216
Pujol, Jordi 112

¡¿*Qué he hecho yo para merecer esto!?* (Almodóvar 1984) 32
¿*Qué tal Teresa?* 73n1
Querejeta, Elías 98
Qué tal Margarita… pero bien 2, 59, 62–9, 73n1, 200, 203
Quintano, José Antonio 163

radical ecology 106–7n22
Ramón Resina, Joan 195
Reina, Charo 132–3, 220
Reina Santa (Gil 1947) 32
religion 26–7
Renoir, Jean 165
Réponse de femmes: Notre corps, notre sexe (Varda 1975) 38

Revenga, Luis 53
Revuelta, Manuel 20
Rita (character) 148, *149*, 155, 161, 163–6, *167*
Rochefort, Christiane 9, 39, 41–6, 48–50, 52, 56n4, 62
Romero, Concha 69, 77
Romero, Pilar 28, *31*
RTVE archive footage 175–8
Ruiz, Emilio *193*, 194–7

Sáenz de Heredia, José Luis 208
Samper, Josefina 177, 196
Sánchez Biosca, Vicente 109
San Sebastián Film Festival (2004) 4, 172
Santa Eulalia, Mary G. 82
Santaolalla, Isabel 153–5, 165, 169
Santiago, R. 84
Sanz, Bernardo 112
Saura, Carlos 23, 53–4, 77, 100, 212
Scholz, Annette 8
script authorship 3
self-referentiality 63–4, 67, 69, 112
Selva i Masoliver, Marta 119, 129
Selva, Marta 5
Sevillano Canicio, Víctor 176
'Shadow Cinema' 61
Silvano (character) 148–9, 151, 164
Sissi – The Young Empress (Marischka 1956) 206
Smith, Paul Julian 176, 178–9
Solà, Anna 5
Soler Leal, Amparo 36n6, 76, 86–7, 89, *95*, 97, 213
Solomon, Stefan 61, 73
soundscapes 25–6
Spain 5, 17, 20, 68, 77, 119–20, 123, 125–6, 133, 175
  authoritarianism in 2, 4, 138
  and the Basques 111–13
  Civil War (1936–39) 6, 26, 54, 126, 150, 184
  and colonialism 149–50, 170
  democracy in 111, 115, 125–6
  divorce in 37, 77

Franco's regime (1939–78) 6, 9–10, 53, 56–7n5, 65, 96–7, 201
National Library (Biblioteca Nacional) 3, 59
street cultures 122, 132
Tejerazo 108, 135, 203
Transition period 6, 10, 53, 77, 79, 85–9, 93, 101, 109, 133, 151, 185–6, 189
  urbanisation of 99–100
Spanish cinema, studies of 4–5, 8, 15
Spanish Ministry of Culture and Sport Database 154
Stoppard, Tom 60
street models *193*, 194
street riots 130, *131*
student demonstrations 40, 63–5, 176–7
Suárez, Adolfo 178, 217
Suárez, Gonzalo 22
subtitling project 4, 12n9, 56n3, 199
Susana (character) 148, *149*, 150, 155–7, 159–60, 164–5, *167*

Taylor-Jones, Kate 90, 106n14
Tejero, Antonio 11n4, 108, 134
television adverts 13n13, 210
Thelma and Louise (Scott 1991) 77, 104n3
Thomas, Sarah 93, 105n7
tía Remedios (character) 87, *96*, 97, 100
time out of joint (destiempado) 86–9, 94–9
¡*Todos al suelo!* 2, 11n4, 203
Toribio, Núria Triana 8, 11n5, 12n10, 56–7n5, 71, 88
Torreiro, Casimiro 120
Torrent, Ana 21, 91, 98
Torres, Augusto 151
Trilateral Commission 137–8
Tuchman, Barbara 118

unfinished works 60
'Unproduction Studies' 60–1, 74n3
Uriarte, Teo 189–90

¡Vámonos, Barbara! (1978) 2, 6–7, 9, 13n15, 69–71, 76–7, 88, 146, 168, 174, 200–1
   Anemnos-en, Bàrbara! 78–9, 83
   car, 215
   and censorship 105n12
   dubbing for 78–9, 83–4, 98–9, 104n5, 105n11, 106n21, 215–16
   as 'first' feminist film 41–2, 57n7, 77, 81, 105n9
   and *Girlhood* 77, 89, 103, 159
   and *Lejos de África* (1995) 152, 159
   and *Margarita y el lobo* (1969) 59
   public screenings 5, 56n3, 57n7, 78–9, 83, 215–16
   related interviews 19, 50, 121–2, 173, 213
   reviewer responses 79–85, 87–8
   see also specific characters

Vaquero, Isabel 117
Varda, Agnès 38, 68, 81
vegetarianism 99–100, 106–7n22
Vernon, Kathleen 84–6, 105n9
Viader, Jordi 88
Vindicación Feminista (Feminist Vindication, 1976–79) 5
Visconti, Luchino 102

Waldo, Kathryn 19, 34–5, 74n5
Webber, Andrew Lloyd 60
'witch hunts' 19–20
women 7–10, 17–18, 26–7, 64–5, 70–1, 199
   at the Film School 18–19, 34
   interviewing 122, 124, *125*, 127–30
Wright, Sarah 91, 98–9

Yoldi, Pili 38

EU authorised representative for GPSR:
Easy Access System Europe, Mustamäe tee 50,
10621 Tallinn, Estonia
gpsr.requests@easproject.com

www.ingramcontent.com/pod-product-compliance
Lightning Source LLC
Chambersburg PA
CBHW051609230426
43668CB00013B/2037